The Coast Time Forgot

The
Complete
San Mateo Coast
Touring Guide

DON WEST
&
JOSEPH W. COTCHETT

Photography
Leslie Cotchett

D0207942

Thornton House
Moss Beach, CA 94038

Coastal Guide Books

©2002 By Don West & Joseph W. Cotchett

9876543210123456789

PUBLISHED
BY
THORNTON HOUSE
P.O. BOX 57
MOSS BEACH, CA 94038

Library of Congress Control No 2002101468

West, Don (Donald Ray), 1928-
Cotchett, Joseph W., 1939-
    Includes bibliographical references and index

ISBN 0-9641243-7-8
    1. Travel 2. Natural History; 3. History

PRINTED IN U.S.A.

Dedication

This work is dedicated to the memory of Marion Shepard West, who drew endless inspiration and sustenance from her hours along the Pacific Coast Highway and deep in the redwood forests. D.W.

This book is also dedicated to my family, wife Victoria and children, Quinn, Camilla, Leslie, Rachel, Charles, their families, my friends and our extended families -- all of whom are committed to keeping the San Mateo coast a special place where environmental values and quality of life will always endure. I could not dedicate my small contribution to the coast without their support.   J.W.C.

Table of Contents

PART I	Introduction	Page 1
PART II	A Brief History	Page 4
PART III	The Esentials - Flora, Fauna And Weather	Page 13
PART IV	The Discovery Hikes	Page 19
PART V	Driving Tours	Page 31
	Coastal Scenic Tour	Page 31
	From the Seashore to the Redwoods & Back	Page 43
	Tunitas Alternative	Page 50
PART VI	Biking Tours	Page 53
	Coastal Scenic Tour	Page 53
	Lobitos-Purisima Tour	Page 61
	Higgins Purisima Tour	Page 65
PART VII	Nature Tours	Page 69
	Butano State Park	Page 71
	El Corte Madera Open Sp. Preserve	Page 79
	La Honda Creek Open Sp. Preserve	Page 88
	Long Ridge Open Space Preserve	Page 90
	Memorial Park of SM Cty.	Page 94
	Pescadero Creek County Park	Page 101
	Portola Redwoods State Park	Page 111
	Purisima Creek Redwoods OSP	Page 119
	Russian Ridge Open Sp.Preserve	Page 127
	Sam McDonald County Park	Page 130
	Skyline Ridge Open Sp. Preserve	Page 135
PART VIII	Walking Tours	Page 142
	Half Moon Bay Walkabout	Page 142
	Pescadero Walkabout	Page 158
	Pillar Point Walkabout	Page 168

Table of Contents
(continued)

PART IX   **The Kids Will Love It**

           (And So Will You)   **Page 177**

Año Nuevo State Preserve   Page 177

Burleigh H. Murray Ranch   Page 188

Fitzgerald Marine Reserve   Page 190

Lintt Trout Farm   Page 191

Pescadero Marsh   Page 191

Pigeon Point Light Stn.   Page 194

Pt. Montara Fog & Light Stn.   Page 197

Sanchez Adobe   Page 198

Sea Horse Ranch   Page 200

Waddell Beach   Page 201

PART X   **Beaches & Picnic Spots**   **Page 203**

PART XI   **Funtime on the Coast**   **Page 221**

Festivals   Page 221

Drama, Music & Talent   Page 229

Eateries   Page 230

Snack Time   Page 239

Shopping   Page 241

Bed & Breakfasts   Page 249

Hotels & Motels   Page 251

Hostels   Page 254

RV Parks   Page 255

Camping   Page 256

PART XII   **Assistance, Practical**

           & Religious   **Page 259**

Without Whom....   **Page 263**

Bibliography   **Page 271**

Acknowedgments   **Page 272**

Index   **Page 273**

Table of Contents
(continued)

Maps

Rancho Miramontes Plat   Page 8
Discovery Site   Page 22
Nature Tour Maps
   Butano State Park   Page 72
   El Corte de Madera Creek OSP   Page 82
   Long Ridge Open Spacxe Preserve   Page 93
   Memorial County Park   Page 96
   Pescadero Creek County Park   Page 105
   Portola Redwoods State Park   Page 112
   Purisima Creek Redwoods OSP   Page 122
   Russian Ridge OSP   Page 129
   Sam McDonald County Park   Page 132
   Skyline Open Space Preserve   Page 140
Walkabout Maps
   Half Moon Bay   Page 143
   Pescadero   Page 159

ABOUT THE AUTHORS

An enduring love affair with the San Mateo Coast is the common denominator among all the contributors to this book.

Don West, author of a half-dozen books and a former San Francisco Examiner columnist and reporter, was first smitten in 1948 on a drive down the Coast Highway. He has been exploring all the coast's byways and wonders since then.

Joseph W. Cotchett, lawyer, author and environmentalist, has considered the coast his home for some 40 years. He has spent a great deal of time preserving the history of the San Mateo Coast, and has served as Chairman of the California State Parks Commission.

Leslie Cotchett, whose photography reflects her passion for capturing the coast's essence, grew up in San Mateo County taking pictures. After attending the University of Colorado and working as a hospice nurse, she has returned to her first love.

The
Enduring Lure
Pulling Us Back To the Sea

*Communing with the vast expanse of the Pacific
is a favorite relaxation from Devil's
Slide (above) to the tip of land
where Sebastian Vizcaino
and his crew saw land
on Jan. 1, 1603*

PART I

INTRODUCTION

One of the very special places on this earth, the Pacific Coast extending south from San Francisco has been rising out of the sea for eons, its mountainous folds and crevices nurturing habitats for all manner of wildlife, flora and fauna. Redwoods, oaks of a half-dozen varieties, pines, madrone, manzanita and fir proliferate. Sea lions contend for space with seals along the beaches while gray whales pass twice yearly on their migrations. Dozens of varieties of birds likewise use the coastline for their winter and spring migrations. Upon their return in May from their Baja California winter homes, pelicans, scaups and cormorants patrol offshore while sandpipers and plovers scour the beaches, avocets and phalarope seek their food in the marshes and sloughs, and terns swoop down into Pillar Point Harbor for their meals.

The mountain range stretching southward for some 85 miles forms a serrated ridge that dares the Pacific's weather vortexes to breach its heights. The resultant mild microclimates created from these contentious currents are far different along

Pigeon Point is great for whale watching.

this coastal plain than inland only a few miles. Spring, summer and fall, the pulsing breezes keep temperatures in the 70's. Even when winter storms press down from Alaska for a few weeks in January or February, rarely do daytime temperatures fall below 50 degrees Fahrenheit. Despite this unique meteorology and geography, and its proximity to the stressful crush of Silicon Valley and the San Francisco Bay Area, the coast remains immune from the suburban and urban ills of the neighboring megalopolis. There are quiet and expansive seascapes and uncluttered mountain vistas. There is space and fresh, untainted air to breathe.

Trails and roads beckon to bicyclists with promises of no reckless auto drivers. There are quiet lanes to stroll, hiking trails – both leisurely and challenging — along the beaches and deep in the redwoods. You may gather driftwood on remote shores. You can even hike up to the crest of Sweeney Ridge and re-live the discovery of San Francisco Bay by Capt. Gaspar de Portolá and his expedition in 1769. Ride horseback. Go camping. Go fishing with experienced sea captains. Play golf on championship courses. Para-sail or windsurf at Waddell Beach. Surf the old fashioned way on the easy sector of Half Moon Bay or, if you've proven your mettle, take on the Maverick's rollers off Pillar Point. Kids young and old can learn the mysteries of shy sea creatures hidden among the rocks and tide pools of Moss Beach's Fitzgerald Marine Reserve. See the seals and sea lions up close at Point Año Nuevo. Picnic at one of a dozen exciting places along the water and in the woods. Discover the foods of the Portuguese who settled Pescadero after operating whaling stations at Pigeon Point, or sample the endless savory specialties of chefs from Pacifica to Half Moon Bay to Pescadero. Art, pottery and creative toys, furniture, clothing and more beckon the shopper.

There are festivals galore. At the annual Halloween affair, the entire countryside erupts into orange-colored streaks, row after row and field after field of pumpkins honor the Half Moon Bay Pumpkin Festival where each year growers from around the nation compete to bring in the largest pumpkin, which seem to get bigger every year. The Tours des Fleurs each July invites public tours of the coast's vast flower-growing operations, a chance to learn the horticultural secrets of the region. The Chamarita Festival in

June colorfully revives the traditions of Azores Island immigrants who settled here. The Artichoke Golf Classic attracts top-notch players every May. The Dream Machines, the Spring Fest, Harbor Day, Annual Chili Cookoff and more galas keep things perpetually lively.

A combination of geographical whimsy, benign neglect in its early European discovery years and some championship conservation efforts in recent decades preserved this wonderland. Geological upheavals restricted access from the first. The main entry from the Bay Area – Highway 92 – meanders part of the way along an old cow path that was the original trail used to drive some of the Franciscans' 50,000 cattle back and forth to Mission Dolores in San Francisco. Early Anglo settlers carved a county from San Francisco and Santa Cruz and called it San Mateo County (after St. Matthew). But the geologic barriers resisted efforts of tanners, loggers and railroader entrepreneurs to exploit the land. And in modern times, a new breed of conservationist champion emerged to protect this unique heritage.

The result of all this has been to create a handy escape hatch for everyone. Go have fun!

Music on the plaza at the corner of Main and Kelly Avenue draws a relaxed and happy crowd to Half Moon Bay.

PART II
THE COAST TIME FORGOT
A Brief History

Gaspar de Portolá's statue
on the Beach in Pacifica,
donated by his Catalan admirers.

Everyone has heroes and the San Mateo Coast has plenty, especially the ones responsible for keeping this wonderland pristine and unspoiled for future generations. Some early credit usually goes to the Catalan adventurer, Don Gaspar de Portolá, who led the first European land expedition up this coast in 1769. Portolá partisans erected a modernistic bronze rendering of the man at the beach in Pacifica to celebrate his efforts. But we differ. Portolá was really an ineffective and hapless explorer. His only big discovery was a complete accident and his primary goal – finding Monterey Bay – eluded him entirely on his first exploration. Because of mistakes on a 177-year-old map furnished him, he walked around Monterey Bay without recognizing it and kept plodding northward. Maybe if he had stayed at Monterey, our coast might be in an even deeper time warp.

We could credit Jose Gonzales Cabrera Bueno, the navigator who drew the faulty map of Monterey Bay for Captain Sebastian Vizcaino in 1602. Vizcaino's crew went ashore there for wood and water during their search for a likely stopover port for the galleons carrying gold from the Philippines to New Spain. They had written glowing reports about the year-round safety of the Monterey anchorage, but Bueno's map had a critical error. Bueno mistakenly mapped a point of land in a northeasterly direction instead of northwest, confusing Portolá's men a century and three-quarters later.

Vizcaino was just one of many mariners who had been up and down this coast for more than 200 years without disturbing the native Ohlone population. Juan Rodriguez Cabrillo breezed past in 1542. In 1579, Francis Drake raided a couple of West Coast ports in New Spain before stopping off in a long cove behind Point Reyes north of here that was later named after the English privateer. Francisco Galli paused to chart Pillar Point in 1585. Sebastian Rodriquez Cermeno sailed blithely past in 1595. Vizcaino stopped off long enough to name Point Año Nuevo, having reached that landmark on New Year's Day of 1603. On the same trip, Vizcaino touched in at Drake's Bay, but a priest on board suggested the place be named after Saint Francis and it became the Port of San Francisco on Spanish maps for nearly two centuries, leading to confusion for later map makers after the modern bay was discovered and settled.

Spanish colonizing stalled in Baja California due to the harsh terrain there, and they probably would not have pushed into Alta California if it had not been for a perceived Russian threat. Explorations by Vitus Jonassen Bering, a Dane in the service of Peter The Great, opened the northwestern shores of Alaska to Russian fur traders and the Spanish were afraid the Russians would try to exploit California as well if it were left uncolonized. Portolá's expedition was supposed to counter that threat. Some theorists trying to explain the two-century delay in finding the true San Francisco Bay and settling the Pacific Coast have suggested that frequent summertime fog hid the area from explorers. But Vizcaino is known to have peeked in the Golden Gate and reported seeing only a vast estuary, probably because Angel Island blocks the view from outside the harbor mouth. And captains sailing difficult-to-maneuver square-rigged barkentines were not eager to explore areas that might be too tough to navigate.

When Portolá's scouts climbed the hill atop today's Sweeney Ridge in 1769, all they saw was a vast estuary and mud flats "as far as the eye could reach." This was the report of Father Juan Crespi, the spiritual leader on Portolá's trek. Thus Portolá and his crew limped back to San Diego, unable to find Monterey Bay and not sure of what to make of the vast estuary that seemed filled with native villages, some not too friendly toward the Spanish intruders. The Spaniards did not return until nearly seven years later, while across the continent the 13 British colonies were declaring themselves the United States of America and adopting the Declaration of Independence. Don Juan Bautista de Anza led an expedition that explored the great bay they would name after St. Francis, and on July 26, 1776 set up an outpost made of tule reeds on a sand hill where San Francisco is now located. Two months later, a primitive chapel that was to become Mission Dolores was set up. As the mission was being built, natives living on the sand hills were forced to flee to islands in the bay when marauding tribes from the San Mateo portion of the peninsula raided and burned their homes.

Friendly Ohlones

The Ohlones on the San Mateo Coast were unfailingly friendly and helpful to Portolá and his hapless explorers. Suffering miserably from scurvy, diarrhea and other intestinal problems, food furnished by the Ohlones invariably cleared up most of the Spaniards' scurvy problems. Native offerings were especially helpful when they stopped on the shelf of land above Point Año Nuevo at a village they called Casa Grande because of a spherical-shaped wooden building large enough to hold all 200 of the town's inhabitants. The huge meeting house was surrounded by smaller individual pyramid-shaped houses made of split pine boards, each

*Gaspar de Portolá had no time to smell the flowers,
worrying instead about getting his expedition's
gear over the top of San Pedro Mountain.*

with only room for one or two people to sleep. Their hosts treated them to honey cakes, greens and gruel made from acorns.

Alongside San Gregorio Creek, they found another village of some 80 Ohlones, but tried to eat the ground acorn meal raw and suffered massive diarrhea onsets. At Purisima Creek, they found a small abandoned village they dubbed Rancheria de las Pulgas because of all the fleas found in the deteriorating grass huts. *Las pulgas*, the fleas, were a recurring pestilence in Alta California. At Pilarcitos Creek near today's Half Moon Bay, native foods, nuts, blackberries and wildfowl furnished by the Ohlones again got the explorers over a bout of scurvy.

The Spaniards in the mid-to-late 18th century still had not discovered the dietary causes of scurvy and Portolá's support ships were forced to return to New Spain because of sickness and death among their crews. Subsisting on a limited and starchy diet, the land expedition members suffered again and again from the malady. But the Ohlones who had lived on the coast for thousands of years enjoyed nature's balanced bounty of sea foods, seeds, nuts, fruit, berries and game – one herd of 50 deer was spotted by

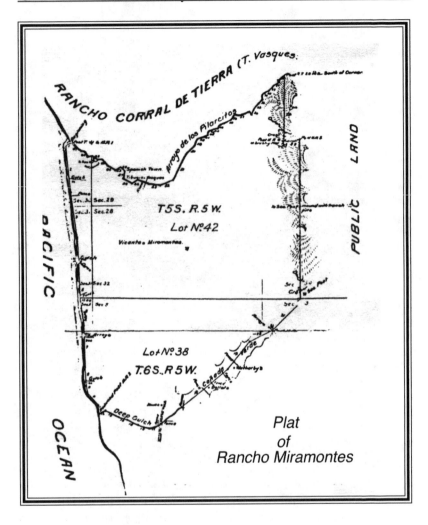

Plat
of
Rancho Miramontes

Portolá's scouts, but they lacked the natives' skills for successfully stalking the animals.

Ohlones maintained summer and winter homes, moving from place to place for their food. All the Coastside streams were alive with runs of salmon and steelhead, albeit hazardous because the natives had to vie for fishing spots with bears. Browns, blacks and grizzlies abounded. Cougars and bobcats were also competitors with the natives for fish and game. Reed boats were used for catching fish and birds among the thousands inhabiting the sloughs and coastal waterways. Occasionally, when one of the whales that migrated annually up and down the coast would wash ashore, the victim of an attack by orcas or simply dying of old age, there would be enough to feed a village for weeks.

Had the natives understood what was in store for them from the people who would come after Portolá when he returned the next year with Father Junipero Serra and Crespi, they might not have been so friendly and hospitable. Their way of life was soon swept away by the fervor of the missionary fathers' determination to convert "the heathens" to Christianity.

The Franciscan fathers established a chain of missions aimed at conversions and enabling natives ultimately to live a sedentary life like the colonizers. While the missions operated, nearly all of the coastal tribes were herded into the system, usually under duress, and taught the ways of farming and animal husbandry. But the tribes rapidly dwindled in number; twice as many natives died as were born in the mission years. When Mexican law disbanded the missions in 1824, most of the lands that Spain had intended to be given to the natives was instead carved into vast ranchos and granted to military and civil leaders.

Although a Coastside land grant was made in 1833 – Rancho El Pescadero granted to Juan Jose Gonzales, a San Francisco Presidio soldier — the first to actually settle on his Coastside rancho was a Presidio soldier who had not been paid in six years, Candelario Miramontes. Miramontes, whose name lives on in a Half Moon Bay street and a road, was a sergeant with a wife and 13 children, and was granted 4,424 acres in 1841. Officially known as Rancho Arroyo de los Pilarcitos, it extended southward from the creek, down to the sea shore and up to the mountain ridge. They built a house on the south side of Pilarcitos Creek, cultivated five acres along the creek and turned his 30 cattle loose to graze. Tiburcio Vasquez (uncle to the infamous bandit of the same name), a former mission official, built a house across the creek from Miramontes' home, but had one of Miramontes' sons live there and run his 4,436-acre Rancho Corral de Tierra Sud. Vasquez' ranch extended northward from the creek to the line of Rancho Corral Tierra de Norte that encompassed today's Montara, Moss Beach and Pillar Point. Rancho San Pedro was granted to Francisco Sanchez who built the adobe house in Pacifica that is preserved as a State Park.

To the south was granted Rancho Cañada Verde y Arroyo de la Purissima, Rancho San Gregorio, Rancho Butano and Rancho de Punta de Año Nuevo. Most of the Mexican rancheros lost their land because of the high cost of clearing titles after the United States bought California as part of the Gadsen Purchase. After their father died, the Miramontes family sold part of their land to repay money borrowed to take their cases before the Land Commission. Vasquez kept his land until 1862 when someone stuck a revolver through the window of a Half Moon Bay bar and shot him. Although a large funeral was held and he was honored as a pioneer, his killer was never apprehended. He was buried beneath the floorboards of the Catholic Church he had built at the edge of the village's cemetery.

The town developed along Pilarcitos Creek was first called San Benito, and later became known as Half Moon Bay. During the gold rush, the Coastside furnished food and building materials as the village of Yerba Buena became San Francisco and spread over the nine sand hills to Daly City. To handle shipping of farm produce and lumber, wharves were built at Pillar Point, Miramontes Point and Montara Beach. At the mouths of Purissima, Tunitas, San Gregorio and Pescadero Creeks as well as Pigeon Point, makeshift rigs were used to load schooners lying offshore. Rancher and lumberman William Waddell built a wharf close to Point Año Nuevo.

Redwoods Into Shingles

Sawmills sprouted like mushrooms after a wet winter along all the Coastside creeks, but the precipitous terrain prevented shipping the lumber over the hill to the main port of Redwood City. Many solved the problem by turning 3,000-year-old redwoods 16 to 18 feet across into shingles for easier shipment. One ancient giant along Tunitas Creek with a 16-foot diameter trunk was eviscerated for 1,250,000 good shingles. Other loggers dragged the wood down the mountain to the ocean, some floating it to schooners offshore and others building special chutes or cables for the task.

Farmers arrived in the 1850's and agriculture evolved from wheat and other grains to row crops such as cabbage, Brussels sprouts, artichokes, strawberries and pumpkins. Floriculture took hold slowly and grew into one of the largest industries with some operators shipping cut flowers all over the United States from here. The long growing season and rich soil enables flower growers to raise many crops each year, and the valleys and hillsides blaze with color nearly the year round.

In the 1920's railroad fever took over the coast and after a lot of promoting a scenic coastal line to Santa Cruz, a road was built around Devil's Slide south of Pacifica and all the way to Tunitas Creek. Large hotels were built in San Gregorio, Half Moon Bay, Pillar Point and Montara. But getting money to push the line further south was stalled by a bank crisis and the project withered away into bankruptcy. The hotels closed and disappeared.

During Prohibition years, the coast's many hidden coves and beaches made it ideal for landing whiskey and wine offloaded from Canadian ships some miles out at sea. Periodic raids by federal revenue agents at the larger hotels usually netted several truckloads of hooch, but most Coastsiders usually looked the other way at such activities, taking a live and let live attitude toward the smugglers and bootleggers.

In the post-World War II surge in the Bay Area, developers began buying up coastal land, talking about building condos all along the coast. Having seen how Southern California "China Wall" developments had blocked public access to the ocean beaches, a "Save Our Shores" movement was organized to place a measure on the statewide ballot. It passed and led to formation of the Coastal Commission, a body that strictly controls development on the coast. With additional pressure from persistent volunteers in such organizations as the Audubon Society, the Committee for Green Foothills, Peninsula Open Space Trust, Sierra Club and others, this coastline has been kept pristine, free from development and in a kind of time warp of its own.

As the moon powers the tidal ebb and flow,
the surf carves the land a grain of sand at a time.

PART III
THE ESENTIALS
FLORA, FAUNA, WILDLIFE
&
WEATHER

Weather on the San Mateo Coast is something only longtime residents fully appreciate and understand. For most folks, Coastside weather can seem capricious if not downright confusing. The first thing to understand is that the topography of the coast and offshore weather systems combine to create a natural air conditioning system in the summertime. When the thermometer is reading in the 90's and 100's just over the mountains to the east, sea breezes and fog keep things in the 60's and 70's on the coast.

Springtime and fall, weather patterns are far more stable and usually result in balmy, clear days that make all visitors start looking for a seaside cottage so they can take up permanent residence. Winter brings the westerlies and southerlies that signal two-to-four-day storms revolving from the Alaskan weather machine sometimes fed by tropical depressions from Hawaii. High surf pushed by the storms pounds the beaches, cliffs and the break-water at Pillar Point Harbor, and then the rain is gone, leaving everything crisp and clean.

Dressing for the unique Coastside weather is simple; wear layered clothing. Always carry light jackets or sweaters that can be donned or doffed as needed. A hat and sunscreen is also advisable even on the occasional hazy day. Sunlight refracted through haze can be tough on most human skin.

The fog bank, which usually sits offshore through much of the summer, can also be useful in gauging what to wear and when on Coastside outings. If the sun has pushed back the fog bank early in the day, chances are the evening will be balmy and clear. But the closer the burnoff comes to noon, the earlier the fog is likely to return. An offshore breeze usually kicks up ahead of the advancing fog bank and one knows it is nearly time to break out jackets and sweaters. Another clue is to note how the errant wisps of fog start building up against the mountains to the east, soon to be followed by the rest of the fog bank. After its arrival, the air is even more exhilarating.

Flora and Fauna

Although the Europeans' occupation of this coast is only a little over two centuries old, there have been major changes to the natural eco-systems of the coast. The redwoods were cut back deeper into the mountains, but the stubborn terrain resisted the loggers' efforts and a few far-sighted people moved early to save some of the best groves. But gone are tens of thousands of tanbark oaks that were cut to furnish hide tanners with their key tanning ingredient. Thousands of live oaks were harvested and turned into charcoal for household fuel by the early to mid 1800's. Oaks and manzanita was also extensively harvested for firewood; the manzanita burls were dug up and used to make tobacco pipes. Most of the remaining live oaks were felled by Americans farmers clearing land for tilling.

Sand hills that once were covered with all manner of greasewood and other scrub brush were likewise cleared and the resultant erosion can be seen again along Highway One.

Efforts to restore some of the woodlands led to planting of non-native species including Monterey pine and Monterey cypress and eucalyptus. In the case of the cypress and pine, their native area around Monterey Bay was extended. But the story of the eucalyptus brought from Australia in the 1840's showed how horticultural fads affected competition for space. The trees were believed at one point to keep away malaria and were planted near swamps, then later promoted as a source of hardwood for furniture. Both the U.S. and California forest services distributed eucaplypts for planting in the 1870's. Stage Road from Pescadero to San Gregorio and beyond contain some of the earliest plantings of eucalyptus. A large grove borders the northern edge of Pescadero Marsh.

The influx of farming activity brought all kind of foreign plants and shrubs to the coast. Milk thistle, quaking grass, wild oats and poison hemlock are just a few of the foreign plants that crowded out native plant varieties. Only recently has there been a push to restore native plants on public lands, especially along the beaches where ice plant and other succulents crowded out native grasses. The native grasses and other plants were the natural feeding and nesting sites for many species of wildlife.

Farming is still one of the main sights along the coast. Coastal shelves and canyon bottomlands raise multiple crops of strawberries, artichokes, cabbages, lettuce, flowers and pumpkins. Hothouses proliferate along Highway 92 east of Half Moon Bay and along Butano and Pescadero Creeks east of Pescadero.

Wildlife

Endangered species like the snowy plover that once numbered in the tens of thousands along the beaches were hard hit by the disappearance of native plants. Replacement of the grasses and shrubs where they once hid their nests helped decimate their population. Completely disappeared are many of the fish species that once laid their eggs along the beaches. The woods were once home to the grizzly, the brown and black bear, but all except the black have been gone for generations. And only a few remain back in the hills. Likewise, the mountain lion has virtually disappeared from the coastal range. Without these predators, the deer herds have grown more brazen and now filter into inhabited areas in search of food.

Only a few mountain lions remain. On the rare occasion when encountering a mountain lion, there are some basic rules to remember: (1) do not run; (2) do not crouch or make yourself smaller and thus make yourself a more likely prey; (3) do not approach the mountain lion. Maintain eye contact with the animal so that it is aware that you know of its presence. (4) Make noise by yelling or shouting. (5) Make yourself larger by raising your arms or a jacket or sweater over your head. The mountain lion may be only curious and lose interest quickly, but (6) watch its stance closely; a crouching position by the big cat could signal an attack. Arm yourself with a tree branch or club and be prepared to fight.

A black bear is much less likely to attack. Bears will usually avoid human contact unless attracted by the smell of food. Keep all food carefully stowed and out of reach, and this lessens the likelihood of a bear incursion.

Precautions

Town and village walkabouts seldom involve dangers beyond looking both ways and waiting until it's safe to cross a street. There is always a handy place to stop for refreshment or sustenance when tired or thirsty. Emergency services are always close by in case of need. But going hiking, biking or otherwise touring the back country will require some basic preparations.

The presence of wildlife and problem plants like poison oak require caution on the part of hikers and picknickers in some of the Coastside woods and canyons and even the more remote beaches. To make your fun trip safe, here are a few suggestions.

First of all, steer clear of all wild animals. Some may be cute, but they are wild and must survive after you leave their habitat. Give snakes their own space and they will leave you alone. On the rare chance you encounter a rattlesnake or are bitten, do not panic. Snakebites are rarely fatal for healthy adults. Do not rush around. Keep the bitten area below your heart. Use your snakebite kit immediately to remove as much venom as possible and get to a doctor as soon as possible.

When going into the back country where you are away from emergency services. You should carry a first aid kit that contains a snake-bite kit, sewing needle and thread, aspirin, antibacterial ointment, antiseptic swabs, butterfly bandages, adhesive tape, adhesive strips, gauze pads, two triangular bandages, codeine tablets, two inflatable splints, Moleskin or

Second Skin for blisters, 3-inch gauze, CPR shield, rubber gloves, and lightweight first-aid instructions. And you should know how to use all items in the kit.

In addition, you should have a compass, whistle, matches in a waterproof container, cigarette lighter, a small signal mirror and flashlight for emergencies.

Other precautions:

• Check the weather forecast. You would not want to be in the middle of a six-hour hike or bike ride and get hit by a gully washer. It spoils all the fun.

• Avoid traveling alone, stay with your partner or party, don't exhaust yourself or other members of your party by going too far too fast. Let the slowest person set the pace.

• Before you leave, find out as much as you can about the route, especially the potential hazards.

• Don't wait until you're confused to look at your maps. The maps in this guide book are only for planning and general informational purposes. Before starting on a long hike, you should have acquired a map from the agency controlling the park or preserve you plan to use. Follow the map as you go along, from the moment you start moving up the trail, so you have a continual fix on your location.

• If you get lost, don't panic. Sit down and relax for a few minutes while you carefully check your topo map and take a compass reading. Confidently plan your next move. It's often smart to retrace your steps until you find familiar ground, even if you think it might lengthen your trip. Lots of people get temporarily lost in the wilderness and survive—usually by calmly and rationally dealing with the situation.

🐛   Tick Trouble   🐛

When hiking in the back country as well as in some of the parks nearby, ticks can be a serious problem. If you hike in any area where deer are apt to have traveled, it is best to take some basic precautions such as wearing long pants tucked into shoe tops. If the weather makes this too uncomfortable, be prepared to remove the little bloodsuckers as soon as possible. Lyme disease, while not as prevalent here as in parts of the northeastern United States can be a problem. It is prudent to treat the potential disease carrier cautiously.

If you find a tick has attached itself to your skin, remove

it as soon as you have the tools to do so. Studies by the Center for Disease Control have shown that it takes 36 to 48 hours for a tick to transmit an infection. The less the tick feeds on you, the less chance for getting an infection.

First, the don'ts: Don't follow the old folklore advice of using a match or petroleum jelly or you may stir the beastie to regurgitate all its poisons at once. For the same reason, don't twist or jerk it around either.

Do shield your fingers with a tissue, paper towel or rubber glove as you use a fine pointed pair of tweezers for the removal. Grab the tick as closely as possible to the skin surface and pull slowly and firmly until it is removed, taking care not to crush the insect. Once removed, place the tick in a sealed plastic bag and keep it in your refrigerator in case the doctor wants to test it for presence of disease germs.

If you are unable to remove the tick whole, make certain all of its parts are removed from your skin. Disinfect the bite area thoroughly. Wash your hands with soap and water. If infection occurs in the wound, consult your physician.

All of the precautions outlined here are suggested so that your hiking experience is a pleasant one.

PART IV

THE DISCOVERY HIKES

This is one of three Coastside trails to the Discovery Site.

Seeing San Francisco Bay almost as dramatically as the first Europeans saw it more than 230 years ago is a great way to pump more fun into an otherwise routinely breathtaking Coastside hike. Following in the footsteps of the Gaspar de Portolá discovery expedition will require considerable imagination, of course, because most of the natural sloughs and estuaries that the explorers saw are now covered with modern changes like San Francisco International Airport, Bayshore Freeway and tens of thousands of dwellings, businesses and industries. If there is a slight haze, just pretend it is caused by campfires from the dozens of Ohlone and Costanoan villages the Spaniards saw that November day in 1769. Hiking to the San Francisco Discovery Site is one outing everyone who loves the outdoors should do at least once.

The official Discovery Site is marked by an imposing piece of granite on Sweeney Ridge (named after one of the historical owners of the hilltop). But keep in mind that it is only an approximation. No one has any more than a vague idea of where Portolá and his men stood when they first saw the bay. We have three versions: one from the leader himself, another from

Miguel Costansó, his engineer, navigator and storekeeper, and another from Father Juan Crespi, the spiritual leader.

Portolá, who did not bother to note his scouts' historic bay sightings until two days later, stated: "We traveled four hours on a very bad road reduced (or eased) by a level canyon part of the way, and stretched before us was a great arm of the sea for 16 to 20 leagues (a league was about three miles in length) that the scouts said was a sheltered port with two islands, we halted without water." A man of few words, he gave no indication of where they were on the ridge.

Costansó was only a bit more detailed in his entry for Nov. 4: "We followed the south shore or beach of San Francisco (they had named their camp after St. Francis) until we entered the mountain range to the northeast. From the summit of this height, we were able to distinguish a magnificent estuary that stretched to the southeast."

Father Crespi, after dutifully reporting they had celebrated San Carlos, whose name was to grace the mission planned at Monterey (when they finally found the place), wrote on Nov. 4: "About one in the afternoon, we set out to continue the journey, following the beach to the north. We entered the mountains, directing our course to the northeast and from the summit of a peak we beheld the great estuary or arm of the sea which must have the width of four or five leagues and extends to the southeast and south southeast." On Nov. 13, the disheartened expedition leaders – not aware they had discovered a hitherto unknown maritime wonder (although not the one they sought) – turned back south still looking for Monterey Bay, which kept eluding them. After enduring a cold, two-day storm, they set out Dec. 9 not far from the very bay they sought but did not recognize, and returned to San Diego.

CAUTION: Hiking to the Discovery Site on a day when fog clings to the ridges is not advisable. A walk in the fog can be a bracing experience, but winds may be stiff on the ridge on foggy days, and when visibility is close to zero, a hiker can easily become disoriented and lost. Besides, you need a clear day to get the full effect of all the sights. And always take a jacket for the chilly ridges.

Discovery Site

There are three ways to directly reach the Discovery Site from the Coastside. We will start with the Baquaino Trail, the one with the least climbing.

This easiest choice has the advantage of eliminating some 600 feet of climbing. It is also the shortest, extending a mere 1.3 miles from the end of Fassler Boulevard.

Getting There
Take Highway One to the Rockaway/Fassler Boulevard signal in Pacifica and turn east up the hill. Follow Fassler all the way to its dead end. There is no signage, nor any off-street parking.

This trail, named after one of Portolá's scouts, is believed to be the final leg of the route taken by the expedition on Discovery Day. It also has the advantage of saving the moment of "Eureka!" until you top the rise, and the bay is spread before you in all its splendor. The other trails are breezier and you get your first look at the bay less dramatic as you see it a long time before arriving at the Discovery Site marker.

Grasslands, rock outcroppings and patches of coastal scrub extend along the trail as it climbs the first 350 feet to the Cattle Hill trail branch to the west. Stay on Baquiano Trail as it curves up the hill to the right. The spectacular ocean and valley views and photographic opportunities are best on a day after rain has cleared away all the haze. In spring, the Discovery hiker is treated to a carpet of yellows and golds of the field mustard, *Brassica campestris,* and lizard tail, *Eriophyllum staechadifolium,* splashed with blues of the silver lupine, *Lupinus albifrons,* and mountain iris, *Iris douglasiana.*

The trail curves around the south side of the mountain and climbs another 245 feet to the crest. And there is what Portolá, Costansó, Crespi and company saw Nov. 4, 1769. Except that the mudflats and estuaries were closer to the hills, and instead of freeways and modern buildings, there was smoke from villages hanging over the land and bayscape.

The trail to the right connects to the south with ones on

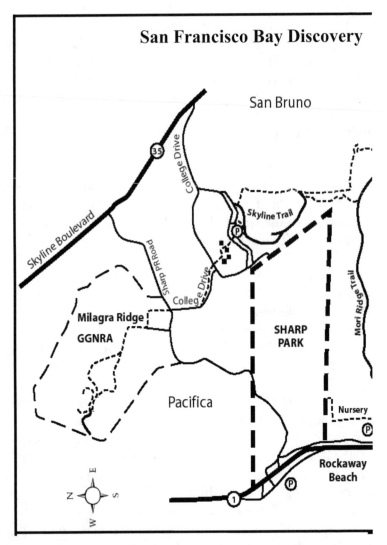

San Francisco Bay Discovery

the San Francisco Water Department's watershed trails but one must have a proper permit to enter.

Mori Ridge

This trail system will give you a workout closer to what the explorers from the Portolá expedition experienced. From their camp alongside today's San Pedro Creek, Portolá sent a group of scouts to see what was over the next ridge. Another group went hunting for meat, which went up a hill much like the one called

Trails Map

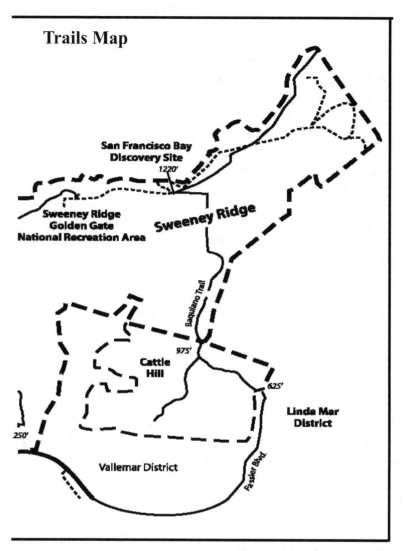

San Francisco Bay
Discovery Site
1220'

Sweeney Ridge
Golden Gate
National Recreation Area

Sweeney Ridge

Baquiano Trail

975'

Cattle
Hill

625'

Linda Mar
District

250'

Vallemar District

Fassler Blvd

the Mori Ridge Trail and returned with exciting news of a vast waterway that they thought natives told them contained a ship (the scouts had misunderstood the Ohlones' sign language and no ship was found).

This trail takes about three-and-a-half hours and is a five-mile round trip that climbs 1,100 feet steeply up the grassy slope of Mori Ridge to matchless views of the coast. Views open out over the Pacific Ocean and northwest to the Farallon Islands, north to Pt. Reyes and Mt. Tamalpais. In the foreground the

Pacifica residential areas contrast with the stark outline of Pedro Point.

The grasslands are bright with flowers in the spring, giving one an excuse to pause in the stiff climb now and then to look more closely and enjoy them more fully. A half hour's hike brings you to scattered old plantings of Monterey pines on an exposed ridge that is often swept by winds and fog.

As you reach the Sweeney Ridge Trail portion of the Bay Area Ridge Trail route, the ridge flattens out and San Francisco comes into view, including the antenna on Sutro Heights and the towers of the Golden Gate Bridge. East are San Bruno Mountain and beyond, the East Bay Hills. At this intersection you bear right (southeast) on the Sweeney Ridge Trail Shortly, you skirt an old Nike missile site with blocky cement buildings and battered fences. The trail continues for a mile on a paved, level road leading to the Discovery Site.

Up on the gentler slope, the brome grass, *Bromus ssp.,* and foothill sedge, *Carex tumulicola,* grasses give way to low bushes. Springtime on the ridge is a riot of white patched with blue of the iris the Indians found useful; by twisting the leaves just right, they had surprisingly strong rope and devised slingshots for hunting small game. There are also the scarlets and yellow of Indian paintbrush, *Castileja spp.;* the golden yarrow, *Eriophyllum staechadifolium,* that blossoms until November; and daisies in yellow, lavender and white; and lots of blooming shrubs. Be careful of the ever-present poison oak; it is red and rose by the end of summer.

Getting There

To reach the Mori Ridge trailhead, go north on Highway One in Pacifica, pass Reina del Mar Avenue signal. Watch for the "Orchids" sign and turn abruptly right into Shell Dance Nursery; continue past the nursery buildings to parking at end of dirt road; going south on Highway One in Pacifica, make a U-turn at Reina del Mar Avenue and go north.

The expedition did not remain long on the ridge to marvel at the view. Disturbed at being so far off course in their exploration, the group descended into the valley that today is flooded by a succession of reservoirs holding the water supply for San Francisco and cities along the San Francisco Peninsula.

Skyline College Route

This 3.6-mile route starts from Skyline College's parking lot Number Two near a pine tree in the back corner. There is a short climb, then a 300-foot drop and a climb out of "The Notch."

After a mile, you join the Mori Ridge Trail as it swings east along the ridge that can be windy and chilly even in sunny weather. You pass the Nike missile site and it is another half mile to the Discovery Site where the Baquiano Trail is met.

A spring-fed marsh and a small reed-rimmed pond is reached at a split in the trail. The route goes left of the marsh and on to the southeast corner of the preserve, where a gate for equestrians (permits required) leads into the San Francisco Watershed. The trail going right at the marsh is an equestrian trail that takes off steeply downhill to stables at the end of Linda Mar Valley.

Getting There: Take Highway One to Sharp Park Drive and turn east up the hill to College Drive signal. Turn right to Skyline College. Turn left to Milagra Ridge.

Milgra Ridge

Milagra Ridge may or may not have been one of the explorers' vantage points, because none of the advance scouts who first saw the Bay kept any log or diaries. From the Milagra Ridge site on a clear day, one can see all the way to where Sir Francis Drake careened one of his ships for repairs in 1579 behind Point Reyes, and all the way to the Farrallon Islands. This hilltop is at the northern end of the long ridge and may well have been used by the scouts. Thorough scouts would have ranged in all directions. We will ever know for certain.

The advantage of the Milagra Site is that it is a leisurely stroll from the parking lot, handy for the less vigorous who still want to enjoy the sights.

Portolá scouts, if they did range this far, probably saw only San Bruno Mountain's raw knob and some of the sand hills of what became the San Francisco Presidio and Mission Dolores.

Taste The Challenge

To re-live what the Portolá expedition experienced, purists may want to test themselves by climbing San Pedro Mountain just as the explorers did on the days leading to discovery of San Francisco Bay. It was late October of 1769. They had been searching in vain for Monterey Bay for months, having left San Diego in July. It has been raining off and on for several weeks. A storm kept them stalled alongside today's Martini Creek. Rations were down to five flour and bran tortillas a day per person and they were thinking of killing one of their mules so the could have meat, but even this was reserved to those ill with scurvy. On top of all these troubles, Portolá himself took ill.   But finally on Oct. 30, the weather cleared and they started out again only to be stalled by high water in the creek and it was almost mid-day of the 31st before they were able to follow a trail made by their *gastadores,* the foot soldiers and grubbers who cleared the undergrowth and heavy rocks for the rest to follow.

After climbing "a very bad road on a very high mountain," wrote Portolá in his journal, they were met by 25 *gentiles,* as he called the natives. From the summit, the explorers finally realized they had travelled too far north. They could see Point Reyes and the harbor now called Drakes Bay, but called San Francisco Bay on Spanish maps of the time. They could see the mouth of what they thought was only an estuary, but would prove to be today's San Francisco Bay. And far offshore they could see the Farallon Islands glistening white with centuries accumulation of bird guana.   After checking their maps, they ruefully decided that they had missed Monterey Bay and were far to the north of their goal. So they went down the north side of the mountain and camped alongside San Pedro Creek near the beach to rest and recuperate for four days. While the others rested, scouts climbed the tall ridge to the east and returned with news of the vast mudflats and estuary on the other side.

McNee Ranch State Park

The trail requires about 3.5 hours round trip and the distance up to the saddle of and back is 6.4 miles. The climb is about 800 feet and leads to connecting trails to Montara Mountain, the ridge trail and another down to San Pedro Valley, treks for the more adventurous. The rugged slopes reach an elevation of 1,500 feet near Montara Mountain's peaks. In addition to being the trail followed by Portolá's party in 1769, it was the route of early wagon roads between coastal ranches. In the 20th century, it was called Old Pedro Mountain Road and carried automobiles until it was abandoned for one carved out on the Devil's Slide route. With Devil's Slide actually sliding slowly down toward the Pacific, plans are in the works for a tunnel through the mountain for Highway One traffic, plans that would not disturb hiking trails on top.

Getting There:
Take Highway One past Montara. An entrance gate on the east side of the highway just north of Montara State Beach leads into park. There is ample parking at beach, on west side of highway. Cross with care.

Follow the cypress-lined trail for a half-mile, then take a left on Old Road, which is less steep than the service road, and therefore much easier for foot and bicycle travel. After about a mile, the trail intersects the North Peak Access Road, and the hiker one can continue upward on it.

From this split in the trail, the vista becomes magnificent. Below are farm fields planted sometimes with artichokes and cabbage, and other times with flowers on the far side of Martini Creek. Montara Peak towers ahead, challenging you with chaparral and wild grasses. The sands of Montara State Beach stretch to the south. Stay to the left for Old Road.

Old Pedro Mountain Road winds around the mountain, jogs left at the Saddle Pass, and continues to a gate marking the park's boundary. From the gate Old Road passes through private property and down to San Pedro Valley. Stay to the right for the trek up Montara Peak. Go another half-mile and the steep North Peak Access Road turns to the right up the mountain to communications installations on its peaks, the route of another trip in the park. For details on this, we go on a trip of discovery to San Pedro Valley County Park.

San Pedro Valley County Park
Jurisdiction: San Mateo County—650-363-4020

Getting There:
Take Highway One to the Linda Mar signal and turn east. Go to end of Linda Mar and turn right to park entrance. A small museum is in Visitor Center.

The park contains 1,050 acres in the narrow valley at the end of Linda Mar Boulevard in Pacifica. It contains trails along San Pedro Creek's middle fork and the steep ridges draining the south fork. The forks are of particular significance because they provide some of the few remaining spawning areas for migratory Steelhead in the county. The Steelhead spawning season is normally from December to February. During the rainy, winter months, a special attraction is the beautiful Brooks Falls, which has a drop of 175 feet in three tiers.

Wildlife is abundant at San Pedro Valley. Park inhabitants often seen are red-tailed Hawks, Turkey Vultures, Quail, Scrub Jays, and Garter Snakes. Those observed less frequently include Deer, Bobcats, Grey Fox, Raccoons, Rabbits and Gopher Snakes.

San Pedro Valley has a significant place in early Bay Area history as the site of Indian villages and although Gaspar de Portolá's camp was closer to the beach, his scouts undoubtedly climbed trails through parkland to the ridges for their first view of San Francisco Bay. There was an early outpost for Mission Dolores in this valley, as was the adobe home of Francisco Sanchez, still standing and now a San Mateo County museum.

The park trails offer a choice between easy, level strolls and some very vigorous climbs to the ridges above the valley. The creeks, which are still spawning grounds for the steelhead trout that migrate upstream to the park each winter, also furnish a substantial part of Pacifica's water supply.

Before setting off on one of the trails, obtain a map of the trails from the Visitor Center.

Facilities: Visitor center, picnic tables and barbecues for families and groups; trails for hikers; self-guiding nature trail, wheelchair accessible. Wheelchairs for day use offered free.

Rules: Open 8 A.M. to dusk; bicycles permitted on Weiler Road only; No dogs; $4 per car fee.

South Fork of San Pedro Creek to the Old Trout Farm

This eight-tenths of a mile loop is a leisurely stroll on relatively level ground that takes no more than a half hour. It follows along the creeks past the Old Trout Farm that was wiped out in a flood in the 1962, marked now by the tanks that were once part of the fishery. Under overhanging trees by the rippling creek, the trail continues for just under a mile. Turn back when you will, or find the Brooks Falls Overlook Trail, where stone steps start up the hillside, and follow that trail back to the picnic grounds.

North Ridge Loop

This is another of the shorter trips for people with only an hour to spare, but who want to get their heart pumping a bit with a climb some 600 feet up the west-facing slope on the Valley View Trail. The trail then drops again to join Weiler Ranch Road farther up the valley. The trek starts by crossing the creek on a bridge from the main parking lot to the left of the Visitor Center. Continue past the group picnic area under the walnut trees. Turn right on Weiler Ranch Road, then almost immediately veer left on the Valley View Trail, which takes off uphill.

There are two picnic tables between the beginning and the end of the Valley View Trail. The Valley View Trail climbs a slope that can be pleasantly sunny and welcome in cool weather. The view to the south takes in Montara Mountain. From the ridgetop, easy switchbacks bring you down to Weiler Ranch Road. For a longer walk you can follow this easy road to the upper end of the valley, where hills rise steeply to Sweeney Ridge a thousand feet above.

Brooks Creek/ Montara Mountain Trails Loop

This is a bit more vigorous, a 2.4-mile loop requiring about an hour-and-a-quarter and involves climbs of some 460 feet.

The hikers-only trail begins beside the restrooms at the picnic area west of the Visitor Center and will take you slowly up the hillside under tall pines, occasional redwoods, and many eucalyptus. When you leave the forest and get out into the chaparral the views across the canyon open up. You will hear the water tumbling down the canyon before you see the falls.

Across the misty, forested canyon there are splendid views of the ocean and the flanks of Montara Mountain. Turn right (east) on this trail and steadily descend around bends and turns to the floor of the park.

South Ridge Loop Trip

This is a three-hour, 800-foot climb up the high ridge on the Hazelnut Trail, covering 4.3 miles by the time one returns on a west-facing slope to the Visitor Center.

One takes the Weiler Ranch Road about a mile up the valley before crossing a bridge over the creek. Follow the trail to the head of the valley, where the Hazelnut turns to the right. It makes a wide swing west, then continues on switchbacks up the canyon wall. After a wide swing east, you zig and then zag up a ridge, gaining 400 feet in elevation.

At the highest point on the trail, there is a gentler grade in tall chaparral of coffeeberry, *Rhamnus californica,*with berries that are edible when they blacken; Montara manzanita, *Arctostaphylos andersonii imbricati*, with its tasty little apples; wild lilac, *Ceonothus thrysiflorus*; and scrub oak, *Quercus dumosa*, and soon one reaches the high saddle between San Pedro Creek's middle and south forks. A huge eucalyptus grove dominates the northwest end of the flat just before the steep grade downhill. The trail then doubles back and forth through a thicket of hazelnut, *Corylus cornuta californica*, the shrub that gives it its name. At the foot of the hillside and across a little meadow behind the Visitor Center, the trail ends.

Montara Mountain Trail

Still more vigorous and time-consuming, this trail leads up the park's ridge for dramatic ocean views. The five-mile round trip requires a 1,400-foot climb and a bit more than three hours and is recommended only for intermediate and above hikers in relatively healthy condition.

PART V
DRIVING TOURS
Coastal Scenic Tour

This is the "must" tour for anyone who loves marine views and wide-open spaces that are a balm to the soul. Driving time can range from one hour to two hours, but figure on adding another hour for stopovers along the way. The soothing quality of the seashore combines magically with sweeping mountain vistas.

Head south on Highway One past the broad expanse that was once part of the original settlement by Candelario Miramontes, a San Francisco Presidio soldier who was given the 4,436-acre land grant of Rancho Arroyo de los Pilarcitos in 1841. He and his wife and 13 children and a neighbor developed the village called San Benito, then Spanishtown and, in the late 1850's Half Moon Bay, the first community on the San Mateo peninsula. Southward, the highway passes Miramontes Point Road and the tour enters the rural landscape that extends all the way to Santa Cruz; our tour takes up only the first 20 miles.

Just past Miramontes Point Road, the roadway dips down through Arroyo Cañada Verde and climbs again onto the bench land where farm crops extend on both sides of the road. A half-mile south of Miramontes Road, watch for a small parking lot on the right for Cowell Beach, named for a banker who obtained the land around it through an 1890 foreclosure of a restaurant owner who had the misfortune to expand during an economic downturn. There is a short half-mile walk to the beach itself. There is a promontory with interpretive signage and a restroom. One can view seals lolling on the beach to the south of the promontory, an area off limits to human visitors. To the north, a stairway leads down to the beach. Tucked up against the tall cliffs, it is one of the more protected of the coast's beaches.

THE LOST VILLAGE OF PURISIMA: Southward on Highway One, you pass Verde Road as it enters from the left; on the southeast corner, there is a large grove of Monterey cypress where the village of Purisima once stood. A large hotel, blacksmith and shops were here until the demise of the railroad. All that remains are the foundation stones of a 17-room mansion

*Kurt Doebbel's 17-room mansion with his
new plantings of Monterey cypress across the road from Purisima
Village and his businesses.*

owned by the wealthy restaurateur who lost his mansion and ranch
to Cowell. Verde Road loops around for some two miles at the
base of the hills and then returns to the Highway.

On your left is an excellent produce stand and Christmas
tree farm where you may want to stop on the return part of the
trip. Off to the west one can see the towers of the marine radio
station KFS, part of the communications system for ships at sea.
On the left as the highway curves around to the right, a pumpkin
farm sits along the banks of Lobitos Creek. A small village called
Lobitos once sat in that draw a bit upstream from the farm, but
disappeared a few years after the railroad. On the right, a sign
indicates Martin's Beach, a turnoff to a secluded beach.

TUNITAS CREEK DISASTERS: The roadway climbs
slightly up and around the headland before heading downhill to
the Tunitas Creek crossing. This small waterway has a history of
failed dreams. Upstream on the Tunitas watershed, several logging companies sought ways to get lumber to San Francisco in
the mid 1800's. One ill-fated solution was to build a chute along
the south-facing cliff on the north side of Tunitas Creek. The

*An 1878 view of Purisima Village
four miles south of Half Moon Bay along Purisima Creek;
all that remains are some of the trees now grown tall.*

chute's designer hoped to use the structure to send the lumber to small schooners anchored at the mouth of the creek. The chute was built, but a winter storm with strong southerly winds tore it down and washed it out to sea. Railroad promoters more than 50 years later went so far as to build a trestle across Tunitas Creek to show investors they were serious about extending the rail line south as far as Santa Cruz, but an economic downturn kept them from mounting rails on the trestle and it was torn down.

    The highway climbs a long hill and drops down to the

This stand between Half Moon Bay and Lobitos Creek is one of the more popular produce stops along the Coastal Highway.

deep arroyo of San Gregorio Creek. There is a nice state beach on the right. State Highway 84 (La Honda Road) goes east from here, too. The village of San Gregorio, now only one store and several private residences, is about a half-mile east, but we will visit this bit of time warp on the return trip.

VALLE DE LOS CURSOS: The Portolá expedition spent three days in this canyon in October of 1769 during the march north that led to their discovery of San Francisco Bay. They camped near a village of Ohlone that sat on the northern bank of the creek. Miguel Costansó, the expedition's navigator, noted in his journal that "the land seemed rich and of good quality; the watering places were frequent and the natives of the best disposition and temper that we had seen." The Ohlone village stood in the midst of a burned off area above the creek. But the Spaniards dubbed it the Valle de los Cursos, because one of their leaders had such a bad bout of diarrhea they had to spend an extra day here to allow him to recover. When the expedition passed through here again on their way south three weeks later, the winter rains had begun and the Ohlone had abandoned the village, presumably to return to their winter quarters east of the coastal mountains.

Highway One climbs out of the valley along the cliffs before heading back downhill to Pomponio Creek and another state beach followed by a longer climb up to a crest above the ocean. At the crest of the bench, there is a view to the south along Pescadero Beach, one of the most fabulous along this stretch of coast. On the left is Pescadero Marsh, a bird lovers' paradise. The parking lot for the marsh is on the right just after crossing the bridge over Pescadero Creek. If you happen to be taking the tour during the spring or fall when birds are migrating, this is a good place to stretch your legs and watch the avian wildlife. The trail passes under the road and out to the edge of the marsh for some excellent views. Have your binoculars and camera at hand for the best sights

Highway One follows the edge of the ocean for another two miles to Bean Hollow Beach where restrooms are available. A large nursery operation is on the left just past Bean Hollow

Pescadero Marsh, nature's avian and marine nursery.

Reservoir. Just beyond the nusery is a sweep of open space that is part of a 1,719-acre acqusition by the Peninsula Open Space Trust; they bid $39 million, topping luxury home developers for the land that links with the group's Cloverdale Coast Ranch buy that is four times as large and extends to Gazos Creek. On the right are a few scattered homes on the beach, most of which were built before coastal protection regulations were imposed.

PIGEON POINT: Some three miles past Bean Hollow is Pigeon Point Lighthouse, named for a schooner, the Carrier Pigeon, that went on the rocks there in 1859. A hostel there is run by Hostelling International - American Youth Hostels and California State Parks, in cooperation with the U.S. Coast Guard. The point has seen many changes since the 1800's when Portugese immigrants operated a whaling station for more than 20 years. A schooner loading facility for shipping lumber and farm produce also ran here before and after the lighthouse was established in 1872. The Peninsula Open Space Trust acquired Whaler's Cove just south of the lighthouse in 2000, blocking a motel project there. Plans are to turn it over to the state for park use. More details on the lighthouse can be found in Part IX of this guide.

Highway One continues south. On the right around the long curve is another farm produce stand open seasonally, and on the left the remains of Campbell Soup's mushroom farm and processing plant. The road swings inland and as the roadway rises just past Gazos Creek, one can see just the tops of the posh camp at Coastanoan at Cascade Ranch. It's so posh that they furnish down comforters in their 88 deluxe tent cabins. If you want to rough it, there are 47 "standard" tent cabins. Or even stay in the lodge portion of the 480-acre enclave.

On the coast side of the highway is the Año Nuevo Reserve, vast sand dunes with lots of trails. Details can be found in Part IX of this guide. The main entrance to the preserve is on the right seven miles south of Pigeon Point.

Two miles further south you will reach Waddell Beach, where on most days from spring through the fall, one can witness some spectacular athleticism by wind and parachute surfers. The area is named for William Waddell, an early lumberman who logged redwoods and firs along the creek that bears his name.

It's only 144 steps to the top of Pigeon Point Lighthouse.

He built a railroad beneath the sheer cliff to transport his lumber to a wharf he built in the lee of the point. The railroad and wharf were torn down years ago.

OFF THE BEATEN TRACK: For the return trip -- after you have relaxed a bit -- turn back north on Highway One. If you are pressed for time, you can retrace your route on Highway One and take in the sights you missed on the way down. The drive never grows stale. But for variety, we suggest an inland swing to get the complete taste of the Coastside; the inland valleys and canyons add a distinct flavor you should not miss.

Past the pick-your-own blackberry patch and the Christmas tree farm, you pass Cascade Ranch, once one of the main coastside dairies and now part of a preserve. The Steele brothers ran one of the first dairies on that property. And one of the family's third generation, Charles, was the first motorcycle patrolman on the Coast Road when it was still just a dirt track. As you pass the grove of eucalyptus trees that hides the Coastanoan at Cascade Ranch, the road drops a bit into the Gazos Creek basin. Slow down and turn east onto Gazos Creek Road. The twisting roadway was originally cleared by Chinese laborers on a path just wide enough for a team and wagons to haul lumber from mills further inland. Now the two-lane, still narrow but a paved road follows the riparian vegetation of alders and willows. Follow the creek for about a mile-and-a-half before reaching a fork where the main pavement turns sharply north. Two sawmills were set up inland another mile or so and worked until 1918. Turn onto Cloverdale Road as it climbs out of the creek's basin and over the hill. All of the land on the left is the Cloverdale Coastal Ranch acquired by the Peninsula Open Space Trust. After about a half-mile, you will pass the entrance to Butano State Park, where you can picnic or hike to your heart's content. More details on Butano State Park can be found in Part VII of this guide. The open space trust donated 905 acres to the state at the entrance to Butano Park in mid-2000. When plans for the ranch are completed, it is anticipated that trails will extend from Pigeon Point and Bean Hollow Beach into Butano Park.

Continue on Cloverdale Road through farm country past plant nurseries that flourish back in the lee of the hill that was

Cycling eastward on Stage Road
in Pescader is a popular weekend pastime.

raised eons ago by seismic activity along the San Gregorio Fault
which rises out of Monterey Bay and runs north-northeast through
here. The road follows along the basin of Butano Creek for a
couple of miles before reaching Pescadero Creek Road just after
passing Pescadero High School on the right. A right turn will
take you into the redwoods and three county parks and finally
out to Highway 84 at La Honda.

PESCADERO DISCOVERY: For this tour, turn west
for the short trip into the village of Pescadero. This village settled
in the late 1800's by people from Italy, Portugal and the Azores is
a great place to stretch your legs and enter another time warp.
Here you have your choice of a couple of good deli grocers or
Duarte's Restaurant's famous artichoke soup and fresh berry pies.
The main village street is called Stage Road. (See Part VIII of
this guide for details of the village.) After your walkabout and
snack, drive north on this paved, two-lane road past the cemetery
and through the arbor of ancient eucalyptus that leads to an old
ranch house where the road turns sharply west. Make a slow turn
so you do not miss seeing the giant sculpted Road Warrior figure

behind the tree in front of the ranch house. The road climbs its winding way through the sand hills.

You are following the little -changed (the pavement is the major one, of course) road that was used by stagecoaches running between Pescadero and Half Moon Bay right up into the early 20th century. That large metal barn on the left below the roadway is a more modern artifact, left over from a short-lived Hewlett-Packard experiment that went nowhere. The road climbs to the top of another hill and heads downward again to the arroyo cut by Pomponio Creek. Pomponio Creek Road goes to the east as Stage Road crosses the creek. Up though the old grove of eucalyptus trees the road climbs to the crest of a hill with a view of the Pacific Ocean, then a slow series of curves down to San Gregorio Creek. About the only traffic on this road comes from the few ranches along the way an occasional adventurer like you.

SAN GREGORIO STAGE STOP: Across the creek and up the short grade, you pass on the left what remains of the old San Gregorio Hotel (vintage 1866). The old service station, also now converted into private residences, started life as a bar. If you are in the mood for strawberries that taste like strawberries, take a right on La Honda Road and go about a tenth of a mile. Stop at the old brown barn where you will find berries to make the taste buds salivate. Go back down La Honda Road, stop at Stage Road and turn right into the San Gregorio General Store. Weekends the place is packed, sometimes for music sessions and other times just for people stopping and chatting at the bar, having a sandwich or browsing through the used and new books and collection of hats and casual clothing.

Continue north on Stage Road about a mile to its connection with Highway One, where you turn right and go down the hill to Tunitas Creek. Just past the bridge, turn right (east) on Tunitas Creek Road and you are back off the beaten track. The road goes past several small ranch houses and barns into open country. Just past a house tucked in a grove of ancient eucalyptus trees, the road crosses the creek. Watch on the left for the intersection with Lobitos Creek Cutoff. Turn left on the cutoff road. It turns back west and then heads slowly northward through brush country and rises past a small ranch and over the hill and downward toward Lobitos Creek. At the bottom of the hill, take the right fork as its goes past Lucy Lane and up the hill.

Verde Road reaches a fork where one branch returns to Highway One and the other goes to the right along the base of the foothills. The view to the west is of farmland reaching down to the ocean. On the right are entrances to a couple of residences perched on the hills above. One of the steel gates leads to what remains of a couple of old oil wells, the only ones to produce appreciable amounts of crude oil. In the early 1920's, a small oil boomlet had drilling rigs all along the coast, but thankfully (for those of us loving clean air and unspoiled vistas) very little of commercial quantities was found. Where Verde Road turns sharply west, you should turn east; this is the connection with Purisima Road. Up the short grade, the road tops a rise above rich farmland on broad shelves along Purisima Creek.

This area was part of Rancho Cañada Verde y Arroyo de

San Gregorio General Store, another popular Coastside tradition that nurtures its links with the past.

la Purissima that was granted in 1839 to Jose Maria Alviso, a Mexican Army lieutenant in Monterey. The influx of European immigrants during and after the Gold Rush brought farmers who tilled the rich bottomlands, raising hay and wheat in the early years. Some ran dairy herds and raised pigs.

The roadway is narrow and dips and rises with the terrain. Ahead rise the steep slopes of the Santa Cruz Mountains. To the north and south the sand hills – green in winter and spring and burnt a pale yellow in summer and fall – slope up sharply.

Some four miles from the Highway One turnoff, the road veers almost in a U-turn and starts uphill. At this curve is the parking lot for the lower entrance to Purisima Redwoods Open Space Preserve, a system of trails that extend to the Skyline. (Details on the preserve can be found in Part VII of this guide).

The steep grade on the road (the name changes here to Higgins-Purisima Road) extends for a mile, twisting and turning on a narrow road bed past driveways to four homes. Upon reaching the top, one has a great view to the south, west and north. It is all downhill for the next 2.5 miles. But use extreme caution, because the switchbacks are tight and there is barely room for two cars to pass.

Near the bottom on the right is the entrance to the Burleigh H. Murray State Park. The trail is a dirt ranch road that follows Mills Creek east southeast into the foothills. Robert Mills, an Englishman who had worked in San Francisco as a glazier, took his earnings, bought 1,000 acres and set up a dairy farm back in one corner of the canyon in 1862, one of the first dairies on the peninsula. (Details on this park can be found in Part IX).

Head west again on Higgins-Purisima Road past a cluster of homes along Arroyo Leon Creek and out into the flat.

This is farming land that was once part of the 4,424-acre Rancho Arroyo de los Pilarcitos granted in 1841 to Candelario Miramontes, a soldier at San Francisco Presidio. Miramontes' family later sold a part of the rancho to James and William Johnston, two brothers from Ohio who farmed the land, slowly adding to their holding until they owned nearly all of the southern half of the Miramontes rancho. The first years were tough ones; most of the calf crop was lost to grizzly bears. James Johnston built the white saltbox house that sits on the left just south of Purisima Road on the edge of a field. The house was

*James Johnston built his saltbox house before any loggers
started cutting redwoods; he floated lumber from a schooner offshore
to build one of the first non-adobe buildings on the coast.*

restored by the Johnston Foundation but is not open to the public despite several attempts to arrange public access.

Just a short distance past the Johnston House, you reach Highway One. Turn right and return to your starting point; it has been 60 miles of seashore, valley and mountain scenery.

From the Seashore to the Redwoods & Back

This two-hour motor tour (add another hour or so for stopovers) is one that will give you an understanding of why northern Californians' love affair with their cars is not likely to wane any time soon. We will go from the seashore deep into the redwood, madrone and oak forests and emerge back at the edge of the Pacific Ocean. The scenery and ambiance is so overwhelming you will want to go back over the 70-mile route again very soon.

As with all the tours, we start from the corner of Highway 92 and the Coast Highway and head south. After the Miramontes Point Road traffic signal, the scenery turns rural. In spring, the hillsides to the east are bright green, but in summer and fall the color is drab, contrasting dramatically with the deep greens of the farms that border the highway. An excellent produce stand run by a local farmer is on the left. The large grove of Monterey cypress on both sides of the highway at Verde Road mark the once thriving village of Purisima, a town that had its own hotel and even a 17-room mansion. The 1922 demise of the railroad that went from San Francisco to Tunitas Creek spelled the end of the village. The mansion owner lost his ranch and home to foreclosure by the bank. A little further along on the left, hidden among the cypress and eucalyptus trees is the remainder of another village; this was called Lobitos (Spanish for "little wolves") after the creek that passes through. On the right are the antenna of Marine Radio Station KFS, part of the maritime communications system. And next on the right is the turn-off to Martin's Beach, a private beach open to the public for a fee. Around the point and down the short grade, the highway crosses Tunitas Creek, the final stop on the ill-fated seashore railroad. All traces of the railroad are gone.

SAINT GREGORY OR A CURSE: Up the grade and over the next hill, you come to the intersection with Stage Road and the scenery is almost alpine in its beauty. The wide valley of San Gregorio Creek hardly seems to fit the name – Valle de los Cursos – that was tacked on by the first Spaniards who passed this way. This was the label applied by the soldiers of the expedition of Don Gaspar de Portolá, who spent three days camped alongside an Ohlone village here in October of 1769. These were two hungry days longer than they wanted, because one of their leaders was so ill with diarrhea. Suffering from low food supplies, he and others in the party had tried to eat acorns raw without processing them the way the natives did. Not until they reached the next village near today's Half Moon Bay did their digestive tracts clear up, thanks to the generous aid from the natives there. The name that lasted was San Gregorio; the expedition's spiritual leader, Fr. Juan Crespi, named the creek and valley after Gregory I, who launched the Catholic Church on its drive to Christianize the Anglo-Saxon tribes in the 6th Century. At the bottom of the hill, there is a fine state beach that is popular with gatherers of driftwood, but you turn east on La Honda Road (State Highway 84), which runs along above the creek.

Just under a mile up the road, you reach Stage Road again, which was once the center of another bustling coastside village. On the right is what was once one of two fine hotels and remains of an automotive service station. On the left, is a large stucco building that houses the only commercial enterprise still running – the San Gregorio General Store. Almost always packed on weekends when music groups are featured, it is more fun during slower weekdays when you can browse undisturbed amongst great book and clothing selections. Drinks and snacks are available, too. As you continue east on La Honda Road, go light on the gas pedal. Someone in the car may be in the mood for fresh, unsprayed strawberries sold in the old barn on the right below the road.

BOOTLEGGERS & ACID TRIPS: The next seven miles eastward passes fields of strawberries, flowers and small horse ranches. Then La Honda Road dips into the redwoods. The road was originally built in 1868 as a toll road to accommodate sawmill owners trying to get their lumber to market. Then it was a farm road. During Prohibition it became a handy thoroughfare for rumrunners. Small boats brought the illegal liquor onto San Gregorio beach. Local men would be paid $25 a night – a healthy wage in the 1920's – to slide the stuff up the beach on sleds and load it aboard trucks. According to Clifford James Walker's definitive book on the California bootlegging years, *One Eye Closed, the Other Red,* one of the key stops along the road was the one run by Apple Jack Gabrielli right in the middle of La Honda Village. Moonshine whiskey was brought in from area stills, too. Apple Jacks is still a very popular place. La Honda is also infamous for another scofflaw – Ken Kesey, the writer. He and his friends spent several months here in the 1960's under the watchful eyes of local narcotics operatives before launching his Merry Prankster expedition (chronicled in Tom Wolfe's *The Electric Kool-Aid Acid Test*). The shopping center just up the hill and across the highway from Apple Jack's has a Merry Prankster Café, a low-key memorial to Kesey's cross-country escapade.

The highway starts its serious climbing just beyond La Honda. The twists and turns will keep the speed down until the curves become longer as the road emerges into the open. This area was heavily logged with the first mill dating from 1853 and some operating a few years into the 20th century. Just as the road

*Munching away in the sun is fun in the redwoods
at Alice's in Skylonda.*

straightens out a bit, Woodruff Creek enters from the right (south). A sawmill operated along that creek from 1898 to 1901, then a grand hotel called the Woodruff Inn was built on the site to accommodate parties from the bayside who came sightseeing and to pick huckleberries in the fall. The hotel is gone now; an illegal liquor still in the hotel blew up in 1923 and the place burned down. A total of eight sawmills operated off and on for some 50 years along La Honda Creek. The second growth forest has only come back in the upper reaches as you near Skyline Boulevard (State Highway 35).

CYCLISTS & OTHER SPEED DEMONS: Skylonda is the little village at the intersection, a popular gathering place for the young motorcycle crowd; on weekends, the cycles are packed into every available parking space. Alice's Restaurant (no relation to the song of the same name) on the northwest corner is popular for breakfast and lunch. Across Skyline, the Four Corners Restaurant and Skyline Trading Post compete to feed the visitors. Cyclists and some sports car buffs once gravitated to Skyline, drawn by some ingrained challenge to test their machines against the curves along the ridgeline, but serious enforcement by the California Highway Patrol brought them under control. Weekdays, however, is still the best time to tour these roads.

Turn right (south) on Skyline Boulevard and go up the hill.

Two miles south, you top the rise called Windy Hill with fantastic views of the South Bay to the east and the Pacific Coast to the west. On clear winter days, you can see all the way to the Sierras. Another 2.5 miles and on the left you will see the entrance to the Fogarty Winery. Across the highway on the right is a great place to buy native California plants – the Yerba Buena Nursery that is open daily. Another two miles further on Skyline, you will see on the right the first entrance to Russian Ridge Open Space Preserve (For more details see Part VII). The southern entrance is around the corner on Alpine Road, another mile down Skyline. Turn right (west) on Alpine Road.

INTO THE REDWOODS VIA OAK & MADRONE ARBORS: This next section of the tour will give the driver a real workout. The roadway is little more than an old wagon track with a thin layer of tar over the top. It twists and turns on such sharp curves that 15 to 20 mile per hour speeds are all that are comfortable. The payoff is the setting, picture-perfect California in every sense. The first mile is through a dense canopy of canyon oaks. A short open break and then go through another series of canopies for another mile before you round a corner that takes your breath away. You seem perched on an eagle's aerie with nothing substantial under you as the coastline stretches away to the northwest. You just automatically stop for a second (hopefully not in the middle of the road) before easing on down the hill where a view opens up to the south. The massive upthrust of Empire Grade looms there. And miles across the chasm to the west another branch of the Santa Cruz range runs north and south only slightly lower than you.

Travel another mile and you come to the fork in the road where the Portola Redwoods State Park entrance way goes to the left and Alpine Road continues to the right. Stay on Alpine Road. You enter another canopy this time one that includes madrone and Monterey cypress with the oaks. Through the trees for a half-mile, there is another left fork. This one goes to Pescadero Creek County Park (For more details see Part VII of this guide) and San Mateo County's Jail Farm. On the right is Buffalo Valley. Continue on Alpine Road as it goes to the right. You are entering an area where more private homes and small ranches are located, and slowly descending to the area where loggers found it more difficult to extract the big trees. Two more slow, twisting miles and you reach the Memorial Grove addition to Sam McDonald County Park. These towering redwoods silence the rest of the world. There are two places to park and rest from all the twisting and turning. Stop and enjoy these ancient giants. Another 1.5 miles through the big trees and you reach another fork in the road. Take the left fork as the road climbs out of the creek basin past the entrance to Sam McDonald County Park. (For more information, see Part VII of this guide.) The road climbs over the ridge into thePescadero Creek drainage.

MEMORIAL TO BRAVERY: The road here is wider and much smoother than Alpine Road as it take a long curving way downhill for three miles. These upper ridges were logged clean years ago. The trees lower down are all later growth. Not until you reach the entrance to Memorial County Park on the left do you reach more giant redwoods. (More details are in Part VII of this guide.) The park was acquired during the 1940's after loggers talked about cutting the rest of the old growth. Despite criticism that the $225 an acre price for the land was too high, the San Mateo County Board of Supervisors approved purchase of the first portion of the park and dedicated it to the memory of fallen soldiers of World War I.

The road follows the creek through the redwoods for more than a mile. Be on the lookout for one-lane sections of the road. Heavy rains sometimes cause parts of the roadbed to slide into the creek, and the one-lane system requires stop signs on each side of the slide. As the canyon widens out, you leave the redwoods and pass small truck farms along the benchland above the creek. As the road reaches the flatland, there is a huge nursery operation on the left, the Pescadero High School and then Cloverdale Road intersection on the left. Continue west on Pescadero Creek Road. As you near the village, there is a large goat farm on the right. Goats have always figured heavily in local economy; the hill to the southeast of town is still called Goat Hill because the animals once ranged over it

Past the goat farm on the right is the area's first school house, which was built in 1875 by John Garretson for his children. It sits next to the Braddock Weeks House, built in the 1860's. Weeks was part owner of Pescadero's first store and raised pota-

*Pescadero Valley, a rich farmland in the delta
of Pescadero and Butano Creeks with village in background*

toes on 100 acres.

PESCADERO PROPER: At the four-way stop sign, you have reached the thriving village of Pescadero. You have been on the road for more than 50 miles. Time to stop, refresh and perhaps take a walkabout. (More details on the village are in Part V). There are great snacks at the markets. Or try any of the food at Duarte's, where there are some great historic photos of the region on display. As one can see from the photos, the village has undergone considerable change even though it still retains a deep feeling for its past. Settled by immigrants from Italy, Portugal and the Azores, it has remained a farming community with crops growing right up to many of the back doors. After your rest and walkabout, continue west on Pescadero Creek Road. About a mile-and-a-half west, just as you pass the maintenace yard on the left, watch on the right for the parking lot for the Pescadero Marsh. This delta where Pescadero and Butano Creeks merge is an especially rich place for bird watching in the spring and fall when waterfowl are migrating. Take your binoculars and hike the trail for a short way for the best views.

Just a ways further west the road dead ends at the Coast Highway. This is where one of the region's most hated men,

Loren Coburn, built a luxury resort. On the knoll to the north-west of the intersection about where a beach parking lot is now located, he built a hotel where few people ever stayed. Coburn, who once owned 90,000 acres in the area, had alienated every-one for years by blocking access to a popular beach where people gathered agates and other pebbles. "Coburn's Folly," as it was dubbed, stood empty for nearly 10 years while court battles raged over public access to the beach. When it finally opened for busi-ness, there were so few customers it was torn down and 174,000 board feet of choice redwood lumber salvaged.

CHOICES CHOICES CHOICES: If you are still in a traveling mood, you may want to turn south on the Coast High-way. It is just five miles to Pigeon Point where there is an unpar-alleled view all the way to Point Año Nuevo. (More information on the two points is in Part IX of this guide).

The other choices include another view of the Pescadero Marsh from the northwestern side. There is a parking lot on the west side of the highway a few hundred feet to the right. By turning north, you can head back to the starting point just 15 miles away. The highway crosses the bridge across the creek then up the hill where vistas open up along the shore to the north. There is a dip down past Pomponio Beach (named for a renegade Yurok hanged by the Spaniards in Monterey for some long for-gotten infraction). Head up over another hill and drop into the San Gregorio arroyo. As you go up around the hill , stay alert. That view all the way north to Half Moon Bay is incomparable, a 9.5-mile panorama of sea, shore and farmland.

The Tunitas Alternative

This alternative is a shorter tour into the redwoods. While the scenery lacks the variety of the other redwoods tour, it has the advantage of paring about an hour off the time consumed, if your schedule is tight.

Follow the instruction outlined in the redwoods tour above, going from Half Moon Bay to San Gregorio through La Honda up to the Skyline. Instead of turning right on Skyline Boulevard, however, you will turn left for the Tunitas Alterna-tive. Turning left, you will follow Skyline as it winds upward for nearly two miles still following La Honda Creek almost to its headwaters. Watch on the left for signs for the Methuselah Tree, an ancient giant the loggers left standing. It is only a few millennia old. On the right as the roadway curves around the 2,417-foot peak of Sierra Morena, you will see the rock wall marking Skeggs Point, a fine overlook parking area. The view is of the South Bay all the way to Mount Hamilton to the southeast and to the northeast to Mount Diablo in Contra Costa county. Across the highway is one of the main entrances to El Corte de Madera Open Space Preserve, some 2,788 acres of redwoods and trails for hikers, equestriens and cyclists. (More information about the preserve is in Park VII of this guide).

TUNITAS TURNOFF: Less than a mile past Skeggs Point, you will reach an intersection with Kings Mountain Road on the right and Tunitas Creek Road on the left. This was the area where teamsters hauling logs over the mountain and down Kings Mountain Road stayed overnight on their two-day haul to Redwood City. The Kings Mountain Inn sat at the northwest corner of the intersection. The Summit Springs House was a half-mile east on Kings Mountain Road. Loggers worked both Purisima Creek and Tunitas Creek slopes over some 60 years from 1853, but hoisting the lumber and shingles as much as 1,000 feet up to the Skyline was a challenge that limited the amount of logging done here. Turn left (west) on Tunitas Creek Road and it immediately begins its steep descent.

On the right is the Purisima Creek Open Space Preserve, 2,633-acres of trails, redwoods and wildlife. The roadway is narrow, dark and winding. Besides an occasional auto, one must be on the lookout for bicyclists. This is a favorite for cyclists who like the challenge of a steep climb, but they often have their heads down as they slowly pump their way uphill.

The woods are a mixture of second growth redwoods, most 12 to 18 inches across, and Douglas fir and madrone packed in so tightly very little sunlight penetrates the roadway for the first three miles. This tunnel-like traverse keeps you focused on the forest itself as you follow the creek's winding way to the ocean.

Due to the difficult terrain here, only five sawmills worked these canyons off and on from 1868 to 1907. A Frenchman from San Jose named Eugene Fromont was the most active, employing as many as 30 men in his mill where Mitchell Creek enters Tunitas Creek. He built the Summit Springs House and had a piece of the Kings Mountain Road toll collection system, but he lasted only 11 years. Some mill operators only lasted three or four years because of all the problems of working here and getting the shingles and lumber to market.

The road suddenly ends its precipitous descent and emerges from the forest on nearly level terrain. This valley and the one to the south along San Gregorio Creek were where the oil companies were seeking a strike in the 1920's, chiefly because oil had been found here at the 125-foot level in 1881, but not in sufficient quantities to be commercially viable. The creek continues on a less sinuous line south-southwest for nearly three miles through scrub brush with alders and willows along the creekbed.

LOBITOS CREEK CUTOFF: Keep an eye out for a small sign on the right marking the Lobitos Creek Cutoff. Turn right on the cutoff road and it soon heads directly west and climbs past a small ranch on the left. From the crest of the hill, it is a short downhill run to Lobitos Creek. The roadway dead-ends at Verde Road. Take a right and wind past the small farms. This is all that remains of the village of Lobitos. Up over the hill through the eucalyptus grove, the road forks, with the left one going to the Coastal Highway, and Verde Road continuing on the right. Stay to the right as the road rises again. On your right a couple of driveways lead to private property; one of them goes to what is left of the only successful oil strike among many searches in the 1920's. In May of 1920, the Coastside Comet had a headline: "Half Moon Bay May Become Oil Center" telling about three oil wells coming in on the John Cuneo property three miles south of town. The oil was found as drillers were seeking water for irrigation of the Cuneo farm. Later stories told of Shell Oil Co. probing the area and exploratory wells being drilled along the Purisima Valley. But the only commercial quantities were found up this hill to the right. A short roller coaster ride down Verde Road, it makes a sharp turn to the left and reaches the Coastal Highway. Take a right and you are back to the starting point in just a few miles and minutes.

PART VI
BIKING TOURS

*Signpost to everywhere. Starting point for the Coastal
Scenic Bike Tour from Montara Point Lighthouse.*

Coastal Scenic Tour

This is only for those hardy and tested veteran cyclists
accustomed to the sound of auto, vans, pickups and trucks

whizzing by the bike lane. Highway One is the scenic route and has a bike lane marked all along its route, even though it is very narrow on some of the hills and bridges along the way.

Although some of the more ambitious cyclists have taken the trip from San Francisco to Los Angeles, we will only concern ourselves with the portion in San Mateo County between Point Montara and Point Año Nuevo. We start southward from the hostel at Point Montara Lighthouse run by Hostelling International - American Youth Hostels and California State Parks, in cooperation with the U.S. Coast Guard. This sits above the ocean just off Highway One in Montara.

The first 2.5 miles are all level, easy traveling as the highway passes through the villages of Montara and Moss Beach. Presumably, if one as spent any time at the hostel, there were probably opportunities to explore nearby Fitzgerald Marine Reserve and the Moss Beach Distillery. If not, plan on coming back and doing so. Two-and-a-half miles south, the land opens up into a flat expanse with Half Moon Bay Airport, a landing strip and facility for storing small aircraft is on the right. This is where the annual Dream Machine festivities are held each April featuring every imaginable kind of mechanical marvel from steam engines to antique cars and aircraft. The airport is also the home of Three Zero Café, voted by locals as the best breakfast spot on the coast. It doesn't look fancy, but has a great menu.

On the left, farmers are still raising row crops just as the Denniston family did here in the 19th century. And there's a produce stand that's open on weekends with fresh fruits and vegetables from the farm. This was all part of the Rancho Corral de Tierra del Norte granted in 1839 to Guerrero Palomares, the prefect of San Francisco Presidio. There's a great view of the start of the Santa Cruz Mountains as they stretch to the south. On the right beyond the airport, Pillar Point rises some 450 feet at the start of the arching beaches that give Half Moon Bay its name. An Air Force radar tower sits atop its crest.

PILLAR POINT HARBOR: Just past the airport, Capistrano Road angles off to the right. Take the turnoff for a quick and pleasant look at Pillar Point Harbor, or stay on Highway One, if you are pressed for time. The little detour takes you past the old Princeton Inn, once a bootlegger's haven and now a fine Italian restaurant called Mezza Luna. Some funky places such

*The Mavericks Roadhouse Cafe celebrates the surfers who challenge
the Maverick Rollers off Pillar Point.*

as the Mavericks Roadhouse Cafe, a surf store and odd shops are
on the left and then the Half Moon Bay Brewing Co., a fine
restaurant. On the right is the harbor, an array of boats, piers and
seabirds. You can't miss the bright orange Barbara's Fish Trap
on the right and on the left Pillar Point Inn as the road curves
back toward Highway One. You pass the main harbor entrance
on the right just before reaching the signal at Highway One.
Heading south, one passes El Granada, the village rising up the
hillsides to the east. This was a town created by the promoters of
the shoreline railroad that extended from San Francisco to Tunitas
Creek and went out of business in 1922. On the right, there is
another inn, and a couple of restaurants, then an RV campground
that is nearly always crowded. Past the harbor's outer breakwater,
there may be surfers waiting for a roller. The roadway climbs a
bit, but not too long a climb to Mirada Road and downhill again.
        BEACH TURNOFF: To avoid the traffic noise and
congestion, at Mirada Road, turn right (west) past the houses to
an open field on the left, which is the entrance to the Half Moon
Bay city beaches, a clifftop trail extends some five miles south to
Poplar Avenue. The trail is shared with hikers and equestriens,
but no autos. To return to Highway One, turn back east on Poplar

through a quiet residential section. At Railroad Avenue, glance right at the first home with an unusual overhang design; this was once the local station for the ill-fated railroad. At Highway One, turn right (south) and use the wide bike lane.

This broad expanse was once part of the original settlement by Candelario Miramontes, a San Francisco Presidio soldier who was given the 4,436-acre land grant of Rancho Arroyo de los Pilarcitos in 1841. He and his wife and 13 children and a neighbor developed the village that was called Spanishtown and then Half Moon Bay in the 1860's, the first community on the San Mateo peninsula. Southward, the highway passes Miramontes Point Road and the tour enters the rural landscape that extends all the way to Santa Cruz; our tour take up only the first 20 miles.

PURISIMA NO MORE: The roadway dips down through Arroyo Cañada Verde and climbs again onto the bench land where farm crops extend on both sides of the road. As Verde Road enters from the left, there is a large grove of Monterey cypress where the village of Purisima once stood. A large hotel, blacksmith and shops were here until the demise of the railroad. All that remains are the foundation stones of a 17-room mansion owned by a wealthy restaurateur. Verde Road loops around for some two miles at the base of the hills and then returns to the highway.

Off to the west one can see the towers of the marine radio station KFS, part of the communications system for ships at sea. On the left as the highway curves around to the right, a pumpkin farm sits along the banks of Lobitos Creek. A small village called Lobitos once sat in that draw a bit upstream from the farm, but disappeared a few years after the railroad. On the right, a sign indicates Martin's Beach, a turnoff to a secluded beach where weekend cabin owners sun themselves.

TUNITAS CREEK DREAM: The roadway climbs slightly up and around the headland before heading downhill to the Tunitas Creek crossing. This small waterway has a colorful history. Upstream on the Tunitas watershed, several logging companies sought ways to get lumber to San Francisco in the mid 1800's. One ill-fated solution was to build a chute along the face of the south-facing cliff on the north side of Tunitas Creek, and use the chute to send the lumber to small schooners anchored

*Gordon's Chute in its heyday in the 1870's
loading produce, grain and lumber
at the mouth of Tunitas Creek.*

at the mouth of the creek. The chute was built, but was a trouble-some way to ship goods. The steep runway created friction that burnt up sleds, sacks and other goods. Finally, a winter storm with strong southerly winds tore down the chute. Railroad pro-moters more than 50 years later went so far as to build a trestle across Tunitas Creek to show investors they were serious about extending the rails south as far as Santa Cruz, but an economic downturn kept them from mounting rails on the trestle and it was torn down.

The roadway is wider now after a CalTrans project was completed in 2001 that expanded the bridge and bike lanes across the creek. But the climb for the next 1.5 miles to the top of the grade is slow and steep. When you reach Stage Road just past the top of the hill, you may want to pause and make a key decision.

STAGE OR NOT TO STAGE: The view from the cor-ner of Stage Road and Highway One makes it a pleasant place to pause while deciding how to direct your route from this point onward. The coastal route from here to Pescadero Beach is a series of long climbs and easy downhill slides – three of them in fact over seven miles – before relatively level cycling is reached again. The rewards are great ocean vistas beyond compare. The downside is narrow bike lanes on some curves and across a couple of bridges. The alternative is the narrow, twisting back way called Stage Road that reaches from here to Pescadero.

Stage Road was originally just that; the road used by the stages that ran from Pescadero to Half Moon Bay. While it is now paved, it follows almost the same alignment as in the days when four-horse teams hauled the swaying stages around the sand hills. Stage Road drops down a few hundred feet and about a mile to the village of San Gregorio. Only the San Gregorio General Store remains in business now with its fun mix of snacks, drinks, books and clothing. Across La Honda Road (Highway 84) a few buildings remain of what was once a hotel and service station, but are now private residences. To the east about a half-mile up La Honda Road, there is a farm where one can buy some of the best strawberries on the coast. Crossing San Gregorio Creek south on Stage Road, one passes several houses and barns and the roadway climbs out of the canyon for about a mile to the top of a hill where there are views out to the ocean. The land off to the right between Stage Road and the shore is another example of the heroic conservation efforts to preserve the open space here. It is now in the ownership of the Peninsula Open Space Trust, preserving the land between San Gregorio and Pomponio state beaches as well as the San Gregorio Creek estuary below the village of San Gregorio. The roadway here is barely wide enough for two autos as it curves downhill through a grove of eucalyptus trees planted in the 1870's past a couple of small farms to Pomponio Creek. Pomponio was a renegade Yurok Indian hanged in Monterey after depredations against Mission holdings. Pomponio Creek Road turns east back into the mountains and Stage Road continues its twisting route southward and up the hill out of the arroyo. Another mile climb to the top and you find a winding path down the hill. The big metal barn below and to the right of the road was once an experimental operation for the Hewlett Packard organization. At the bottom of the hill, slow down as you approach the farmhouse or you will miss seeing the weird metal sculpture behind the eucalyptus tree on the left just

A favorite bike lane north on Stage Road from Pescadero goes through some of the oldest eucalyptus on the Coastside.

before the road turns sharply right.   The thing looks like a prop out of the "Road Warrior" movie and is made of all sorts of junk iron. The road now heads straight down the arbor of 100-plus-year-old eucalyptus trees into Pescadero where you will have a nice choice of a grocery store snack or a full meal at Duarte's.

STAYING ON THE COAST: If you choose to remain on Highway One, after resting at Stage Road, head downhill for the curving mile to San Gregorio Creek and the state beach. The bridge across the creek is narrow, so watch out for careless drivers; you may have the right-of-way, but a careless driver can wipe out a nice trip. The climb out of the canyon is just about a half mile and then you have a nice level jaunt for a ways before heading back downhill to Pomponio Creek and another state beach followed by a longer climb up to a crest above the ocean. The view to the south from this crest is one of the most fabulous along this stretch of coast. At the crest of the bench, there is a view to the south along Pescadero Beach. On the left is Pescadero Marsh, a bird lovers' paradise.

As you pass Pescadero Creek Road on the left, you have a choice of the two-mile pedal into Pescadero village and refreshments there or continuing on your southerly way.

Highway One follows the edge of the ocean for another two miles to Bean Hollow Beach where restrooms are available. A large nursery operation is on the left just past Bean Hollow Reservoir. On the right are a few scattered homes on the beach, most built before coastal protection regulations were imposed. Some three miles past Bean Hollow is Pigeon Point Lighthouse and another hostel run by Hostelling International - American Youth Hostels and California State Parks, in cooperation with the U.S. Coast Guard. If you plan to spend the night there, you may want to postpone your visit to Año Nuevo until the next day. A trip to the Point Año Nuevo and back will be about a 14-mile round trip. (Details on the Pigeon Point hostel are found in Part IX of this guide.)

The point has seen many changes since the 1800's. Portuguese immigrants operated a whaling station here for more than 20 years. A schooner loading facility for shipping lumber and farm produce was also run here before the lighthouse was established in 1872.

If no room is available at the hostel, there is a campground some 2.5 miles south on Highway One; it is called Costanoa at Cascade Ranch and has a combination upscale campground with 88 deluxe tent cabins equipped with down comforters for those not into roughing it, and 47 standard tent cabins. This is all set on 480 acres next to the proposed Cascade Ranch State Park and across Highway One from the Point Año Nuevo Reserve.

The trip to Año Nuevo Point is a seven-mile trek on a nearly level bike path along open fields with vistas of beaches and mountains. (For details on the park, see Part VIII of this guide.)

Lobitos-Purisima Tour

This tour can be taken using one of several different combinations of quiet country roads and trails in the Purisima Open Space Preserve. The shortest of the portions is about 14 miles, while the longest is about 19 miles to complete the tour. We will begin with a look at the shortest of the choices.

All of the choices start at the same place – at the corner of Highway One and Verde Road south of Half Moon Bay. The nice thing about this tour is there is a good stretch for warming up before the first tough hill. Verde Road heads east for about a quarter of a mile, then turns sharply south; follow the pavement as it parallels Highway One up a short grade past one of the most productive produce farms in the county. A one tops the rise, there is a nice view of the coast to the west. The poles and radio tower on the edge of the cliff to the west belong to Marine Radio Station KFS. On the left are the bare sand hills covered with grass. If you blink, you may miss the driveway on the left with a very formal steel gate and sign; this protects the entrance to San Mateo County's only operating oil wells. These are all that is left of a hopeful little oil boomlet of the 1930's when rigs were testing the coastal depths from here to Butano Creek. This was the only place where oil was available in commercial quantities and then barely that, so drilling rigs disappeared. The farmers did not get rich on oil royalties, but the rest of us got a rich heritage in unspoiled scenic beauty and clean, fresh air.

Shortly, the road comes to a fork with the one on the right going back to Highway One and the one on the left heading uphill through a eucalyptus grove. Take the left fork up the hill. At the top of the hill, one passes the first of what is left of the old village of Lobitos that existed when the railroad extended from San Francisco to Tunitas Creek a couple of miles south. Now, only a couple of residences and three farms are all that mark the location of a once-bustling tourist stop until the railroad went broke in 1922 after only a few years in operation. The plan had been to extend the line all the way to Santa Cruz along the coast, but lack of funds stopped the line at Tunitas, and an economic downturn killed off the line entirely.

The road twists down to Lobitos Creek where just past Lucy Lane (on the left) another fork is reached. The right fork returns to Highway One past one of the most popular pumpkin farms on the coast. Take the left fork up the steep hill on the Lobitos Creek Road. The roadway is narrow and the curves tight, so watch for careless auto drivers at all times; traffic is light, so some forget they are not the only people on the planet. After a short climb, the road drops on a gradual slope past a small ranch on the right and then into wilder terrain and finally connects with Tunitas Road. At the fork with Tunitas Creek, turn left (east). The road turns gradually northeast on fairly level terrain for more than three miles along the course of Tunitas Creek. Oil was discovered back here in 1881, but not in commercial quantities. Where Mitchell Creek enters from the right, the road becomes more steep and starts a steeper climb into the woods.

This is on the eastern edge of Rancho Cañada Verde y Arroyo de la Purissima that was granted in 1839 to Jose Maria Alviso, a Mexican army lieutenant at Monterey. On the banks of these two creeks is where one of the early logging operators worked; Eugene Fromont, a Frenchman living in San Jose in 1867, bought 750 acres of the old rancho for $25,000 and set up a mill that employed 30 men. From 1868 to 1879, Fromont's efforts to get his shingles and logs to market led to extension of this road from the Skyline to the coast plus creation of a hotel and two settlements on the Skyline. Most old growth redwoods were too large to haul to the Redwood City embarcadero, so they were cut into shingles. One huge old beauty with a 16-foot trunk was said to have produced 1,250,000 shingles. Five different logging operators worked these woods until 1907 leaving today's mixture of madrone and second growth redwoods and firs.

As the roadway climbs past Mitchell Creek, the climb becomes very steep and the walls of the canyon begin to close in as they rise precipitously on both sides. After about a mile-and-a-half of steep climbing, there is an entrance on the left to the Purisima Creek Redwoods Open Space Preserve. Here one goes

The Tunitas Creek sylvan arbor makes a vigorous but cool climb for cyclists with the stamina and fortitude.

from paved road to a dirt pathway called Grabtown Gulch Trail. The trail is named after one of Fromont's settlements, or at least what it was eventually called. As part of his varied enterprises, Fromont built a hotel called Summit Springs House and a small settlement of his workers grew up there. Having been built on Fromont's land, most were shanties that would be thrown up quickly and just as quickly deserted, only to be "grabbed" by a newcomer needing shelter. Thus people dropped the Summit Springs name in favor of Grabtown. The trail winds through the woods downward to Purisima Creek in about a mile. Turn left on Purisima Creek Trail as it goes west and emerges after about another mile at the western entrance to the preserve.

On emerging from the preserve, turn left on the paved road. This is Purisima Road and heads west paralleling the creek. The roadway gradually climbs and one has a nice view to the left of the farmland running along a fairly level bench above the creek. The hills rise steeply to the north on the right. As the roadway nears the summit there is a spectacular view of the Pacific shore from Miramontes Point on the north to Seal Rock in the south. Then it's a short downhill run to the starting point.

The Purisima Creek Trail Extension

If the cyclist is more ambitious and enjoys huffing and puffing all the way to the top of Tunitas Creek Road at the Skyline, one can add another three miles to the tour. The roadway is dark and winding upward for another mile-and-a-half. Though auto traffic is light, one must be careful of the careless ones. At the top of the climb is another entrance to the Purisima Creek Redwoods Open Space Preserve.

The pathway on the Purisima Creek Trail heads almost due west as it descends through the trees to the western entrance to the preserve. This alternative keeps the heart pumping at top speed for an additional three-quarters of an hour, and one has the chance to commune more deeply with more redwoods.

The Harkins Ridge Extension

Okay, so you've made it to the top and you want to cool down a bit more slowly before heading back downhill. Here's the way:

Turn northwest on Skyline Drive for nearly two miles of pleasant pedaling (if you don't mind the heavier auto traffic whizzing by) on a relatively level terrain. On the left, you will come to another entrance to the Purisima Creek Redwoods Open Space Preserve. Just beyond the entrance is a handy grocery store where one can buy a fine snack or refreshments, if your body is crying out for sustenance by this time.

Upon entering the preserve, the cyclist is now on a dirt path. Take the first left onto the Harkins Ridge Trail. The path and ridge is named for George Harkins, a longtime logger who lived alone in his cabin on the ridge until he died in 1931. It was said that Harkins was so adept at his job that he could move and maneuver huge logs singlehandedly just using a leverage device called a jackscrew. The trail follows an old fire road down the ridge and descends more than 1,300 feet in a little over two miles, the sharpest drop coming after about a mile and a half on the ridge. The ridge is mostly covered by chaparral with a few tan oaks and bay laurels growing on the steep mountainside. From the ridge, one can see Whittemore Gulch off to the right. A series of sharp switchbacks drop the trail down to the creek level and the preserve's western entrance. Out onto the pavement of Purisima Creek Road, one heads west to the tour's starting point.

Higgins-Purisima Tour

This is an 11.3-mile loop that is mostly along a quiet, but narrow country road that can be taken in either direction. One way has a shorter, but steeper climb, while the other has a greater marine view on one of the legs.

There is also the option of a three-mile round trip detour onto an old ranch road for a peek at what's left of a 19th century dairy operation that is now a state park. The Burleigh H. Murray State Park winds along Mill Creek from grove to grove of eucalyptus trees before reaching the old barn where three generations of farmers milked cows before the land was donated to the state.

We will follow the loop that takes the shortest uphill run – about a mile rather than two-and-a-half miles. Start from the corner of Highway One and Purisima Road (next to the fire station) and go south on Highway One to Verde Road. Turn east on Verde Road.

The grove of cypress and eucalyptus trees at the southeast corner of the intersection is all that is left of the lost village of Purissima. A wealthy restaurateur, Kurt Doebbel, built a mansion and planted the cypress trees around the main house for a ranch that covered more than 1,000 acres. During an economic downturn, Doebbel borrowed from Henry Cowell, a lumberman and banker, and was unable to repay the loan. Cowell foreclosed on the ranch in 1890. It became Cowell Ranch and Doebbel faded from the history books. All that remains of his 17-room mansion are the foundation stones.

Keep going east past the grove. Where Verde Road turns sharply south, cyclists should continue east; this is the connection with Purisima Road. Up the short grade, the road tops a rise above rich farm land on broad shelves along Purisima Creek. Be on the lookout for traffic, because there are people traveling to and from several homes up this canyon plus cars on their way to the lower entrance to the Purisima Creek Redwoods Open Space Preserve.

This area was part of Rancho Cañada Verde y Arroyo de la Purissima that was granted in 1839 to Jose Maria Alviso, a

Mexican Army lieutenant in Monterey. The influx of European immigrants during and after the Gold Rush brought farmers who tilled the rich bottomlands, raising hay and wheat in the early years. Some ran dairy herds and raised pigs.

The roadway is narrow and dips and rises with the terrain. Ahead rise the steep slopes of the Santa Cruz Mountains. To the north and south the sand hills – green in winter and spring and burnt a pale yellow in summer and fall – slope up sharply.

Some four miles from the Highway One turnoff, the road veers almost in a U-turn and starts uphill. At this curve is the parking lot for the lower entrance to Purisima Redwoods Open Space Preserve.

The road's steep grade (the name changes here to Higgins-Purisima Road) extends for a mile, twisting and turning on a narrow roadbed past driveways of four homes. Upon reaching the top, one has a great view to the south, west and north. It is all down hill for the next 2.5 miles. But use extreme caution, because the switchbacks are tight and there is barely room for two cars to pass each other. Drivers tend to adopt the middle of the road as their natural territory.

Near the bottom is the entrance to the Burleigh H. Murray State Park. The trail is a dirt ranch road that follows Mills Creek east southeast into the foothills. Robert Mills, an Englishman who had worked in San Francisco as a glazier, took his earnings, bought 1,000 acres and set up a dairy farm back in one corner of the canyon in 1862, one of the first dairies on the peninsula. The dairy was in operation for three generations before the land was donated to the state. The trail rises slowly by some 600 feet to the dairy center, passing huckleberries, blackberries and a rich mass of riparian foliage on both side of the creek. The return to Purisima Road is back down the same dirt road.

Head west again on Higgins-Purisima Road past a cluster of homes along Arroyo Leon Creek and out into the flat.

This is farming land that was once part of the 4,424-acre Rancho Arroyo de los Pilarcitos that granted in 1841 to Candelario Miramontes, a soldier at San Francisco Presidio. Miramontes' family later sold a part of the rancho to James and William Johnston, two brothers from Ohio who farmed the land, slowly adding to their holding until they owned nearly all of the southern half of the Miramontes rancho. James Johnston, who paid Miramontes $14,000 for 1,200 acres, built the white saltbox house that sits just south of Purisima Road on the edge of a field. The house was restored by the Johnston Foundation but is not open to the public despite several attempts to arrange public access.

Just a short distance past the Johnston House, is the end of the loop. The cyclist who stayed on the route covered 11.2 miles, while anyone who added the side trip to the old dairy ranch totaled 14.2 miles. A good workout!

An Almost Level Stretch

This is a trail for cyclists (hikers and equestrians use this trail, too) who want a pleasant ride through the woods without a lot of huffing and puffing. It starts at the northeastern entrance to the Purisima Creek Redwood Open Space Preserve from Highway 35. Take Highway 35 (Skyline Boulevard) east from Highway 92 to the top of the first hill. Just past the grocery store is the preserve entrance.

This is the starting point for a round trip of about five miles that is a pleasant mix of forest and open hillside views stretching out to the Pacific Ocean. The ridge can be windy, so take along a sweater or windbreaker jacket. Water and a snack would be sensible, too.

Follow the wide path originally used as a fire patrol road; it is called the North Ridge Trail and winds through the redwoods, dropping some 400 feet in elevation in the first three-tenths of a mile. There is a left fork for the Harkins Ridge Trail that one should bypass unless a more vigorous workout is sought. Stay on the North Ridge Trail as it curves around a knoll and a half-mile later is another fork for the Whittemore Gulch Trail that drops down in a series of switchbacks from 1,600 feet to 1,000 above sea level. In wet weather, this trail is usually closed.

Stay on the North Ridge Trail. For the next 1.2-miles, the path is fairly level and the vistas open up to the north and west to some spectacular coastal scenery. Bay laurels, *Umbellularia californica,* can be seen down the steep slopes. Springtime, of course, brings all manner of wildflowers, but many of the hardier thistles and ceonothus retain their blues and pinks well into late summer.

The last few hundred feet of the trail drops another 200 feet. Retracing the path after a nice rest to enjoy the view, and perhaps a snack; the view is of the forest, a mixture of tan oaks, *Lithocarpus densiflorus,* madrones, *Arbutus menziesii,* and live oaks, *Quercus agrifola,* leading to the taller Douglas firs, *Psuedotsuga menziesii,* near the top. The last half-mile is a gradual climb of 400 feet back to the preserve entrance. There's a restroom and telephone available there.

More Bike Tours in the Woods

For cyclists who like the deeps woods and challenges of canyon trips, see the complete guide to the Purisima Creek Redwoods Open Space Preserve in Part VII. There are bike trails available in nearly all the public state and county parks and open space preserves.

PART VII
NATURE TOURS

CANYON & HILLSIDE HIKES

Tucked into the canyons and hills rising from the San Mateo Coast is a greater choice of scenic thrills and hiking challenges than in nearly any other area in the world. The canyon trails through the redwood, fir, oak and madrone forests on the western slopes of the Santa Cruz Mountains, the chain that extends from the San Francisco Bay Discovery site south past the Santa Cruz County line, is a wonderland for hikers, bicyclists and equestrians.

There are 11 preserves covering 23,654 acres just minutes from the hubbub of four million people of the San Francisco Bay Area, all offering a near wilderness experience of peace and tranquility. In addition, there are another 1,150 acres of trails tucked between Pacifica subdivisions where one can trace native paths that were followed by the first European explorers. Or, if one is really adventurous, there is the 200-mile-long Bay Area Ridge Trail that extends along the coastal upthrusts. On the canyon trails, the hiker walks amongst both second growth timber of all kind and redwoods nearly 1,000 years old, and can pause to inspect the plants the Ohlone people harvested for centuries for food, medicine and fishing aids.

We have listed the parks in alphabetical order for handy reference and detailed some of the best trails. Due to changing conditions on some of the trails, it is advisable to check with the authorities responsible for maintaining the park or open space preserve before leaving.

In the deep canyons, this authority could be the California Department of Parks and Recreation or the San Mateo County Parks Department. Most of the preserves on the western slope of the Skyline are run by the Midpeninsula Regional Open Space District. See official telephone number and web site address for each park and preserve.

SUGGESTED AID: To help identify the plants and trees you encounter, there is a slim volume, *Plants Of The Coast*

Redwood Region by Kathleen Lyons and Mary Beth Cuneo-Lazano published by Looking Press, 21600 Big Basin Way, #5, Boulder Creek, CA 95006, which has great full-color illustrations that are ideal for a nature reference.

Butano State Park

Jurisdiction: California State Parks
Tel.— 650-879-2040. Web site: htttp://cal-park.ca.gov/
Getting There
There are two access points from the San Mateo Coast off Highway One. Take the Gazos Creek Road at Coastal Access Point south of Pigeon Point one mile and follow Gazos Creek Road for three miles northeast to Cloverdale Road; or take Pescadero Creek Road through the village of Pescadero to Cloverdale Road and follow Cloverdale to the park entrance.

The 2,200-acre park features miles of hiking trails, 21 drive-in camp sites and 18 walk-in camp sites. Restrooms with running water are provided. There are no showers. Guided nature walks and weekend campfire programs are offered during the summer.

Butano State Park covers a secluded redwood-filled canyon that was once part of Rancho Butano which was granted in 1838 to Ramona Sanchez that extended to the ocean at Pigeon Point. The point was named after a ship called the Carrier Pigeon went aground in a fog before a lighthouse was built there. Before the Mexican government carved out the rancho, the lower portion of the area was used as grazing land for the Santa Cruz Mission. Prior to that, the Ohlone Indians roamed through the creek's watershed harvesting all the edible nuts and berries that proliferate here and fishing the stream that was home waters to steelhead trout and salmon. The nuts of the chinquapin, oaks and bay trees along with the blue elderberries were staples of the native diets; some were used medicinally and for aids in fishing.

Soon after the Americans took over the territory in 1848, logging began on the western slope of the San Mateo Coast, but it was 1873 before the first and only shingle mill was built along Little Butano Creek. No competitors came along, because all the shingles had to be hauled all the way down to Pigeon Point and loaded aboard schooners bobbing in the surf offshore. The Jackson family settled on the northern side of the canyon, and the Taylor and Mullen families had settled on the southern, or Goat Hill, side. Together with Purdy Pharis, who bought the mill in the 1880's, the settlers logged the redwood forest in the canyon bottom until about 1895, taking all but a few of the forest giants. In the 1940s, logging of giant Douglas firs took place.

Timothy Hopkins, son of Mark Hopkins of "Big Four" railroad fame, later acquired the property and left it including most of the Butano and Little Butano Creek watersheds to Stanford University. The land was broken up and sold subsequently in the 1950s to private parties. In 1961, due to efforts of a conservationist lobbying campaign, Butano State Park became part of the state park system.

From the park entry, a paved road runs about a mile along the canyon floor, leading to the Ben Ries Campground, which was named after the park's first ranger. The road continues for another mile into the canyon, but is unpaved and available only for service vehicles and hikers. The other trails in the park all are narrow and for hikers only.

Rules: Trails open dawn to dusk; no bicycles or horses; dogs on leash allowed in campground but not on trails. Camping reservations advised from April 1 through Labor Day by calling Destinet; day use and camping fees.

Maps: California State Parks, Butano State Park, USGS topo Franklin Point.

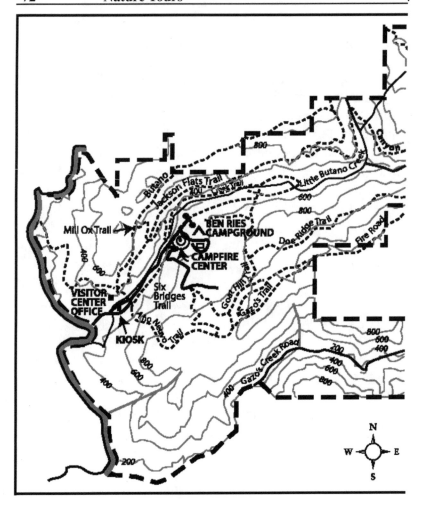

The Warmup:
Little Butano Creek Trail

This hike is just the ticket to unkink citified muscles -- an hour-and-a-half stroll along the valley bottom through the quiet redwood forest without a lot of climbing. The elevation gain is only about 30 feet and covers only a little more than two miles of easily travelled trail that makes for pleasant walking.

Go northeast from the entrance or take the unpaved maintenance road from the Ben Ries Campground. The old wooden flume on the north side was built early in the 20th century to carry water from a small upstream dam to irrigate fields in private lands farther west. Follow the Little Butano Creek Trail

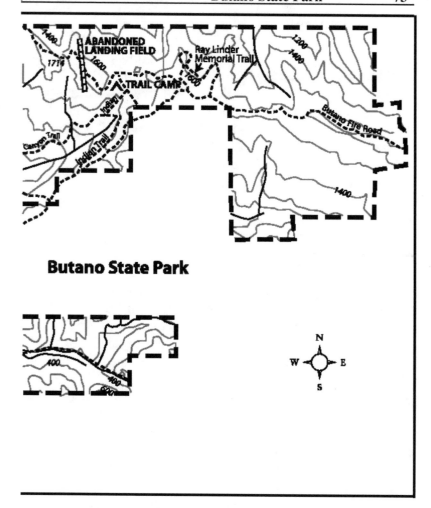

Butano State Park

east up the creek. Second-growth redwoods and even a few giants spared by the loggers make this a shady and relaxing trail. Evergreen needles carpet the path as it winds down to the creek where redwood sorrel grows in the deep shade.

You will pass a water treatment plant building. At a small dam on the creek is a building where water is pumped from the creek to this treatment building for campground and ranger residence use. Across Little Butano Creek on a footbridge, the trail turns downstream on the north bank past large redwood stumps and smaller redwood trees. Flowers peek from among low-growing bushes in season. At various times of the year, one can see the white blossom of the Western coltsfoot, *Petasites palmatus*; the wake robin, *Trillium ovatum*, sports a three-petalled white flower atop three spade-shaped leaves with fuzzy undersides; or the pink-petalled bead lily, *Clintonia andrewsiana* that brightens the shade in late summer with neon-blue berries. Beware of the omnipresent poison oak, *Toxicodendron diversilobum*,; learn to recognize its reddish wrinkled, three-lobed green leaves and give it a wide berth. Several small bridges take the path back and forth over the creek several times. Note the huge redwood burl near the junction of an unused trail just south of one of these crossings.

Natives found beneficial uses for parts of nearly all the forest and hillside plants seen by hikers on these paths. The coltsfoot leaves, for example, dissolve into pure salt when placed on a redwood burl over a hot fire. But of all the forest plants, that bane of the careless hiker, poison oak, has one of the most fascinating histories. Evidently having evolved an immunity to the plant over their centuries here that European races never enjoyed, the Ohlone used the plants stems for basketry, juice of the leaves as tattooing dye, and even boiled the stems, leaves and roots for medicinal purposes including an antidote for rattlesnake bite. But, as they say on the boob tube: "Don't try this at home!" You probably lack the protection of the Ohlone immune genes.

Passing numerous side creeks bridged by boardwalks you reach a very boggy area where the odiferous skunk cabbage, *Lysichiton americanum,* grows. This yellow-flowered, yellow-green-leafed plant is found in only a few localities in the Santa Cruz Mountains, always in wet ground near perennial springs. From the bogs, the trail crosses to the south side of the creek, and 100 feet farther along reaches a paved road where there is a pull-out for a few cars to park. Just ahead and downstream is the junction with Jackson Flats Trail, then returning to the entrance station. The 400-foot or so climb on the Mill Ox Trail has a reward -- a tunnel tree that easily accomodates children and other adventurers. Or, if you're lazier, stay on the paved trail and head back to the campground.

The Grand Tour

Take a sandwich and water along if you tackle this series of trails that touches all the park's habitats. The tour covers a little more than 10 miles and climbs 1,000 feet. You could be gone for five to six hours.

Start at the Jackson Flats Trail from the entrance parking lot and head north through second-growth Douglas fir and live oak. The grade out of the creek basin is gradual as the trail climbs the north side of the valley. After 10 minutes or so, the trail widens to an old road paralleling the paved road below. The trail soon narrows to a single track. Past a series of flat, swampy areas – important winter breeding grounds for newts and home to marsh plants such as skunk cabbage, *Lysichiton americanum,* and horse tail, *Equisetum ssp.* -- one crosses the Mill Ox Trail, which comes up from the valley floor and joins the Butano Fire Road above.

At the junction where the Jackson Flats Trail veers left to join the Butano Fire Road – some three miles out – take the Canyon Trail to the right to circle around the head of the valley. Here the trail has climbed about 650 feet to an elevation of about 850 feet and the vegetation changes from the firs and redwoods to knobcone pines, *Pinus artenuatus*; oaks of many varieties, manzanita, *Arctostaphylos ssp.*; California nutmegs, *Torreya californica*; and golden chinquapin, *Castanopsis chrysophylla*. There are lots of chaparral, *Pickeringua montana,* too. The ground here has changed to shale and sandstone and is much drier.

Nearly all the plants here were harvested by the native Ohlones with each clan having gathering rights to specified territories. The chinquapin produces a sweet tasting nut hidden inside a burr-like pod that the natives roasted and ate; the squirrels, jays and other nut-gathering forest creatures now depend on them for sustenance. The pines have tiny nuts that can be freed from the cones with heat. The nutmeg (no relation to the spice tree of the same name) also has a large nut, but it was more popular for its super-sharp needles that were used for cosmetic tattooing of natives faces and torsos.

The Canyon Trail circles in and out of numerous small draws where smaller redwood and fir trees exist in the protected canyons. Mainly, this is chaparral country, accompanied by more nutmeg, manzanita and possibly a canyon live oak, *Quercus chyrsolepis,* also called the maul oak because the wood is so hard that pioneers made maul or mallet heads from them. Working up and down this slope to the junction with the Indian Trail, the hiker will have gone nearly six miles to reach an elevation of 1,250 feet from the 250-foot altitude at the start.

There is a good spot for lunch just past the Canyon/Indian Trail junction. Cross Little Butano Creek to a mossy sandstone seat. This quiet streamside feels refreshing and cool on a hot day. This area — fewer humans are ambitious enough to climb this far—often has signs of animal visitors. Bobcat or gray fox tracks and scat can be seen at times. Here you are at the edge of chaparral with plenty of tan oak, *Lithocarpus densiflorus*, and huckleberry, *Vaccinium ovatum*.

If you want to add a side trip, the Canyon Trail goes left to the trail camp, situated in a grove of second-growth redwoods and Douglas firs. It has eight primitive camp sites with rustic tables and stools, built and maintained by volunteers. There are pit toilets but no water. Campfires are not allowed. From this trail camp you can stroll on the nearby Ray Linder Nature Trail, which is three quarters of a mile long.

After only a half-mile the Indian Trail ends at the Olmo Fire Road, on which you also can reach the trail camp by a roundabout route. The fire road is wide on the ridge, with spectacular views to the south, west and north. After a third of a mile, one reaches the Doe Ridge Trail on the right and dips back into redwood and fir-forest, winding gently down to a junction with the Goat Hill Trail. If mileposts were used, this would be mile 8.3 from the start of the trip. The Goat Hill Trail goes right downhill to its junction with an unnamed trail leading to the Ben Ries Campground, and go left to the campground.

To complete the entire 10.3-mile tour, go past the park office and join the Six Bridges Trail through riparian vegetation along Little Butano Creek and its north-flowing tributaries. There actually are six bridges amid the maples, alders and herbaceous plants in this is sensitive habitat. Please stay on the trail. Note one huge fir tree that managed to survive the axe during earlier logging. Or you could also save this stretch along Six Bridges Trail for a relaxing stroll for a hot day.

Sightseers' Heaven

The Año Nuevo Trail climbs the south rim of the park for great views and diverse vegetation, requiring an ascent of some 750 feet over three miles that will take more than two hours.

Take binoculars and a camera to get the full benefit of this hike.

Take the Año Nuevo Trail on the south side of the park that goes left of the small nature center. The trail crosses Little Butano Creek on a bridge, passing the Six Bridges Trail on the left. Climb uphill through riparian vegetation and spring-fed plants such as thimbleberry, *Rubus parviflorus, var. velutinus,* and wild cucumber, *Marah organus.* Red elderberry, *Sambucus callicarpa,* bushes are covered with white panicles of bloom in the spring and bright inedible berries in fall. The Californios who lived on Rancho Butano and neighboring ranchos harvested the wild cucumber nuts for the children to use in marble games. Taking lessons from the natives, the rancheros boiled the plant's leaves as balm for sores, especially saddle sores on their horses and mules. Thimbleberry fruit was a favorite seasonal treat and used in making jams; early settler women rubbed the leaf of the plant on their faces to give cheeks the rosy look modern women achieve with rouge.

As the trail climbs, the hiker can see through the trees all the way to the ocean. Long clusters of lichen on tree branches are products of the frequent ocean fogs that roll into this canyon. There is a handy bench to rest from the climb and enjoy the view to the west. From this vantage point one can see where Butano Creek emerges from its canyon and then turns sharply north before joining the main Butano Creek; together they flow a bit farther north before going west to the ocean. Paralleling Little Butano Creek, the seasonal stream, Arroyo de los Frijoles, goes west northwest to the Pacific Ocean, its flow dammed into two little lakes for irrigation. The alignment of these streams has been diverted by a 400-foot-high ridge called the Mesa, apparently some prehistoric action by the San Gregorio Fault, which rises off the seabed in the submarine canyons of Monterey Bay and travels almost due north inland along the coast. Though relatively low, this mesa tends to block some of the summer fogs and strong ocean winds from reaching Butano State Park. This ridge forms the centerpiece of a 5,600-acre property that may become public open space linking Butano Park to the Coast, if acquisitions now in the works are completed.

The trail continues on short switchbacks and then a longer stretch to reach the Año Nuevo Overlook bench. This viewpoint is at 980 feet, and at one time commanded a nice view of Año Nuevo Island, but now is somewhat obscured by growing forest. It takes about 40 to 50 minutes to climb to this point.

Continuing east along the ridge through a fir forest, the hiker will reach the Olmo Fire Road. The trail along it has been cut into a shale bank. Past an unmarked trail to the right, the hiker reaches an intersection of the Goat Hill Trail Extension to the left and the Gazos Trail to the right. Go right (northeast) although the trail entrance is a little obscure, and travel on the Gazos Trail, paralleling the Olmo Fire Road but much above it. This is a sort of dipsy doodle trail along the ridge with splendid views of the Coastside to the west and of the canyon of Gazos Creek to the south.

On the south slope of the ridge, the shale formation is broken into small chips and nurtures knobcone pines, the very territorial chamise, *Adenostoma fasciculatum,* whose leaves leach a mild toxin into the soil to block encroaching neighbors, and bracken ferns, *Pteriim aquilinum,* that natives uprooted to use for basketry pattern making. Views to the east are of the forested Gazos Creek canyon. At the Olmos Fire Road and where the Gazos Creek Trail end, take the road left and downhill steeply through fir forest. Don't miss the giant fir with an 8-foot-thick trunk and four large trunks growing from it. In a half-mile, take the Goat Hill Trail connection downhill to the right, and descend on its right-hand branch about a mile to reach the maintenance road next to Little Butano Creek. From here it is only a little over a mile return to camp, or take the Little Butano Creek Loop back.

El Corte de Madera Creek
Open Space Preserve

Jurisdiction: Midpeninsula Regional Open Space District— Tel: 650-691-1200. Web site: http://openspace.org/

Getting There
From the Coastside, go south on Highway One to Highway 84 (La Honda Road), East on La Honda Road to Skyline Drive, northwest for 3.7 miles on Skyline for the first of three entrances: (1) at gate CM03 (Gordon Mill trailhead). Just 0.7 of a mile on is gate CMO2 (Methuselah Tree trailhead). There is only limited parking on the west side of the road near preserve gate. Still another mile on the east side of Skyline is Skeggs Point Caltrans Vista Park at Skeggs Point, walk 100 yards north and cross road to preserve entrance at gate CMO1.

Once part of the eastern end of Rancho San Gregorio that was granted by the Mexican government in 1839 to Antonio Buelna, A San Jose Presidio soldier, the 2,788-acre El Corte de Madera Creek Open Space Preserve lies west of Skyline Boulevard between Star Hill, Swett and and Bear Gulch roads. El Corte Madera Creek rises from springs near the Skyline and flows between high ridges on the west side of the preserve, to be joined by its main tributary, Lawrence Creek, which flows through the southeast side. The preserve, from its 2,417-foot-high point, Sierra Morena, to the canyon where the creek leaves the lower boundary at an elevation of 700 feet, is a place of high ridges and precipitously steep, deep canyons. From some of these high ridges, views between the trees of the Coastside and the ocean are breathtaking.

Aptly named, El Corte de Madera (which literally means

cut or chopped wood) Creek was a magnet for early lumberjacks and millmen. Loggers arrived along its watershed in 1859 and within only a few years there were nine mills cutting down redwoods and chopping them into shingles that were hauled over the ridge and down grade to Redwood City. Logging of the old forest continued into the 20th century, and second-growth forests have been cut sporadically since then. After the Midpeninsula Regional Open Space District acquired these lands in 1985, even limited timber cutting ceased by 1988. While telltale signs of the loggers can still be seen along certain roads, second-growth forest of redwoods and Douglas fir now covers the canyons and ridges.

All trails except the foot trail to Sandstone Formation are open to bicyclists and equestrians as well as hikers. During the rainy winter season, some of the trails are impassable and are closed. These include the Methuselah, the Leaf and Virginia Mill trails. El Corte de Madera Creek cannot be crossed on the Virginia Mill Trail during heavy rains, and there is slide danger in the area as well. Always check with the district office before setting out on any of these trails after a heavy storm.

Rules: Open dawn to dusk. No dogs. Stay on the designated trails.

Sandstone Formation, Vista Point and Shady Valley Loop

This tour combines old logging roads and new trails for a nearly five-mile overview of the preserve's northern trails. Only a small rise of 300 feet will be experienced on the return end. About two-and-a-half hours of leisurely walking will be needed to complete the journey.

From the Skeggs Point entrance parking lot, take the patrol road (not the gated, paved road on the left). The path veers uphill and around a sharp bend. At this bend the road splits, its two branches being old logging roads that now serve as trails. Stay left on the upper road for this trip. This is the Tafoni Trail, which takes its name from the unique sandstone formation that is the highlight of this hike. The return portion of the loop will bring the hiker back over the lower road, El Corte de Madera Creek Trail.

Continue on the Tafoni Trail for 1.2 miles around a hillside that skirts the north side of a ridge and rises gently to reach a multiple-trail junction. One trail goes to the left, back toward the Methuselah Tree on Skyline; the middle trail, the Fir Trail, bears slightly right (west) to the Vista Point; and the third trail, the Tafoni Trail, on which you have been traveling, goes right to the Sandstone Formation.

It is well worth the side trip for the beautiful views of the Coastside and ocean. Take the Fir Trail for 0.3 mile to a fork. Take the trail on the right, signed Vista Point, that goes to the end of a ridge, and through the rapidly encroaching trees on the slope below you can see the sweep of grasslands down to the Coast. There is an ideal place to picnic and rest in the shade of some young Douglas firs. Chaparral, tan oaks, *Lithocarpus densiflorus*, whose bark fueled a burgeoning leather tanning industry for three decades, and madrones, *Arbutus menziesi*, that gnarled reddish-trunked tree that served Ohlones and settlers alike for centuries, all border the wide trail that circles the vista point.

While the stately redwoods and Douglas fir captured the imagination and stirred the cupidity of the early loggers, it was the less impressive madrone that provided humans with necessities for thousands of years. The bark that is shed serpentine-like from the trunk every summer was gathered by Ohlones and boiled with its leaves into a tea that calmed upset and diarrheic stomachs or stirred into a paste used to heal wounds. The salmon-colored berries announce their ripening in late summer with an acrid fragrance; and they can be stored through the winter as a food source when other supplies run short. The natives shared their madrone secrets first with the Spanish missionaries and then with early Anglo settlers.

Retracing one's steps, the path reaches the multiple-trail junction passed earlier; bear left on the Tafoni Triail toward the unique Sandstone Formation. Only 200 yards from the junction, there is a narrow hikers-only footpath on the right that leads down to the outcrops. You will soon see the unique cliffs jutting up some 50 feet above the wooded hillside. Mother nature has created a chemical mix of rainwater and carbon dioxide from the air to sculpt a fantasy honeycomb surface on the rocks. The weathering comes from a weak acid created by the elements that slowly erodes the calcium-carbonate cement and binds the individual sand grains in sandstone. Please resist the urge to climb on these rocks, because the fragile structures are easily damaged.

    Return on the short, narrow footpath to the Tafoni Trail and turn right (northwest) downhill on it for nearly a mile under oaks and firs to the end of the road. Here the hiker will meet the El Corte de Madera Creek Trail. Turn right (north) on it; the other segment of this trail goes sharply left downhill and west to another park entrance. On the El Corte de Madera Creek Trail, the path winds gently downhill (east) along a forested hillside past numerous burned-out redwood

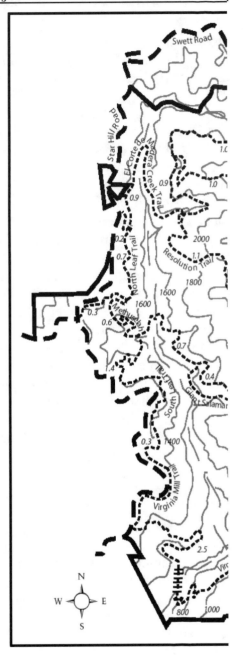

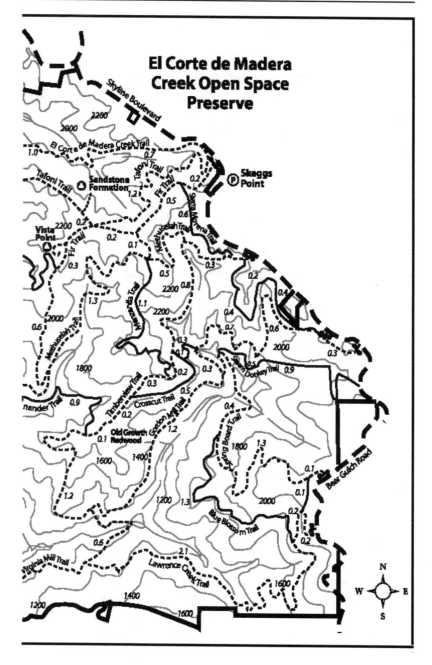

stumps, some of them remnants of giant trees that stood across what is now the trail. Walk through a former tree trunk for an eerie communion with the past. Young redwoods are taking over in the tan oak forest, and the trail winds among them down the ridge.

Along the small creek that is dry most of the year, one quickly reaches the upper part of the preserve's main creek, El Corte de Madera. This area is the site of one of the earliest sawmills in the canyon, a water-powered mill operated by Ambrose Saunders from 1865 to 1868. Saunders sold out to Charles Hanson, who had cornered the shingles market, and John Ackerson, a Redwood City lumber dealer and the county's first sheriff. Hanson was responsible for getting La Honda Road (now Highway 84) built as a means of getting his wood products to market. Purdy Pharis, who owned a total of seven shingle mills in one place and another also had a mill in the area. In most years this creek still has a trickle of water in late August. Many moisture-dependent plants thrive here — brilliant scarlet monkey flowers, *Mimulus cardinales*, tiger lilies, *Lilium pardalinum,* with their purple-spotted orange petals tightly drawn back to attract birds and insects to their pulpy anthers merrily dancing at the end of light filaments. In late summer, tall elk clover, *Aralia californica*, are topped with puffs of tiny, delicate white flowers that ripen into dark berries loved by forest birds.

Turn right (east), and uphill toward the preserve entrance. Although young redwoods grow in this valley, as one ascends the old logging road that is the continuation of the El Corte de Madera Creek Trail, firs gradually replace the redwoods. And you are soon back at the parking lot.

The Resolution Loop

This hike is a little more strenuous, involving a 480-foot loss and then a climb of the same altitude over more than five miles. Set aside at least three hours for the trip.

This also leaves from the Skeggs Point parking area and is a kind of reversal of the Tafoni Trail trip on a little different path near the bottom. After just a hundred yards on the service road, veer off right on the El Corte de Madera Creek Trail and follow the old logging road on the north side of the creek's headwaters. Keep watch for the trail's left jog as it leaves the creek canyon and begins a long, gradual ascent around the nose of the ridge surmounted by the Sandstone Formation. Rounding this ridge and heading south, the hiker meets a fork where the

Tafoni Trail goes left (south) uphill, and the El Corte de Madera Creek Trail continues right and slightly downhill. The downhill route is taken here.

The trail goes first south and then west through a forest that is relatively open. Look uphill as you round a nose of the ridge, you can see a huge sandstone outcrop, a smaller version of the one on the Tafoni Trail.

At the foot of a wide ravine, the El Corte de Madera Creek Trail turns abruptly right (west), rounds the shoulder of a ridge, and drops down to a trail junction in a small clearing. Now it turns left (south) onto the Resolution Trail, leaving the creek. The trail climbs gradually up a west-facing ridge along some of the largest redwoods on the preserve. The best trees are downhill from the trail and in ravines where there is more water.

The trail got its name from a 1953 tragedy. It was the site of the crash of a plane called the Resolution after one of Captain Cook's four ships that explored the Pacific. Everyone on board the plane died when it crashed en route to San Francisco International Airport.

Beyond this point the trail continues gradually uphill, bends into a ravine where dense stands of tall firs and redwoods flourish, then reaches a west-facing chaparral thicket. If the day is clear, one can look out to the Coast. At the junction with Fir Trail, turn left into conifer woods. Take this trail left (northeast) and follow it past the junction with the trail to the vista point and on to the multi-trail junction. Here there is a choice of either picking up the Tafoni Trail, on which one can visit the Sandstone Formation, or head northeast back to gate at Skeggs Point.

The Good Workout Loop

This trail system will take up to six hours during which you cover nine miles, descend and then regain 1,600 feet of altitude as you swing around the southeastern limits of the preserve.

Choose between two starting points: the parking lot just west of Bear Gulch Road on Skyline, or the Methuselah Tree parking lot another half mile to the west on Skyline. The path briefly follows the Sierra Morena Trail to an old timber haul road that is now a patrol road that goes to the left. This trip follows the broad, well-compacted old logging road for 1.8 miles, dropping about 200 feet to Timberview Trail. Taking the trail left for another two-tenths of a mile, there is a short path to the left into a grove containing an ancient giant redwood that survived the loggers' axes. Back on Timberview, continue past the turnoff to Great Salamander Trail, a multi-use path that heads west; continue the slow descent, losing about 600 feet down to the Lawrence Creek bridge.

Timberview Trail continues past the bridge southwest following the creek's clear waters cascading over glistening rocks and idling through deeper pools. After little more than a half mile the hiker comes to the junction with Virginia Mill Trail (to the right) and Lawrence Creek Trail (to the left). It was about here in 1899 that loggers returned after a hiatus of about 30 years to find new ways to get the rest of the trees out of the canyon. G.P. Hartley, a former county superintendent of schools, and Hugh McArthur, who had worked at mills in the mountains for years, set up the largest shingle mill ever seen on the peninsula, but still had to haul their loads out of the canyon one at a time. Just down the creek, three men from West Virginia set up the Virginia Mill and built a rail-lift to haul lumber, not shingles, to Starrs Hill Road to the west. From there it was an easy run to Skyline for tandem wagons pulled by eight mules and then the two-day trip downhill to market. From 1900 to 1906, as Frank Stanger reported in *Sawmills in the Redwoods,* the Virginia Mills shipped seven million feet of lumber out of the canyon before running out of trees to harvest. Nothing remains of either of the old mills now; the second growth forest has covered the scars well, returning it to a wooded wildlife haven.

From the fork, taking a left on Lawrence Creek Trail, the hiker begins a long 2.1-mile climb up the side of a ridge near Bear Gulch Road, a gain in elevation of more than 1,000 feet. Near Bear Gulch Road, some of the older and larger firs rather edge out the redwoods. Here there is a short steep climb to gate CMO5 at the road; one can skip the left path to Blue Blossom Trail, another multi-use path and continue on a hikers- only path, Spring Board Trail twists and turns while dropping back another 200 feet lower. If one chooses Blue Blossom Trail, the way is along a ridge with views across the canyon The next 1.3 miles follow paths through a second-growth forest with frequent breaks on little flats along the way that open up views across the canyon.

The Blue Blossom and Spring Board trails join for nearly a half-mile to the junction with Steam Donkey Trail (named after the steam engine that replaced oxen as a means of dragging logs through the canyons). Take a right on Steam Donkey for a half-mile to a three-forked junction. Take the middle path as it heads north, then curves around to the east to pick up the Ridge Trail as it heads on a winding way northwest then north to return refreshed by the long outing.

Alternate Workout Loop

If you want to see how a forest restores itself in just a little less than a century and walk where loggers extracted the last of the big trees from El Corte Madera Creek, follow the first half of the Workout Loop outlined above right to the junction of the Timberview Trail with Lawrence Creek Trail and Virginia Mill Trail. Be warned that this alternate will add several miles and a couple of hours to the hike, so get an early start.

At the Virginia Mill/ Lawrence Creek junction, take the right hand Virginia Mill Trail west southwest as it follows Lawrence Creek to a point just below its confluence with El Corte de Madera Creek Trail. This not a route to be taken during wet winter months, because high water makes it impossible to cross. During late summer and early fall, however, it is just a step across El Corte de Madera Creek and then a twisting 800 foot climb for about a half mile out of the canyon to a east-facing slope of second growth timber and then along the ridge north, the trail weaving with twists and turns from centuries of seismic and geologic working of the landscape. A little over three miles along the top of the ridge, the hiker reaches the junction with the Methuselah Trail. At this juncture, the hiker is either 3.2 miles or 4.5 miles from the end of the trail, depending upon which way is chosen.

The Methuselah Trail is the shortest of the two, but has the disadvantage of another dip of about 400 feet and then a climb back up of that same 400 feet plus a gradual climb over a mile-and-a-half of another 300 feet. Continuing on the left over the North Leaf Trail has less climbing up and down, and leads to the sandstone cliffs along the Tafoni Trail as well. It is a three-mile hike along the twisting ridge trail to the Tafoni Trail junction. A right turn on the Tafoni trail takes the hiker to a point under the sandstone cliffs where a path leads to a closer viewpoint for the unique result of nature's mix of elements. From the sandstone cliffs to the Fir Trail junction is just a half-mile, then a other mile on Fir Trail to Skeggs Point. What a workout! And what a wonderland!

La Honda Creek
Open Space Preserve

Jurisdiction: Midpeninsula Regional Open Space District — 650-691-1200. Web site: http://openspace.org/

Getting There: On Skyline Blvd go 2 miles northwest of the Highway 84 intersection and turn south on Bear Gulch Rd. Go 0.5 mile down the narrow, winding road, turn left on private Allen Rd and go 1 mile to locked gate at preserve boundary. Directions for opening this gate are included in permit. A designated parking place is 0.2 mile beyond gate.

La Honda Creek Open Space Preserve is one of the least developed of all the preserves and is accessible only with special permit from the Midpeninsula Regional Open Space District. The present entrance via Allen Road is through private property and no riding or hiking is permitted on it. The district acquired the 2,043 acres of steep forest slopes and grasslands with two small private parcels in the middle of the acreage. While the preserve's most northwesterly corner is only a few hundred feet from the southeastern corner of El Corte de Madera Open Space Preserve, there is a sizeable acreage of private land intervening. Only a few trails on the upper part of the preserve are open at this writing and none contain loop routes. All are dead ends that must be retraced to their starting points. The trails lead to a couple of vista points on one side, to a giant ancient redwood on the other and two trails that go for a short distance and stop at gates. The preserve takes in a sweep of meadow descending from private Allen Road south along the canyon of La Honda Creek to its intersection with Weeks Creek. The eastern slopes of the preserve are heavily forested; the central and western parts are steeply rolling grasslands, with the drainage basins of Harrington and San Gregorio creeks in the near view, and the Pacific Ocean far to the west.

This land between Harrington and La Honda Creeks was the scene of intensive logging from 1855 to 1910. A dozen mills worked the slopes and deep canyons, moving from one location to another when the trees gave out or a dispute arose over land ownership. Boundary disputes over the line between the old Rancho San Gregorio and U.S. government land sometimes interrupted operations. The government land could be bought for $1.25 an acre, but some operators paid $2,000 to $3,000 for 160-acre parcels said to be part of the land grant property.

The trail described here is not signed, but it takes the visitor to remarkable vistas, lovely meadows and handsome forests in this preserve.

Rules: At this writing the preserve is open by permit only, which can be obtained from MROSD office. No bicycles or dogs permitted.
Maps: MROSD map La Honda Creek O.S.P, USGS topos Woodside and La Honda.

Bird's-Eye View of the Coastside

This trail offers a three-mile, hour-and-a-half hike that descends the meadows to the lower end of the preserve and returns across the pasture and through the woods on the west side of the preserve with only a 300 foot drop, then gain in altitude.

From the designated parking area walk east on the paved road up a rise through a redwood grove and past a little clearing edged with a few Douglas firs of magnificent proportions. The road soon veers south to a barn and a private residence. An enclave of private property is uphill from the road. Leave the paved road and go right down a ranch road between the barn and a corral, then go up through a wooden gate to a meadow beyond.

A few steps from the gate along the ranch road one of the most dramatic vistas of the Coastside ranches and ridges opens up. A sloping pasture is edged on the east by tall, dark oaks, firs and redwoods. To the south you can see the hills along San

Gregorio Creek and forested Butano Ridge. Far west is the gleam of white surf and the Pacific Ocean beyond. After less than a half-mile, the trail enters a patch of forest at the foot of the meadow. Here are a few towering old redwoods bypassed in early logging. There were seven shingle mills along La Honda Creek in the mid to late 1800's.

The trail emerges quickly into a lower meadow and to more views. In spring these grasslands are bright with all kinds of wildflowers. There are no trails here, only a dense forest on one side, or on the other a precipitously steep hillside that falls off into the canyon of Harriington Creek. There are a number of good picnic sites in the meadow.

Return to the upper meadow, where the path crosses to a service road on the west side of the preserve. Watch for the path across the pasture about halfway up the hilltop. The path heads west, descending gradually down a ridge to pick up a service road, which the hiker then will take uphill.

This road winds through a succession of woods and clearings gives you a chance to enjoy the variety of oaks, madrones, firs and redwoods along the way. Stumps of four and five-foot redwoods cut in early logging when compared to second-growth trees speak to the ages of the vanished ancient giants. Another half hour of hiking takes one out on a hillside clearing below a ridge and above a wooded canyon that drains into Harrington Creek. Around a bend is the parking area.

Long Ridge Open Space Preserve

Jurisdiction: Midpeninsula Regional Open Space District — 650-691-1200. Web site: http://openspace.org/

Getting There: From Highway 84 and Skyline Boulevard go south some 8 miles. The preserve is on the western slope with 2 parking areas; one is near the northern edge of the preserve, and the other is about 2 miles further on Skyline and has more limited space.

This 1,551-acre preserve is dedicated to Mary and Wallace Stegner, avid conservationists who helped preserve this striking sweep of California open space. Stegner was the Pulitzer Prize winning author and longtime Stanford writing program head who nurtured such literary talents as Ken Kesey, Larry McMurtry and many others. A stone bench beside one of the trails contains the dedication. The preserve extends for three miles along the crest of the Santa Cruz Mountains just west of Skyline Boulevard offering dramatic views westward across open grasslands and wooded canyons.

The headwaters of Slate Creek and Peters Creek run from the hillside down into the canyons of Pescadero Creek County Park and Portola Redwoods State Park. Twelve miles of trail in this preserve include connections to the neighboring parks as well paths up to Long Ridge and across high grasslands. A 3.4-mile segment of the Bay Area Ridge Trail crosses the preserve and a segment of the Ridge Trail now connects Long Ridge to Skyline Ridge Open Space Preserve to the northwest.

Grassy hills fall away precipitously from the crest of the ridge and clumps of spreading canyon oaks, *Quercus chrysolepsis*, dot the hilltop. Due west in the great redwood canyon of Pescadero Creek is Portola Redwoods State Park. Its east boundary adjoins this preserve, reached via the Ward Road Trail.

Through an Oak Forest

This is an easy one-hour, two-mile stroll through a fine oak forest and across windswept meadows. The walk starts from the southern entrance on the Hickory Oaks Trail. In 100 yards, the Hickory Oaks Trail turns right under wide-spreading trees that were prized by the natives for the acorns that furnished easily stored winter food and prized by early settlers for the hard wood that made wagon wheels and farm implements such as mallet heads. Beyond the grove and uphill to the left (west) a side trail leads to a meadow, rimmed with handsome trees and dotted with great, sandstone outcrops that once rested on the ocean floor, now raised some 2,000 feet by the ever-pressing Pacific tectonic plate. The side trip rewards the hiker with views down Oil Creek from the top of the meadow. A panorama of successive forested ridges stretches as far as the eye can see. Returning to the road from the north side of the meadow, continue for an easy 15-minute walk under more oaks before rejoining the wide Hickory Oaks Trail to climb over rolling pasturelands. After a half-mile the hiker reaches the junction with Long Ridge Road and retraces the path to the parking lot.

Downhill to Portola Redwoods State Park,
Or Testing the Legs and Lungs Overnight

The easiest way is to arrange to have a car waiting at the bottom of the hill – Portola Redwoods State Park is on the end of this jaunt – or do it the challenging way by hiking the seven miles downhill and camp overnight in Portola Park, returning with a 2,290-foot climb uphill the next day. Either way, it requires planning and making arrangements. The overnighter requires camping reservations. The downhill run-only will require a friend to pay the $3 parking fee and patiently await the hiker's arrival.

Start from the south entrance on Skyline Boulevard, take the Hickory Oaks Trail northwest along the route to the Long Ridge Road junction. Turn left (west), go 0.3 mile and turn southwest on Ward Road to begin the descent along this wide old ranch road. Off to the east is the ridge where Highway 9 winds its curving way unseen down along the west boundary of Castle Rock State Park. To the southeast are the deep, wooded canyons of Oil and Waterman creeks.

Descending steadily, the trail reaches a broad plateau where the Ranch Spring Trail circles the site of a ranch owned by the Panigetti family. The loop trail swings around the plateau and into woods of black oak, *Quercus kelloggii,* and Douglas fir, *Pseudotsuga menziesii,* passes an old spring and returns to the main trail. After another mile, the trail reaches the gate of Portola Redwoods State Park. Bicyclists and equestriennes are not permitted past this point. Hikers continue downhill, winding around the southeast-facing slope. After passing an abandoned farm site on the left, the path enters the shade of an evergreen forest, and goes up a little rise. On the right will be the marked trail to Slate Creek and Portola. After descending steps cut into the steep hillside, the path crosses Slate Creek to follow it through the redwoods.

In less than a half-mile is a large rustic sign declaring that William Page had a mill at this site. This was his second mill that was opened in 1875, his first being on Peters Creek. A lunch stop

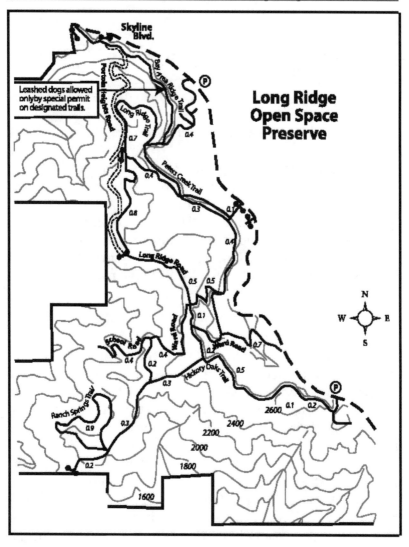

here will give one time to ponder how Page hauled his lumber
out of this canyon up to Skyline to connect with his own
thoroughfare, Page Mill Road, which is a public road today. At
the junction with the Peters Creek Loop is the Slate Creek Trail
Camp, which would be the layover for overnight hiker.

For the downhiller, continue 1.3 miles to the Slate Creek
and Summit trails junction. Take either trail for about a mile hike
to the park visitor center, where your friends await your arrival.

Memorial Park of San Mateo County

Jurisdiction: San Mateo County – 650-363-0212; reservations – 650-363-0212.
Web Site: http://www.eparks.net/parks/

Getting There: Take Highway One to Highway 84 (La Honda Road); go east to Pescadero Road and turn right (southeast) on Pescadero Road, go past Sam McDonald Park and go about 4 miles to sign on left pointing straight ahead (west) to Memorial Park and another small street sign marking Wurr Road; go past the Wurr Road sign and go straight ahead (west) 1 mile to the park entrance on the left.

This park deep in the redwood country is a reflection of how early the conservation heroes emerged on the San Mateo County Coast. Logging was about to resume on the upper end of Pescadero Creek when Roy W. Cloud, the county superintendent of schools in the 1920s, stepped forward to help make this the county's first public park. While visiting the old Wurr School in this remote area, Cloud was enchanted by the beauty of the forests and streams surrounding it. In the Spring of 1923, he urged the County Board of Supervisors to buy land for a park here. After studying possible sites, a citizens committee recommended that the County buy 310 acres for $70,000, the beginnings of today's Memorial Park. It was named in honor of the San Mateo County men who lost their lives in World War I. Timber surrounding this area was logged in the late 1800's and early 1900's, both for redwood lumber and the bark of the tan oak tree. Four small sawmill sites are either on or adjacent to the present park boundaries and another half dozen close by along the creek.

Only its remote location far from markets – lumber and shingles from the mills here had to be hauled down to Pigeon Point or used locally – kept the amount of logging at a relatively slow pace. The last mill still operating in the early 1930's turned out caskets for a San Francisco mortuary. By that time, roads to the bay side of the peninsula made transport a bit easier.

During the Depression, Memorial Park set up a project camp for the Work Projects Administration created by President Franklin D. Roosevelt. WPA crews built many of the park's existing restrooms, roadways and picnic sites.

As the population climbed in the San Francisco Bay Area, the popularity of the park grew so rapidly another 190 acres were added to Memorial Park, and additional park sites were added until it became the center of some 10,000 acres that include the Portola Redwoods State Park and the Pescadero and Sam McDonald County park with links to nearby Butano and Big Basin state parks.

This complex of three county parks is connected to a network of trails linking open space preserves and parks in neighboring counties. Immediately upstream on Pescadero Creek is the 2,800-acre Portola Redwoods State Park, making a total of more than 10,000 acres of redwoods, fir and oak groves available for public use and enjoyment. In addition, two long trails join these parks to other public open spaces. The 6.8-mile Basin Trail extends from Portola Redwoods through Pescadero Creek Park and on an easement through private lands reaches Big Basin Redwoods State Park in Santa Cruz County. Another long-distance trail links the Old Haul Road Trail in Pescadero Creek Park with the Slate Creek Trail in Portola Redwoods State Park, which connects to the Ward Road Trail in Long Ridge Open Space Preserve on the Skyline ridge and will provide backpacking routes that will challenge sturdy outdoor enthusiasts

In addition to the redwoods, Douglas fir, madrone , *Arbutus menziesii*; manzanita, *Arctostaphylos ssp.;* and several varieties of oak, the common plants that may be found here are huckleberry, *Vaccinium ovatum*; poison oak, *Toxicodendron diversilobum*; many varieties ferns; redwood sorrel, *Oxalis oregana*; and horsetail, *Equisetum*. Animals seen in abundance are Steller's jays, acorn woodpeckers, western grey squirrels, raccoons, and banana slugs.

Pescadero Creek, which is fed by several smaller streams such as Bloomquist, Hoffman, McCormick, and Peterson creeks in the park, is a winter home for steelhead trout as they migrate

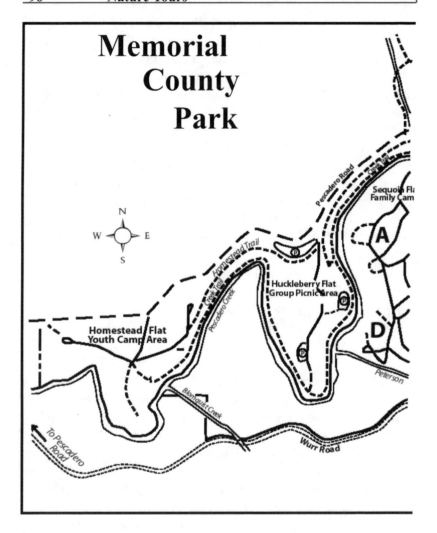

Memorial County Park

upstream to spawn and then move back to the sea in the spring.

The summer temperatures are mild, cooled periodically when fog drifts in from the ocean. In winter, the air is crisp and the ground and plants are moist. The yearly rainfall averages 40 inches and winter frosts are frequent.

Memorial Park Facilities

Memorial Park is open year-round for camping, picnicking and youth group activities. Family picnic sites are located at the east end of the park. They are filled on a first-come, first-served basis.

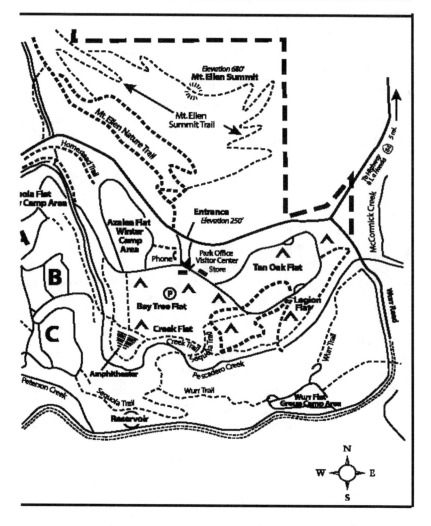

Memorial Park has two large family camping areas. The 156 campsites are assigned on a first-come, first-served basis. Sites are available for up to two weeks. A maximum of eight people are accommodated per site. There is water and shower facilities, and firewood is sold. The showers are coin operated – 25 cents for two minutes. A limited number of sites can accommodate recreational vehicles up to 35 feet in length. A dump station is available for registered recreational vehicles. A camp site availability line is available at (650) 879-0212.

There are six youth group areas (Homestead Flat Areas 1- 6) available for day and/or night use. They are available by reservation for organized youth groups.

Four reservable group picnic areas accommodating 50 to 300 people (Huckleberry Flat Areas 1 - 4) are found in the eastern part of the park. The sites have water, tables and barbecue pits. The areas are available by reservation.

Two group camping areas are located in the Wurr Flat at the southeasterly portion of the park. Each area (Wurr Flat #1 and Wurr Flat #2 accommodate 75 people) and are available by reservation.

An amphitheater is located at the center of the park. There is seating for 300 plus a fire pit and stage. The amphitheater is available by reservation.

A camp store open Memorial Day through September offers camping supplies, groceries, wood, ice, sandwiches, ice cream, candy, and soft drinks. It is located near the park entrance in the picnic area. There is also an interpretive center located next to the park office. Open daily, May-September, the center has natural and historic exhibits and game boards.

Regular campfire and naturalist programs are held during the summer months. A park naturalist leads evening campfires, nature programs and walks on various trails. Pamphlets are also available for self guided walks on the Mt. Ellen Nature Trail. During the summer months, a swimming hole is created in Pescadero Creek just east of the amphitheater. Memorial Park is open every day of the year including all holidays. It opens daily at 8 a.m. Closing time varies by time of year; in the summer months, closing time is 8 p.m, while in winter it is 5 p.m., and in the fall 7 p.m.

Rules: Open 8 A.M. to sunset. No dogs; no ground fires allowed. Reservations required for all organized youth groups, regardless of size or activity, group camp sites and picnic areas, trail camps and Jack Brook Horse Camp. Reservations are not accepted for family camping and picnicking. Fees.

Mt. Ellen Trails

For a tour of a mixed evergreen and chaparral environments plus views north to Mindego Hill, hikers are offered a choice of a one-mile Nature Trail Loop that rises a mere 200 feet in elevation, or a 1.6-mile, 430-foot climb to the summit of Mt. Ellen. The longer trail takes about an hour and a half to the summit.

Cross Pescadero Road opposite the park entrance; take the hikers-only trail uphill to the first junction. Turn left (northwest) onto the Nature Trail and follow the numbered posts that point out the significant trees, plants and terrain you pass through, as well as describing the animals and birds that inhabit the park. While the signs help, if the hiker has a copy of *Plants of the Redwood Region*, in hand, one gets a deeper appreciation of what is being viewed. Stay on the Nature Trail and ignore the junction where the Pomponio Trail goes left. It is at the next junction that the Summit Trail goes left to reach the top of Mt. Ellen. If the hiker chooses to stay on the Nature Trail, it zigzags around several switchbacks to the next junction, turn right and go past the first Nature Trail sign to return to the park entrance.

Hikers choosing the Summit Trail would be well advised to take the route on an early morning or late afternoon jaunt for the added pleasure of bird life toward the end of the hike. During those hours, many species of birds can be heard calling, and if one pauses for a time beside the trail, they can be observed in trailside bushes and trees. The path climbs up and around switchbacks through the forest where lupines, *Lupinus ssp.*, blossom from March to August in shades of blue and lavender and the sticky monkey flower, *Diplacus aurantiacus*, has bright yellow blooms through July. There is a left turnoff for the Pomponio Trail, which follows a narrow path along the southwest-facing hillside up to a high western viewpoint and provides a return down a broad service road. If the hiker continues on the Summit Trail, it zigzags uphill to a fenced opening with a view north through the trees to Mindego Hill's grassy south side. The path goes down and up on the ridge for 500 feet to another clearing with a worn sandstone base and a limited view.

From here it's downhill all the way, winding around many bends, switchbacking out into open grassland, and then back into an oak forest where the bird life can be seen at the proper hours. After passing the Nature Trail junctions, it is a quick descent through the redwoods to the Pescadero Road crossing and the park visitor center.

Tan Oak Nature Trail

This informative trail covers four-tenths of a mile and is accessible to wheelchair users and sight- and hearing-impaired persons. The start of the trail is just north of the parking area from the Tan Oak Flat picnic area. A green rope looped through sturdy posts guides those with sight impairment.

This short trail shows the secret of the redwoods' long life and how plants adapt to the redwoods' dense shade. See the park's tallest and oldest tree and stop at a meditation grove to admire a ring of ancient, burned-out redwoods.

West Side Loop Trip on the Creek and Homestead Trails

This is an easy hour-and-a-half, relatively level stroll that meanders along and across Pescadero Creek and returns under stately redwoods. This hike can be done only in summer or fall because the portable bridges over Pescadero Creek are removed during the rainy season. From the park office follow the park road to Tan Oak Flat and take the Creek Trail on its east side. Shortly make a sharp angle and the Creek Trail begins its westward sally. Follow the trail past Legion Flat to the beach where Pescadero Creek is impounded for a swimming area in summer. This point can also be seen by descending the wide stairs off the service road as it bends east.

From the beach area, take the trail along the bluff to the amphitheater, descend to the creek on steep steps or circle around the amphitheater and pick up the Creek Trail going north. In times of low water, one can descend the steps to the creek, cross it on a portable bridge or hop across on rocks, and continue downstream under overhanging willows and tanbark oaks. At the Sequoia Flat camp sites, follow the road east to ford the creek that flows through a culvert. On the north side of the creek the trail narrows to only 12 inches and traverses a steep, moist bank. When it crosses a wooden foot bridge over a small creek, a look upstream shows Pomponio Falls tumbling down the bank.

Next, a steel bridge spans the creek, reached by climbing wooden steps up the hillside. Across the bridge will be at Campground B, where there are restrooms and a phone.

Return to the Creek Trail on the west side of the bridge and follow it around two bends to the Homestead Trail where the return leg of this loop trip begins. The Creek Trail often washes out in heavy winter rains, in which case take a trail across the picnic area to the Homestead Trail. Huckleberry bushes, *Vaccinium ovatum*, and many varieties of ferns follow the trail.

Where a sign points across Pescadero Road to the Pomponio Trail, the hiker has an option of continuing on Homestead Trail or adding the 3.5-mile Pomponio Loop. This Pomponio Trail commemorates a Native American turned "desperado," said to have holed up in this area in the 1820s and whose specific misdeeds have been lost in the archives. A rebel from the harsh mission system, Pomponio was hanged in Monterey in 1824. Pomponio Creek, which flows from the heights northwest of the park to the Coast, the beach there and the long Pomponio Trail are all named for this colorful rebel.

If the hiker chooses to continue on the Homestead Trail one soon reaches the Azalea Flat campgrounds and the service road, from which one can return to the amphitheater and go on to Tan Oak Flat. To add a short loop after this trip, you could descend to Pescadero Creek from the Creek/Tan Oak Nature Trail junction, turn left (east) on the Wurr Trail and wander through the redwoods on the south side of the creek. The path goes north past an ancient barn, crosses the bridge over the creek and immediately enters the park on the Creek Trail again.

Pescadero Creek County Park

Jurisdiction: San Mateo County – 650-363-0212; reservations – 650-363-0212.
Web Site: http://www.eparks.net/parks/

Getting There: Take Highway One to Highway 84 (La Honda Road); turn east to Pescadero Creek Road; at Alpine Road intersection turn left on Alpine Road and follow to park entrance.

There are 6,486 acres here that tie Memorial and Sam McDonald parks together, and takes in seven miles of Pescadero Creek as it twists through the canyon formed by Towne and Butano ridges. Fed by 19 smaller seasonal streams that tumble down the steep sides of these ridges in wet weather, Pescadero Creek County Park forms the centerpiece of the park system. More than 40 miles of trail reach its highest points, follow its creekbeds and penetrate its extravagant forests. When combined with the adjacent lands of Portola Redwoods State Park, this vast open space is ideal for long, strenuous hikes and horseback rides. Trails leading to the banks of Pescadero Creek offer short jaunts for casual walks. The canyons are heavily forested, especially on north-facing, 2,000-foot Butano Ridge, while the southwest-facing slopes of 1,200-foot Towne Ridge offer pockets of grassland with inspiring views in all directions. Also offered here are trips that sample Pescadero Creek Park's splendid, more remote, near-wilderness areas.

This land here saw only light use during the Spanish and Mexican occupation from the 1770's to 1848. Natives from the Ohlone tribes had for centuries roamed the canyons, harvesting plants, nuts and berries, and taking trout and salmon from the creek. After the gold rush, early settlement by north Americans was limited to only a few farmers and loggers.

The scene of only sporadic logging efforts since 1856 due to its location and shipping difficulties, the area experienced a resurgence of lumbering interest following the 1906 earthquake and fire that destroyed much of San Francisco. Hauling the wood to the bay side of the peninsula was still slow, tough work. A team of six horses pulled wagons with 6,000 feet of lumber to La Honda the first day, then up the grade to Skylonda and down the mountain, all for the sum of $48 for the four-day, sometimes five-day (in bad weather) round trip; and the teamster had to feed and lodge himself and his livestock, and repair and maintain his wagons from that munificent sum.

Facilities include trails for hikers and equestrians; trail camps require permits obtainable from the Memorial Park office.

Rules: Bicycles on Old Haul Road only. No dogs, no fires. Maps: San Mateo County brochure Pescadero Creek County Park, USGS topos La Honda, Mindego Hill and Big Basin.

The Picnic Trails to Pescadero Creek and Worley Flat

This is the ideal path to take for a backpack picnic to an easy destination for families with young children. The creek is only a mile down the trail. It is another half-mile to Worley Flat with only a 50-foot rise along the creek trail, and barely 100 feet to the flat.

For the most fun, select a sunny day, pack a picnic lunch that's easy to carry, take along extra socks and extra clothing – the kids will want to splash in the creek. Start from the Hoffman Creek Trailhead at the Wurr Road entrance to the park. Cross the bridge over Hoffman Creek past a few picnic tables and the kiosk on the left. Follow the wide, unpaved Old Haul Road. This road/trail runs up and down through a clearing and a former orchard, then dips into redwoods on an easement through adjoining private lands. Stumps of old monarchs logged years ago still stand beside the trail showing the size and grandeur of the ancient forest. Some trees are hollow and others are blackened by long-forgotten blazes.

About a half-mile through the cool forest, the trail passes Piney Creek, which leads to a Pomponio Trail turnoff on the left. Along the creek, deciduous alder, *Aldus rubra,* and California box elder, *Acer negundo, spp. californicum*, hug the water. Cross a portable footbridge (removed at high water) over Pescadero Creek. Either picnic in the shade by the creek or go on to the sunny meadow at Worley Flat, just another 10 minutes up the Pomponio Trail.

This is a popular picnic stop where the creek rolls over scattered rocks, laps at mossy stream banks and bathes the trunks of the alders and elders arching overhead. The kids can entertain themselves for hours here. Then it's an easy hike to the flats; return on the maintenance road.

Brook Trail Loop for Coastal Views

Set aside at least five hours for this climb of about 650 feet out of the creek canyon to explore sunny meadows and enjoy wide views.

Take along a map from the San Mateo County Parks and Recreation Department because this trip meets many trail junctions that may not be well marked. It is possible that undergrowth may have obscured one or two signs or another may be missing. Start at the Hoffman Creek Trailhead on Wurr Road and follow the directions to Worley Flat. Continue on the Pomponio Trail past the wide meadow and curve right (east) across its north end. At the far side of the meadow follow the Pomponio Trail left onto a graveled tread. Go uphill through oak woodland. Soon you cross the former Jones Gulch Trail, and take the foot trail down a long stretch. In springtime the sunny patches will bloom with the blues of the mountain iris, *Iris douglaiana*; and the wood rose's pink petals turn in the fall to deep red urn-shaped hips the natives used to brew tea. The iris, while poisonous, had its uses, too; the leaves were stripped and twisted into strong twine used for animal snares. The trail switchbacks descend to the creek.

Another trail junction is reached after 1.6 miles. The Pomponio Trail goes right and the Jones Gulch Trail goes left. Take the left and cross the Jones Gulch Bridge -- the Brook Trail Loop starts. This is truly a magical part of Pescadero Park. Under the towering redwood trees in the creek canyon carved out of Butano sandstone, can be seen little waterfalls dropping over fallen logs, five-finger ferns, *Adiantum pedatum var. aleuticum*, and moss carpeting the creek's high banks. Pink-flowered redwood sorrel, *Oxalis oregana*, adorn the forest floor.

After another 500 feet, bear right on an unpaved patrol road. The unmarked Jones Gulch Trail, crosses Towne Creek in a culvert, goes 300 feet further on the patrol road, and turns sharply left. Slowly climbing through a forest of ancient and second-growth trees on the west side of the Brook Trail Loop, one will see new trees sprouting from fallen ones and tanbark oaks growing out of sawn-off redwoods. About midway up the mountain, the trail narrows and skirts a deep ravine, then makes 10 or 11 switchbacks through mixed forest to a clearing mostly covered with chaparral, *Pickeringa montana*, a hardy plant whose underground root system enables it to survive wildfires. From this vantage point, one has a view into the deep, heavily wooded canyon of Towne Creek. To the south lies Butano Ridge rising above the Pescadero Creek Canyon.

After more switchbacks through a mixed forest of fir, oak species and madrone, *Arbutus menziesii*, the trail crosses a gentle grassy slope with a view of the Skyline ridge. Trail signs point south to destinations in Pescadero and Memorial parks and east to the Hikers Hut and the continuation of the Brook Trail Loop.

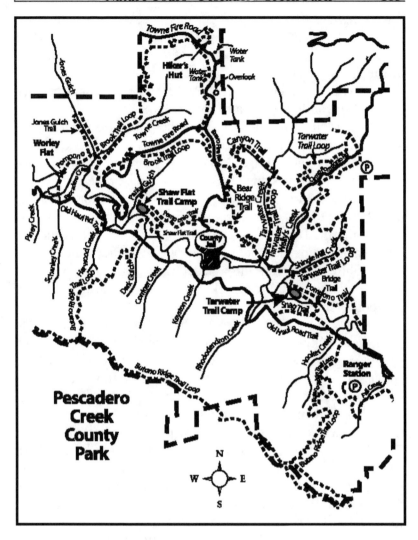

Pescadero
Creek
County
Park

In a few steps the trail reaches a wide, unpaved road, which can be taken. Or the hiker can stay on the foot trail that parallels this road around the head of the Towne Creek canyon. The hiker is now in Sam McDonald County Park.

In about a half-mile there will be a left turnoff sign (north) to the Hikers Hut. Follow the trail for a quarter-mile uphill into the woods to a cabin that has an incredible view of the coast. Thanks to one of the Coastside's heroes, Ollie Mayer, and a dedicated team of Sierra Club volunteers, the hut was brought from Denmark and assembled on this park site in 1977. This hut can be reserved for an overnight or a weekend by calling the Loma Prieta Chapter of the Sierra Club. The visiting day hiker is welcome to sit on a log seat in front of the hut and enjoy the vista of Butano Ridge and Pecadero Creek canyon.

After a rest and snack, return to the Brook Trail Loop and proceed downhill through a fir forest. When the trail crosses the patrol road, climb to a ledge where there are two picnic tables and another fine view of southwestern San Mateo County's beautiful evergreen forests. Next take the narrow foot trail through quiet redwood groves on the west-facing side of the canyon. Go past the Towne Fire Road crossing, and at the next junction angle sharply right to stay on the Brook Trail Loop. For approximately a half-mile the Brook Trail Loop levels off, paralleling the fire road. Then it joins the road for about 500 feet, after which it goes right, uphill, and zigzags through deep redwood forest to another trail junction, where the Brook Trail Loop goes right onto the Pomponio Trail heading north.

Shortly the path crosses another fire road, the Jones Gulch Trail, and continues to Grangers Bridge across Towne Creek where a sign shows the elevation is 270 feet. From this bridge, one has a view upstream of the confluence of Towne and Jones Gulch creeks. Little waterfalls drop into a pool shaded by huge redwoods, its banks festooned with a variety of ferns. Just a bit farther is the Pomponio/Brook Trail junction where the Brook Trail Loop began. The creek tumbles over a sandstone shelf, bounces off a fallen tree, and continues on its way to join Pescadero Creek. The hiker bears left on the Pomponio Trail retraces a few switchbacks uphill, crosses Worley Flat, and heads southwest to the ford of Pescadero Creek. That leads to the graveled Old Haul Road, where after a turn to the right (west) one returns to the Hoffman Creek Trailhead.

Thar's Tar in The Water

There are two choices for exploring Tarwater Creek, a seasonal stream that earned its gooey name much like the Pennsylvania creek that ultimately made J.D. Rockefeller super rich. Globs of petroleum-based tar ooze from the ground in one of the swampy portions of the creek. The difference here, fortunately for nature lovers, nothing of commercial value was found beneath the ooze. Big oil has been pushing for decades to drill in the marine canyons offshore that are downstream from this telltale glob, and so far conservationist friends in Washington, D.C. have been able to prevent such an environmental disaster, but that is a different story. Our focus is the creek and the choices offered around it: either a 3.5-mile, two hour jaunt on Tarwater Trail itself, or a five mile, three hour hike to the creek and then up the canyon sides.

Let's look at the shorter trip first. Again, there are two choices. If one has made proper reservations at the Memorial Park office and camped at Tarwater Trail Camp, one may start the hike there by taking the Bridge Trail west to the Tarwater Trail, across Camp Pomponio Road and follow it northeast along the west side of the creek. Or take the reverse route.

Reversing Directions

The starting point for the reverse route is the parking area about two-thirds of a mile from the park entrance off Alpine Road. Looking north from this vantage point, one can see about three miles to the south side of 2,143-foot Mindego Hill. From the parking lot, cross the road and take the designated Tarwater Trail Loop northwest about a quarter-mile through open grassland and follow the trail along a narrower path into a woodland of mixed oak varieties and bay trees, *Umbellularia californica*. Emerging from the woods, follow the east edge of a long meadow, then cut across and skirt the forest above a branch of Tarwater Creek. Continue around a huge, lone redwood and watch for a side trail cutting over to a small building with a corrugated tin roof under a cluster of tall eucalyptus trees, known as Tie Camp. This is all that remains of the Moore, Fisher and Troupe sawmill operation that cut redwood trees into railroad ties here in 1915 and 1916 to feed a small railroad-building boom.

The main trail zigzags downhill through the redwoods past a wallow dug up and rooted in by wild pigs. If you happen to spot any, do not challenge these unpredictable descendants of European pigs that were brought here for sport hunting. Their razor-sharp teeth can be dangerous. At its junction with the Canyon Trail the narrow Tarwater Trail Loop widens, and you bear left (south) to continue this trip.

Before doing so, take a brief side trip up the Canyon Trail

where the path crosses the main trunk of Tarwater Creek. There one can observe globs of thick, shiny, iridescent material. That's the tar that gives the creek its name.

Double back to the wide Tarwater Trail Loop, turn right, walk the gentle rise and continue south about one mile through sizable redwoods above the east side of Tarwater Creek. Huckleberries, *Vaccinium ovatum,* with their white blossoms in spring becoming sweet blue berries in fall; and in May and June the mountain iris, *Iris douglasiana*; and year-round the deer fern, *Blechnum spicant*; five-fingered fern, *Adiantum pedantum ssp. Aleuticum,* and other varieties line the trail's edge. At the next junction, go through a gate in a split-log rail fence onto Camp Pomponio Road and turn left following the road (also the Pomponio Trail here) for about 200 feet. Then veer off right onto the narrow Pomponio/Tarwater Trail Loop. With another gate on the left, go right onto an unpaved road -- still the Pomponio/ Tarwater Trail Loop -- in a small clearing bordered by tall California wild lilac, *Ceonothus thyraflorus.*

Across Wally's Creek is the hikers-only Shingle Mill Creek Trail that goes into a dark grove of second-growth redwood trees. This area, easily accessible to logging through the 1960s and early '70s, has grown tall and dense since then. Huge stumps encircled by new growth are clues to the size of the ancient trees. Follow Tarwater Trail east northeast as it parallels Shingle Mill Creek for more than a half-mile and then crosses the stream and climbs atop the ridge. The banks on the right side of the road are chalky limestone deposits. Higher up the trail, there is a tremendous old redwood more than 12 feet in diameter with a burned-out heart and two huge elbow-shaped limbs high above the ground perched at the top of the steep hillside on the left. Soon the trail reaches the parking lot where the hiker began.

Circling Tarwater Canyon

To add another hour and an extra two miles and more scenic views to the hike, follow the Canyon Trail branch from the junction of the Tarwater and Canyon trails. Take the Canyon Trail as it descends to the Tarwater Creek crossing. There in the swampy area, you can see the traces of tar that give the creek its name. From there, the hiker has a climb of several hundred feet on a narrow trail, closed to horses in wet weather. Switchbacks go past a few pools in the creek, a huge logjam and a marshy spot where wild boars like to root for their dinner. The trail makes a long climb south and then round a sharp switchback where there is a view north through the trees to Towne Ridge.

About an hour from the trailhead, the hiker turns left on Bear Ridge Trail through a forest with a high canopy. Swing along on this trail up a little rise and then downhill to intersect the Bravo Fire Road before picking up Bear Ridge Trail on the left again. The trail clings to the side of the deep Tarwater Canyon, passing through big Douglas firs, then crosses to the ridge's west side.

At the next trail junction, turn left (southeast) on the Pomponio Trail. To the west, this trail reaches the eight Shaw Flat Trail Camps, which require reservations through the Memorial Park office. There are restrooms, but campers must carry their own water, food and sleeping bags. Non-campers follow the Pomponio Trail downhill into a huckleberry hollow and then out to the paved Camp Pomponio Road. There a big sign announces that the county jail (a men's correctional center) is just west of there, and only official visitors may enter. The hiker goes left, following the road across a steel-trussed bridge over Tarwater Creek, climbs up a short hill, and turns left (north) around a split-rail fence onto the wide, west leg of the Tarwater Trail Loop. And returns on the trail described earlier.

The Day-Long Workout On Butano Ridge Trail

This hike is ideal for the experienced hiker who wants to spend a day communing with nature while testing stamina and physical conditioning. This takes at least eight hours, covers nearly 13.5 miles and involves climbs totaling 1,750 feet.

Almost the entire hike is within Pescadero Creek County Park, but the starting point is in Memorial County Park. Start from Hoffman Creek trailhead, reached from the parking lot on Wurr Road about a quarter-mile off Pescadero Creek Road. Remember to take extra sweaters, a windbreaker and plenty of water and food for this trek.

Follow the Old Haul Road for 1.5 miles past the crossings of Schenly and Harwood creeks passing from time to time through dense groves of red alders, *Alnus rubra,* that the Ohlone used in many ways. Basketry was the main use; roots were striated and made into thread, and the inner bark turned into dye by boiling until soft, chewed and then spat intro a woven bowl as a dye solution. The orange dye turned a deep brown with age. Stately redwoods stand as sentinels along the bottom of Pescadero Creek canyon.

Ignore the two trails that cross to the north side of the creek—Towne Fire Road and the Shaw Flat Trail— leading to the Shaw Flat Trail Camp on the Pomponio Trail. Just opposite the Shaw Flat Trail is the entrance to the western leg of the Butano Ridge Trail Loop. Turn right (south) as the trail goes up and around ridges, between giant redwoods, past burned-out shells of huge old redwoods and continues zigzagging upward for nearly two miles. About two-thirds of the way up the mountain, the path turns southeast until finally reaching the road on the ridge top, the Butano Ridge Trail Loop. Turn left. The road continues up and down for more than two miles. The Butano Ridge Trail Loop angles sharply uphill to the east. Where the trail levels off there is a turn right (east) and under tall redwoods and Douglas firs until reaching a massive sandstone wall, at least 30 feet high.

Just beyond this exposed sandstone is the Basin Trail sign on the right. From here it is 5.5 miles to Big Basin Redwoods State Park and 21 miles to Waddell Creek. This trip, however, take the sharp left to the Butano Ridge Trail Loop and a series of switchbacks go downhill into a lovely evergreen forest.

At the junction continue on the left fork, the Butano Ridge Trail Loop. The right fork, the Portola Trail (also called the Basin Trail) will reach the Old Haul Road about a mile farther east and across from the trail into Portola Redwoods State Park. Continuing on the Butano Ridge Trail Loop, one goes into a damp little glade, then descends to a flatter area near the Old Haul Road. At the junction with this road are several California wax myrtle, *Myrica californica,* with their long, glossy, narrow leaves.

Take a left on the wide, graveled Old Haul Road and follow it uphill past Hooker Creek, the Snag Trail to the Tarwater Trail Camp on the right and Rhododendron Creek on the left. At the sign for Keystone Creek, the hiker may see a small waterfall upstream in a shady ravine. Then, just past Dark Gulch, one reaches the other leg of the Butano Ridge Trail Loop on which the climb to the ridgetop began. Retrace the trail back to the Hoffman Creek Trailhead.

Portola Redwoods State Park

Jurisdiction: California Parks and Recreation
Telephone: 650-948-9098. **Web Site:** http://www.cal-parks.ca.gov/

Getting There: From Highway One and Highway 84 (La Honda Road), go east to Pescadero Creek Road, turn left on Alpine Road and go to turnoff to state park.

This difficult-to-reach park is only for the adventurous who enjoy the deep woods and who believe getting there is half the fun. Access requires miles of slow twisting and turning on narrow Alpine Road, then another three miles down grade on the park entry roadway. Though it is barely wide enough for two cars, it is paved all the way.

Portola Redwoods State Park rests at the base of Butano Ridge and offers miles of hiking trails through some of the largest redwoods in San Mateo County and links with neighboring parks and preserves in San Mateo and Santa Cruz counties. This 2,800-acre plus park adjoins San Mateo County's 8,027-acre complex of Pescadero Creek, Memorial, and Sam McDonald parks. On its northeast corner it abuts Long Ridge Open Space Preserve, which lies along the crest of the Santa Cruz Mountains amid thousands of acres of contiguous open space. With the opening of the Basin Trail in 1995 connecting Big Basin State Park to the south, and the Butano Fire Trail Extension, there are almost limitless choices for extensive backpacking trips between Portola Redwoods State Park and other state and regional parks in the area.

There are also shorter, more leisurely walks through the woods on trails starting from the park office and on short nature trails around Pescadero Creek. There are three picnic areas with tables and barbecues, two group camps, and 67 camp sites (nine of which are set up for RV'ers — 21-foot maximum for trailers and 24-foot maximum for motorhomes – without hookups), all on a first come, first served basis. Restrooms and coin operated showers are available. The hiking trails range from the shorter to longer loop trips up to 13 miles long, and still other trails that

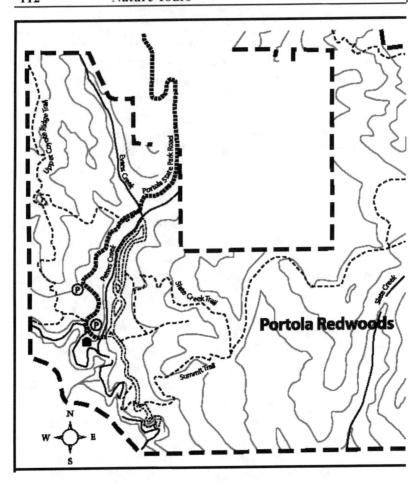

Portola Redwoods

connect to adjoining parks and open space preserves.

This was originally home to the Ohlone natives who spent summers on the coast and in fall gathered nuts, berries and other useful plant products on trails along the creeks. Few Spanish or Mexican loggers wandered this deep into the woods. After the United States annexed California in 1848, it took more than a decade for settlers to arrive. The first known settler in this area, Christian Iverson, a former Pony Express rider, arrived in the 1860's and built a small redwood cabin on a high bank above Pescadero Creek. The Loma Prieta earthquake of 1989, hit the old structure hard and refurbishing the cabin is still not done.

Although loggers came to this area in the 1850's seeking wood to build and then rebuild San Francisco after the 1906

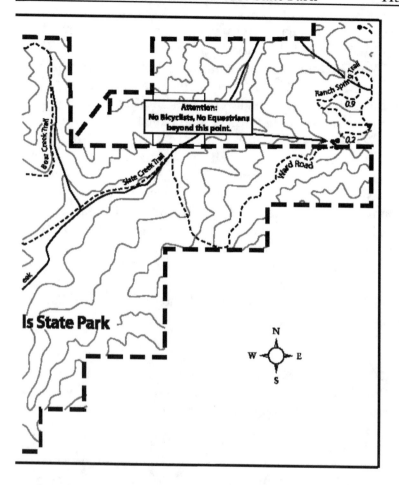

Attention:
No Bicyclists, No Equestrians
beyond this point.

Bear Creek Trail

Slate Creek Trail

Ranch Spring Trail

0.9

0.2

Ward Road

ls State Park

N
W — E
S

earthquake and fire, most worked the lower end of Pescadero Creek at first. In 1865 William Page developed a mill on Peters Creek, which was moved to Slate Creek in 1875, the latter being within today's park boundaries. He had a road built from old Mayfield in today's Palo Alto, Page Mill Road, which is still in use on the east side of Skyline Boulevard. The west side portion of the Old Page Mill Road Trail twists two miles downhill through Skyline Ridge Open Space Preserve and may continue as a public trail to the Peters Creek Loop in Portola Redwoods at a future date. Loggers cut the giant redwoods along the streams and hillsides and made them into shingles and shakes, then hauled them by mule teams over the Skyline ridge to the Embarcadero in present-day Palo Alto.

After logging activity waned, San Francisco residents established summer retreats along Pescadero Creek. In 1924, a San Francisco Shrine group purchased 1,600 acres in this area that were bought 31 years later by the State of California. The Save-the-Redwoods League donated additional acres during ensuing years, swelling the park to to more than 2,800 acres.

The park's visitor center features exhibits of the outstanding natural features of the park. Freeze-dried specimens of many animals and samples of trees, flowers, and shrubs are displayed in life-like settings. The many campsites for families, groups, and backpackers willing to walk to trail camps are very popular during summer, especially on weekends. Between Memorial and Labor Day weekend camp sites are booked well ahead. Spring, summer, and fall are the best times for hiking, picnicking, and camping. Parking is available for day hikers near the park office and convenient to all the trailheads. Parking and camping fees are charged.

Rules: Hikers only on trails. Bicycles allowed on Old Haul Road Trail in adjacent Pescadero Creek County Park. No dogs on trails; allowed on leash in camp and picnic areas. Fishing prohibited in order to protect native steelhead trout population.

Maps: Portola Redwoods State Park brochure, USGS topos Mindego Hill and Big Basin.

Short Nature Walk Along Pescadero Creek

This is a three-quarter-of-a-mile loop that will acquaint children and adults alike with the forest eco-system using a $1 guide and map from the Visitor Center. Take Sequoia Nature Trail from the side of the Visitor Center. The numbered sign posts coordinated with the park brochure provide an easy, short-course about the flora and geology of the forest.

The walk can be extended for another mile-and-a-half on the connecting Iverson Trail. Go around the Nature Trail Loop past posts numbered 8, turn right and then left and follow the trail to Iverson Trail and go left. Iverson Trail climbs with switchbacks through redwoods of all ages -- some burned but still living, others with hollow cavities in their trunks -- to two overlooks above Pescadero Creek.

At the next junction, there is a choice to make: either take a left on an unnamed trail to cross Pescadero Creek and return to the park office. Or by going 0.15 mile straight ahead, the sightseer can cross Fall Creek on a little bridge and continue right to Tiptoe Falls. Here this lively creek drops over a shelf of sandstone into a quiet little pool in a basin flanked on two sides by high rock walls clothed with overhanging ferns, shrubs, and trees. Upstream in a narrow canyon the creek splashes over a jumble of fallen logs.

Return to the main trail by going to the right up a bank and through a grove of widely spaced, second growth redwoods. Beyond is a group of ancient stumps with notches cut for inserting the springboards on which early loggers balanced to fell these huge trees. Shortly the Iverson Trail crosses a bridge over Iverson Creek and goes uphill to the park service road. Step onto this road and turn left (north) to see, beside the trail, timbers remaining from Christian Iverson's 1860s cabin. To return to the park office, go left on the trail just beside a road barricade, descend along the east bank of Pescadero Creek, and then cross it on the service-road bridge. Follow the paved road back to the park office.

Two More Shorties

1. **Old Tree Trail:** This a short walk of just over a third of a mile up a slight rise to an old redwood that was probably only a sapling when Christ was born. The tree is some 12 feet across and stands 298 feet tall. The trail starts near the end of the service road just south of the Visitor Center.

2. **The Doggie Walk:** Here's one where you can take the pooch for a stroll – on the leash, of course. This is a mile loop through the mixed evergreen forest on Upper and Lower Escape Roads along Peters Creek. Start on either one just past the campgrounds.

Coyote Ridge Loop Trail

This is a two-mile loop with some 650 feet of climbing and could take an hour-and-a-half. It starts from the park office and goes left on the entrance road for about 30 feet. Turn left on the Iverson Trail, and in 0.1 mile turn right onto the Coyote Ridge Loop Trail. Across a paved road leading to the walk-in camp sites the path switches back uphill through oak and bay tree forest. There are burnt trunks on still-living trees, and several redwoods have developed double trunks, all part of nature's adaptation to the cycle of forest fires. In spring the trail is lined by two-eyed violets, *Viola ocellata*, and redwood violets, *Viola sempervirens,* and western wake robin, *trillium ovatum.* Climbing steadily, the trail reaches the junction of the two Coyote Ridge trails (elevation 960 feet), where the hiker goes right and begins the descent.

Numerous switchbacks lead to a little meadow where wildflowers often bloom until late summer. Beyond the meadow, climb three steps cut into a tree fallen across the trail. Then, in a deep ravine, cross a plank bridge over a little creek that splashes into a pool about 20 feet left of the trail. Abruptly the path drops down to the main park road, crosses it, descends wooden steps to a bridge over Evans Creek and shortly crosses the longer Peters Creek bridge. At the junction with the Slate Creek Trail (east) and the Upper Escape Road, turn right (south) on the Upper Escape Road through a fine redwood grove and follow the road back to the campground and on to the park office.

Summit and Slate Creek Trails Loop

This is another hour-and-a half jaunt that climbs some 550 feet and covers 2.5 miles, or 3.7 miles if one wants to add a side trip to the Big Tree.

It all starts at the bridge over Peters Creek just east of the Visitor Center. Turn right past the amphitheater where the road becomes a service road for park vehicles only. On the right take the trail that leads to Tiptoe Falls. After 0.3 mile through thick huckleberry, *Vaccinium ovatum,* the trail returns to the service road and continues to an opening overlooking Pescadero Creek 200 feet below in a sheer-sided canyon. Just beyond, the path re-enters the forest on a trail where more huckleberries are interspersed with graceful ferns of several varieties, long-leafed iris, *Iris douglasiana,* and creeping snowberry, *Symphoricarpus mollis,* a member of the honeysuckle family. Its cousin, the common snowberry, *S. albus,* was regularly trimmed in the fall by natives so its light-weight stems would grow back straight enough the following spring to be used as arrow shafts.

The trail passes several double-trunked redwoods and one huge old-growth redwood before crossing the service road to the Summit Trail. As the trail gains elevation, redwood trees are being edged out by tan oak, *Lithocarpus densiflrous*, live oak, *Quercus agrifola*, madrone, *Arbutus menziesii*, and some Douglas fir, *Psuedotsuga menziesii*. Heading steadily upward the path rounds below a ridge and then goes atop a narrow ridge where pink-petalled California roses, *Rosa californica*, bloom on small leafed, thorny bushes in summer. Then, as the trail curves east, one sees south to densely forested Butano Ridge. Here is a good rest stop, just a few feet from the 950-foot summit.

To take the return leg of this loop trip, turn due north on the Slate Creek Trail; the path on this is west-facing ridge twists back into the heads of ravines, around bends, and deeper into redwood forest. Stay left and go due south at the trail junction sign indicating the campground to the right, following along a narrow trail with mossy banks. The ridge goes through the redwoods for another half-mile. At the next junction one can take the Old Tree Trail left (east) for a half-mile round trip into a quiet canyon to see a grand old redwood giant.

If one chooses the Old Tree side trip, return to the Slate Creek Trail junction, continue straight ahead to the service road and go to the right on it to the park office. If the Old Tree side trip is bypassed, turn right (west) at the Old Tree Trail junction and go less than 0.2 mile to the park service road and then right to the park office.

Peters Creek Loop

This is the trip that takes the hiker deep into the woods the loggers could not reach. The 1,000-foot climb and terrain will be evidence enough of why the old trees still stand. Plan to start this 13-mile trip early in the day, take plenty of water and food. This is an eight or nine-hour day trip and the hiker should allow ample time to negotiate the steep climb out of Peters Creek on the return leg. There is also the option of spending the night at Slate Creek Trail Camp, three miles from the park office and doing the seven-mile loop up and down to Peters Creek on the second day. Camp sites must be reserved by calling the park office ahead of time.

Take the Summit Trail from the service road south of the

Visitor Center to its junction with the Slate Creek Trail. From this junction at 940 feet, go right (northeast) along an east-facing ridge under a high forest canopy of redwoods, Douglas firs, and occasional oaks growing in more open zones. In many places the trail passes through a leafy, green canyons of tall huckleberries, *Vaccinium ovatum*. As the trail gradually gains in elevation, it turns around to the north-facing slope and in 1.3 miles reaches Slate Creek Trail Camp. There are six separate camp sites with picnic tables screened by low native shrubs sitting under high madrones, *Arbutus meniezii*, and tan oaks, *Lithocarpus densiflorus*.

Take the Bear Creek Trail as it goes north, an old jeep road that climbs around a west-facing knoll, swings east, and then north again up a steep canyon above a seasonal creek that is a tributary of Slate Creek. In a few places, fallen trees or big boulders may create detours. The trail eventually rises from under redwoods to more open country where firs, oaks and bays thrive. The old road ends at about the 1,380-foot level.

From this point a narrow trail enters a high wooded bowl. Under tall Douglas firs and a dense tangle of berry vines, the path veers a bit west, and emerges among drier foliage made up of hardy manzanita, *Arctostaphylos ssp.*, chinquapin, *Capatanopsis chrysophylla,* and some knob cone pines, *Pinus attenuata*. This is the highest point of this trip, about 1,440 feet. The trail next goes through a forest of spindly Douglas fir proceeding up and down a southwest-facing ridge to an opening high on its north side with views of Peters Creek Canyon.

The downhill leg of the trip starts on a foot trail that can be slippery if the litter fall is damp or the soil muddy. On foggy days, moisture drips from trees overhead and the air is heavy with the odor of bay leaves crushed underfoot. Steadily downward goes the trail, zigzagging into and around ravines on a west-facing slope. After crossing a little plank bridge over Bear Creek, make a sharp turn left (west), along a side slope above the creek thickly covered with ferns of all kinds, redwood sorrel, *Oxalis oregana*, and trailing yerba buena, *Satureja douglasii*, another source of tea for natives and early settlers alike.

On the return the steepest part comes first—an elevation

gain of 760 feet in about a mile. After reaching the trip's high point, it is almost all downhill, allowing the luxury of enjoying the trees, flowers, ridges and canyons.

Purisima Creek Redwoods Open Space Preserve

Jurisdiction: Midpeninsula Regional Open Space District — 650-691-1200. Web site: http://openspace.org/

Getting There: This preserve has several Coastside entrances; the quickest access is to take Highway One to Higgins Purisima Road just south of the HMB fire station. The road narrows several places while climbing and then dropping to a sharp curve at Purisima Creek where there is limited parking at the entry. This entrance also can be reached from the intersection of Highway One and Verde Road that runs into Higgins-Purisima Road.

This 2,633-acre treasure of redwood forests, clear-flowing streams, steep-sided canyons and long ridges has some of the most scenic of all the coastal and mountain vistas, but it will take stamina and endurance to gain them. Rugged terrain and long climbs make it a place to find both quiet seclusion and escape from the noise of exurbia. New trails and old logging roads form a 21-mile trail network.

Facilities: Trails for hikers, equestrians and bicyclists; one trail for the physically limited, with picnic tables, restroom and special parking. Equestrian parking.

Rules: Open dawn to dusk. No bicycles on Soda Gulch or North Ridge foot trail. No dogs allowed.

Map: MROSD brochure Purisima Redwoods O.S.P, USGS topo Woodside.

The preserve extends eastward for three miles to the 2,000-foot-high crest of the Santa Cruz Mountains. Three ridges climb to the Skyline dividing the preserve into two main canyons trending westward. Between Harkins and Tunitas ridges flows Purisima Creek, the centerpiece of the preserve. It was along this creek that loggers and shingle cutters started harvesting redwoods that were hundreds of years old, first for buildings in the newer village of Half Moon Bay. Because of the rugged terrain, half of the eight mills along the creek cut shingles that were easier to transport.

Purisima Creek, a meandering, year-round stream fed by many tributaries, flows west for three miles through the preserve past large second-growth redwoods, then through rolling grasslands to the 2,200-acre Cowell Ranch, finally reaching the ocean in a waterfall over sandstone cliffs. Whittemore Gulch, between Harkins Ridge and an unnamed ridge to the north, has a seasonal creek that flows through a wooded canyon to join Purisima Creek near the preserve's western entrance. This is where the first sawmill on the coast was established in 1854.

Redwood logs were far too large to drag up the steep canyons to the bayside market. Many devices were tested to overcome the problem. One, devised by Purdy Pharis, used a cable to operate a tramway rising one thousand feet from the creek to the ridgetop. There was little need for lumber on the Coastside and attempts to ship to San Francisco with all manner of chutes and other jury-rigged devices usually failed. Instead the trees were cut for shingles, which pack animals could haul out of the gulches over steep, winding trails.

Only a few primeval redwoods remain; one said to be 1,200 years old. Purisima also harbors one of a few remaining critical habitats of the marbled murrelet, a small, seagoing robin-sized bird now on the list of threatened species; they nest high up in old-growth trees away from predators.

Near the headwaters of Purisima Creek, a fire in November of 1880 swept over 2,700 acres all the way to Tunitas Creek and Summit Springs, wiping out buildings, lumber mills and storage sites on the mountain. Nature has healed the scars in the century and a quarter since.

Some of the most challenging hikes on the Peninsula are up Purisima's canyons and back down its ridges. The old county road, now the Purisima Creek Trail, rises along the creek from the lower end of the canyon to Skyline Boulevard. Some narrow trails are exclusively for hikers, others on logging roads are also open to horsemen and bicyclists. There is a quarter-mile Redwood Trail for the physically limited that wanders through tall redwoods along the Skyline ridge. Several turnouts have picnic tables where one can look out toward the shore.

Purisima Creek Trail

If you decide to do this round trip using three of the trails to go up to the ridges and back down again, plan on taking about six hours to travel the 8.5 miles. A climb of some 1,600 feet is involved and then a descent of about the same altitude over switchbacks. If you can arrange a shuttle from the top, the time required is about four hours and a six-mile, mostly gradual climb.

The first mile or so of the trip is less strenuous, giving the muscles time to warm up. It is cool and heavily wooded. In springtime, streams trickle down the canyon sides into Purisima. Flowers bloom at every season. Immense redwoods remain near the creek here at the lower end of the preserve. On the north side is a grove of memorial trees, dedicated by a contributor to the Save-the-Redwoods League, which helped purchase this beautiful preserve.

The trail follows the old county road and is close to the creek, with stair-steps up the canyon over rocks and under bridges of fallen logs. Some stumps, still rooted, are sprouting new shoots.

Less than a mile up the creek, there is a trail off to the right across the creek – the Borden Hatch Mill Trail named after mill operators from the 1800's. The trip can be used to shorten the hike or take a sightseeing jaunt up the Bald Ridge Trail past the site of Grabtown, where loggers and team drivers paused to "grab" a bed and bite to eat as they journeyed over the mountain. This look will take the hiker back to the creek via Grabtown Gulch Trail and a return westward.

This trip adds 1.4 miles to the trip, making a loop of 8.8 miles, or can be used as a way to have a shorter jaunt and still see some spectacular views. As an add-on, it has the advantage of doing the serious climbing at the beginning of the trip.

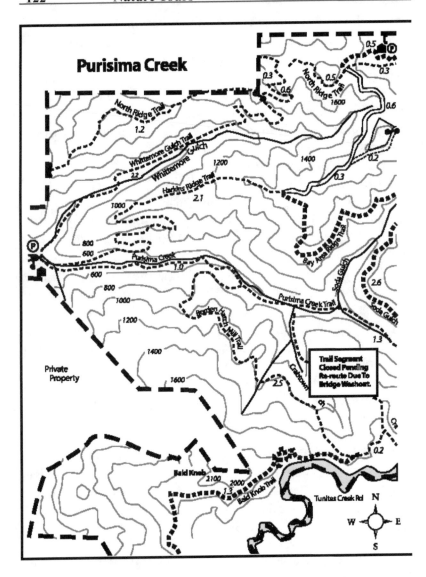

Purisima Creek

For those hikers who intend to go the entire distance, continue up the Purisima Creek Trail to its junction with the Soda Gulch Trail. About a mile a half past this junction is the eastern entrance to the preserve and the parking lot, if a shuttle ride awaits. For the intrepid, long-distance hiker, take a left on Soda Gulch Trail and across Soda Gulch Creek and up to Harkins Ridge Trail. Take a left here.

The trail follows an old fire road down the spine of Harkins

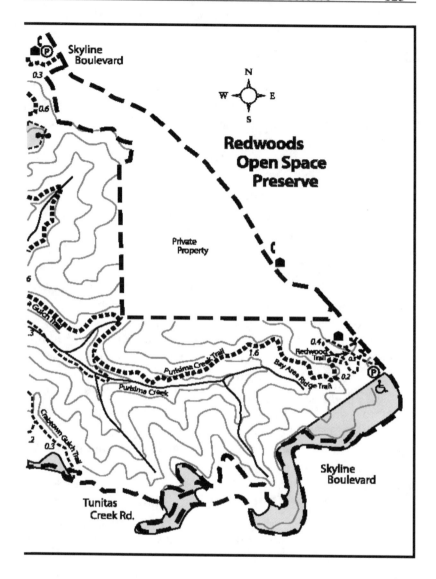

Ridge and descends more than 1,300 feet in a little over two miles. The ridge is mostly covered by chaparral with a few tan oaks and bay laurels growing on the steep mountainside. Small stands of firs and redwoods on the north side of Harkins Ridge provide late afternoon shade. From here one can see Whittemore Gulch off to the right.

Back down to the canyon and creek, find a spot to rest. You have earned the pleasure of the creek's clear waters and the light filtering through the redwood trees. As you quietly commune with nature, remember the few hard working far-sighted conservationists that preserved this wonderland.

North Ridge

One trip that will give a good workout takes 4.5 hours to travel nearly seven miles, dropping and then regaining 1,600 feet from the north ridge top to the west entrance to the preserve. This hike descends to Purisima Creek first by way of the North Ridge, then connects with the Harkins Ridge trail and returns up the Whittemore Gulch Trail.

The hikers' foot-trail zigzags a half mile down the mountainside under Douglas firs, *Psuedotsuga menziesii*, wide-spreading tan oaks, *Lithocarpus densiflorus*, madrones, *Arbutus menziesii*, and a scattering of live oaks, *Quercus agrifola*. If the day is clear, the views west present a sweep of the San Mateo coast from Half Moon Bay north and south. Start from the north Skyline entry on the service road. The foot trail intersects the service road and all users go south on the Harkins Ridge Trail. On a plateau, this path overlooks a steep canyon among clumps of sizable redwood trees and a thick stand of Douglas firs.

After another half-mile or so around the canyon's face, the route turns right on an old fire road down the spine of Harkins Ridge and descends more than 1,300 feet in a couple of miles. Chaparral predominates here, but tan oaks and bay laurels, *Umbellularia californica*, can be seen on the steep mountainside. Small stands of firs and redwoods on the north side of Harkins Ridge give late afternoon shade. From here we glimpse the Whittemore Gulch Trail, the route of the climb back to the ridge.

The descent continues on the Harkins Ridge Trail past the Soda Gulch Trail that goes south to meet the Purisima Creek Trail in the canyon below. On Harkins Ridge, the knolls are densely covered with Warty-Leaved ceanothus, *Ceonothus papillosus*, which forms a showy blue cloud in March and April.

Four switchbacks lead downward into the relaxing shade of the Purisima Creek redwoods and along the creek for a half-mile. Just a few steps before the bridge to the south side of the creek, the Whittemore Gulch Trail junction leads to the right.

About 300 feet beyond the bridge is the preserve gate at Higgins-Purisima Road. You could leave a car here and avoid the hike back up the mountain. Before leaving, step down to the creek to see its pools and cascades at close range.

The Whittemore Gulch Trail takes a 3.5-mile return to the Skyline ridge. This trail's soils are heavily eroded, and it is usually closed in wet weather to bicyclists and equestrians, who must return on the Harkins Ridge Trail. In the lower gulch, redwoods that escaped during logging days have now grown to magnificently large trees. Alders, *Alnus rubra,* and big-leaf maples, *Acer macrophyllum,* grow among the redwoods and venerable Douglas firs, and the canyon is lush with ferns.

The trail leaves the canyon after a mile-and-a-half, and zigzags more than a mile up the mountainside, crossing a thickly covered chaparral slope. Be wary of the poison oak that dominates the hillside, its fall colors brilliant reds and oranges. At the old jeep road, the North Ridge Trail turns right. At the trail junction, hikers turn left into the forest on the half-mile foot trail on which they trip started. Bicyclists and equestrians must continue uphill on the North Ridge service road for a third of a mile.

Grabtown Gulch and Bald Knob Loop Trip

Another alternate hike takes in the southern ridge tops of the preserve, descending through the hardwood forests of Grabtown Gulch to the Purisima Creek Trail and returning on the Borden Hatch Mill Trail to Bald Knob. This 7.5-mile loop takes about three hours and descends some 1,200 feet to the creek then back up 500 feet to Bald Knob.

To find the trailhead, turn west off Skyline Boulevard just opposite Kings Mountain Road on Tunitas Creek Road. Go two miles to a brown metal gate on the right. There are several turnouts for limited parking on the road downhill from the entrance.

This trail starts off gently over a little rise, staying along the flank of the ridge – possibly where the village of Grabtown was located. There are some private residences to the left just outside the preserve. Keep to the right at the first little clearing, and continue to a larger opening in the forest, which was a center for logging operations. All traces have disappeared. At this clearing trails take off left and right. Take the right hand fork, the Grabtown Gulch Trail; you'll return up the left hand trail, the Borden Hatch Mill Trail.

About a 1.5-miles down Grabtown Gulch Trail one goes through Douglas firs and young redwoods that are beginning to overtake the tan oaks and madrones that sprang up after previous logging. From openings in the trees it is possible to look out to the ocean—sometimes dramatically shrouded in fog.

The trail continues downhill, cutting first east across the ridge and then reverses itself to descend a very steep slope into Grabtown Gulch. Here the path is lined with a variety of ferns, and the creek is well below the trail. Continuing on the creek's shady east side, one can see can orange tiger lilies in midsummer, some as big as three feet high.

Just where Grabtown Gulch Creek flows into Purisima Creek, the trail crosses a reconstructed old logging bridge. This the widest part of Purisima Canyon where shingle mills once flourished.

Follow the canyon to a trail on the left that climbs south on the ridge west of Grabtown Gulch. This is the Borden Hatch Mill Trail, named after George Borden and Rufus Hatch, who were the second set of sawmill operators in the canyon, buying out the first operators in 1865. This trail gains the 1,000 feet plus of elevation that was lost down to the creek. It goes more than two miles up the north-facing side of the mountain below Bald Knob. Across a tributary of Grabtown Gulch, sometimes quite damp in winter, the trail connects with the old patrol road out to Bald Knob, closed at the preserve boundary. To reach the new trail, for hikers only, go left (east) at the old patrol road junction and continue about two-tenths of a mile toward the Grabtown Gulch Trail. An abruptly sharp right turn takes the hiker onto the new Bald Knob Trail and goes west along the southern border of the preserve.

The trail threads through tan oaks and young, second growth redwoods. Bald Knob's summit is soon visible through the trees. Around the south side of Bald Knob, redwoods give way to firs, some of giant proportions amid several huge stumps.

Through a dense grove of chinquapins, *Casatanopsis chrysophylla,* struggling for light in a tall fir forest, the trail emerges onto grassy slopes dotted with young trees. Welcome one of the most glorious vistas on the Coast. You are at the steep upper end of Irish Ridge which divides Tunitas Creek from Lobitos Creek. The view to the south and west sweeps the west side of the Santa Cruz Mountains sloping down to the shore, with the Pacific Ocean spreading out to the horizon. You have just walked the south side of Bald Knob, where a dense grove of young firs is flourishing. The rough, gravel track down Irish Ridge is used for patrol only.

As one strolls back along the Bald Knob Trail, a look down slope (south) to an open, brushy area reveals the rooftops of private homes in the Kings Grove community. At the junction of this new trail with the Borden Hatch Mill Trail go east and continue about 0.2 mile to the Grabtown Gulch Trail. Go right (south) and return to the wide forest opening near Tunitas Creek Road and out to parking along this road.

Russian Ridge
Open Space Preserve

Jurisdiction: Midpeninsula Regional Open Space District — 650-691-1200. Web site: http://openspace.org/

Getting There: From the junction of Skyline Road and Highway 84 (La Honda Road), go southeast some 7 miles to Rapley Ranch Road; access to preserve is from two points, one from the Caltrans Overlook on the left 2 miles from Rapley Ranch Road and the other access is at Alpine Road just off Skyline.

Russian Ridge Open Space Preserve's 1,580 acres lie along the west side of Skyline Boulevard for about three miles north from the Page Mill/Alpine Road intersection through the Mt. Melville area and extend southwest into the deep canyons of Alpine and Mindego creeks. Trails run along the ridge-top parallel to Skyline Boulevard, and the routes lead through beautiful wooded canyons, and old ranch roads descend the west slopes. Spectacular views east of San Francisco Bay and Mt. Diablo. West to the ocean an expanse of ridges greet the visitor. Strong winds that bring clear skies can also carry dense fog, especially in summer.

Bay Area Ridge Trail Hike

Choose this hike on one of those super-clear days when clouds, fog and haze have been swept away by winds or rain. Take along water and lunch and your binoculars. The views around all points of the compass are unbeatable, sweeping from the Sierras to the Farallons. The round trip is nearly six-and-a-half miles, so plan for at least three hours to be able to enjoy the sights.

Start from the Russian Ridge parking area at the northwest corner of Skyline Boulevard and Alpine Road. Climb the steep rise to the ridge. After a long switchback, the one trail leads left (south) to a trailhead on Alpine Road. Ignore that trail. Continue along the Bay Area Ridge Trail route, go 0.2 mile the next junction and can go right to the summit of Borel Hill (2,572

> **Facilities: Trails for hikers, equestrians and bicyclists. Rules: Open dawn to dusk. No dogs permitted.**

feet above sea level). From Borel Hill trail on a clear day in winter, with binoculars you can see the snow-capped Sierra Nevada through the gap of Niles Canyon to the northeast and the Farallon Islands to the west. The Ridge Trail curves north into the head of a swale, then bends west past sandstone outcrops that frame views to the south and west.

To complete this Russian Ridge segment of the Bay Area Ridge Trail, the path follows the Mindego Ridge Trail left (south) and then continues right (north) on the Ridge Trail. The trail gradually ascends the west side of the ridge. To the west stretch ranchlands, creek canyons and ridges, and the ocean beyond.

Southwest is Mindego Hill, said to have been formed more than 100 million years ago in a volcanic event. Continuing another half-mile along the Ridge Trail toward a group of radio antennas, one reaches a junction where the 0.6-mile Hawk Ridge Trail leads left (west) and then south, downhill. This trail offers a shorter return to the starting point. From this junction north to Rapley Ranch Road, the Ridge Trail is open to hikers and equestrians only. Bicyclists can return south on the multi-use Hawk Ridge and Alder Spring trails and retrace their route back to the Alpine Road/Skyline Boulevard parking area.

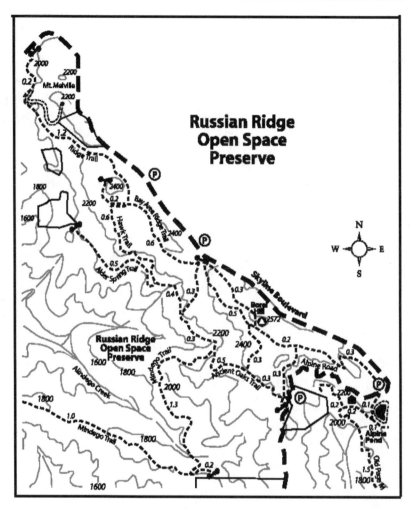

If one takes the northward Ridge Trail route, it winds in and out of woods with views alternating between east and west. A wooden deck appears beside the trail, a likely spot for a sheltered lunch stop. Return to the Hawk Ridge Trail junction and take the Hawk Ridge and Alder Spring trails back to the Mindego Ridge Trail. Turn north on it and retrace the trail to the starting point.

Mindego Creek to the Slopes of Mindego Hill

This is a three-mile trip out to Mindego Hill and a three-mile return over the same path that takes some three hours, drops 400 feet and then a return climb of the same elevation.

Start from the Caltrans Vista Point parking lot, cross Skyline Boulevard and go through the gate onto the old ranch road that heads downhill. It passes both the Bay Area Ridge and Hawk Ridge Trails and turns southeast. It descends through grasslands and soon turns into a canyon shaded by canyon oaks, *Quercus chrysolepsis*, madrones, *Arbutus menziesii*, and Douglas firs, *Pseudotsuga menziesii*. After about a half an hour the trail emerges into open pasture again, looking out across forests toward Mindego Hill. The grassland below the road has several ideal sites for a picnic stop.

A few minutes walk farther down the trail leads to a little flat beside a tributary of Mindego Creek. On one side of the flat, pasturelands furrowed by a century of grazing cattle rise steeply. Continue across the creek and go up over a little ridge and down to another branch of the creek. From here there is a brief climb to another ridge overlooking the canyon of Alpine Creek and the ridges to the south. A private road on the left, where public access is prohibited, leads out to Alpine Road. Follow the trail northwest on the narrow ridge toward Mindego Hill. Immense canyon live oaks, *Quercus agrifola,* line one side of the road. A mile walk along the ridge brings you to the fenced boundary of the preserve on the lower slopes of Mindego Hill. Turn back at this private property-line fence to retrace your steps to the Skyline.

Sam McDonald County Park

Jurisdiction: San Mateo County – 650-363-0212; reservations – 650-363-0212.
Web Site: http://www.eparks.net/parks/

Getting There: Take Highway One to Highway 84 (La Honda Road and turn east to Pescadero Road. Turn right on Pescadero Road and go 1.2 miles past the Pescadero/Alpine Road junction.

This 1,003-acre county park, part of the Pescadero Creek County Park complex, lies on both sides of Pescadero Road near La Honda.

The park is named for Sam McDonald , an African-American man who went to work at Stanford University as a teamster, and rose in over 50 years to become Superintendent of Athletic

Grounds and Buildings. He began buying land in the La Honda area in 1917 and eventually owned more than 400 acres along Alpine Creek in the northwest corner of today's park. Upon his death in 1957, he willed the land to the university and a year later San Mateo County purchased it. In 1976 the County bought additional acres plus the 37-acre Heritage Grove.

The 400 northeast-facing acres that drain into Alpine Creek are mostly redwood forest. Abundant here are huckleberry, *Vaccinium ovatum*; miners lettuce, *Montia perfoliata*; California hazel, *Corylus cornuta ssp. Californica*; and lots of redwood sorrel, *Oxalis oregana*; all plants used by natives and pioneers alike. The berries became pies, the lettuce and sorrel eaten in salads, the nuts of the hazel roasted and eaten or ground into meal. On the southeast side of Pescadero Road are the sunnier grasslands and mixed oak and madrone woods on south-facing Towne Ridge. On the north side of this ridge, the 38-acre Heritage Grove sits on the banks of Alpine Creek. There are fine old-growth redwoods and a healthy second-growth redwood and fir forest. Parklands stretch from the grove west to Pescadero Road.

Facilities include trails for hikers and equestrians, picnic sites, group camp sites reserved especially for youth groups, Hikers Hut and Jack Brook Horse Camp. Restrooms are located at the park office and in camp sites.

The Appetizer Big Tree Trail

This is an ideal loop to work up an appetite before a picnic at one of the tables in the redwoods, one that takes only about 30 to 45 minutes to go a mile with a slight climb of 200 feet.

Start from the southeast side of the parking area on a trail through the trees that quickly emerges at Pescadero Road. Cross to the other side (careful of traffic) and step onto the Big Tree Loop Trail, part of the Towne Trail leading to Pescadero Park. The uphill trip portion begins under second-growth redwoods already towering 150 feet skyward. Pass a road to private properties inside the park, and continue to a park sign on the right that points to the Heritage Grove Trail and right to the Big Tree Trail. Take the right fork uphill on a shady north-facing slope.

Continuing uphill, the trail bends south and then slowly descends west past a big green water tank. Paralleling the Towne Trail service road, it heads downhill left (southeast), descends

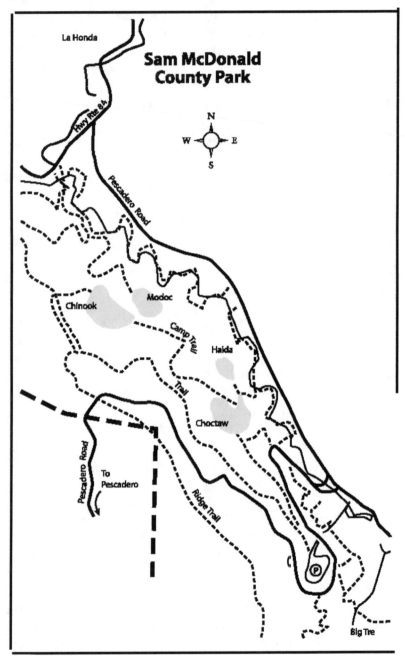

some steep steps, goes around some switchbacks and finally reaches the Big Tree. Fire-scarred and open on two sides, this venerable giant is alive and well after centuries. When redwoods burn, they tend to sprout from the base nurtured by naturally enormous water basins in their roots, which often accounts for the multiple fused trunks. This is a great place to stop for a picnic lunch at a nearby picnic table. Across Pescadero Road there are other tables under the trees that offer a pleasant place to reflect on the wonders of these magnificent trees.

Loop Trails North from Park Office

This is a leisurely hour-and-half stroll through the forest with the potential for another mile on the Ridge Loop if the hiker is inspired. The change in elevation is only about 300 feet, so there's not a lot of climbing.

Start to the right of the park office and walk immediately uphill under beautiful redwood trees. At the first junction turn left on the foot trail that winds up and down past many burned-out shells of giant redwoods and some splendid living trees. Some of these oldest trees are fire-scarred and others are hollow and yet still living. Graceful ferns flourish in this shady forest

After 1.3 miles there is a junction. Take the Forest Loop Trail (north), joining the unpaved service road for a short, steep downhill stretch. On the right there will soon be a small sign pointing right to continue on the 2.6-mile Forest Loop Trail, which

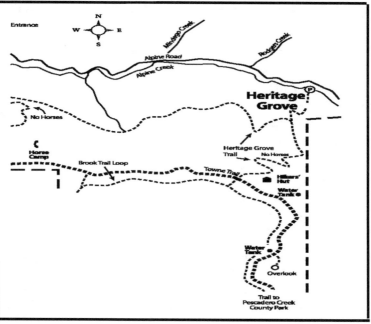

goes east to the Chinook campsite. The service road is a longer loop north past the park's water-storage tank. It goes up, down and around bends heading north, then east to the banks of Alpine Creek. Stay on the road and as it turns south it climbs out of the creek canyon. Lovely five-finger ferns, *Adiantum pendatum var. aleuticum,* drape the trailside, and Western wake robin, *trillium ovatum,* bloom until the end of May, comfortable in this moist, shady environment.

About a half-mile after turning due south you enter the Modoc group camp site, where there are picnic tables, barbecues, restrooms and a little circle of log seats for evening gatherings. Follow the paved park road here past other group camp sites and at the Forest Loop Trail leading off the road on the right, follow the path uphill to the junction where this loop started.

Heritage Grove Loop

This is a longer workout, two-and-a-half hours, a climb of some 550 feet to Towne Ridge, a five-mile hike through the woods and then the wonder of the Heritage Grove. Take the Heritage Grove Trail after crossing Pescadero Road, not the Towne Trail. The path wanders among widely spaced redwoods and Douglas firs, dips into little ravines, crosses a stream with a little waterfall known as Gorge Creek and crosses a seasonal creek.

Where the trail bends north, Alpine Creek can be heard pouring over rocks and fallen trees at the bottom of the slope. Note the stumps of cut redwoods with slots for springboards on which the early loggers stood to use a two-handled saw. After 1.2 miles, there is a sign on a redwood post pointing left to the Heritage Grove. Five minutes more and the hiker is on the fenced flat where the largest and best trees remain. Beyond and down the trail are two bridges over Alpine Creek and a small parking area on the creek side of Alpine Road.

Return to the grove, and then turn left (due south) at the redwood signpost to begin the climb to Towne Ridge and the Hikers Hut. From here to the ridge one passes through a mixed forest of oaks, bays, maples, and some Douglas firs. Around a wide turn is a knoll where the canopy is high above the ground and the undergrowth is a tangle of vines of different berry and honeysuckle varieties. Up on the ridge-top grasslands, a short trail leads through the woods to the Hikers Hut on a path that leads to neighboring Pescadero Creek Park. This short detour offers a wonderful view across Pescadero Creek Canyon and up to Butano Ridge, you can return to the Towne Trail and go west three-quarters of a mile to the Jack Brook Horse Camp.

From the horse camp trail take the Towne Trail (service road) along the west side of a redwood-filled canyon. Proceed downhill to the junction of the Forest Loop Trail. Turn right and wind up and down along the 1.3-mile trail on the north-facing ridge to the park office This adds about three miles to the hike, compensating with a fine overview of Sam McDonald Park.

Skyline Ridge
Open Space Preserve

Jurisdiction: Midpeninsula Regional Open Space District — 650-691-1200. Web site: http://openspace.org/

Getting There: From Skyline Boulevard and Highway 84 (La Honda Road), go south to the Alpine Road junction. There are two trail entrances: (1) On northwest corner of Skyline Blvd/Alpine Road intersection. Park here for trail entrances: (a) through an immense underpass leading to Alpine Pond for hikers and wheelchairs only, (b) 400' down Alpine Road on left for bicyclists and equestrians, and (c) northwest uphill to Ridge Trail in Russian Ridge Preserve. (2) On Skyline 3/4 mile southeast of this intersection.

This 1,612-acre preserve lies along the western crest of the Santa Cruz Mountains in the heart of thousands of acres of public open space. Russian Ridge, Coal Creek, Monte Bello, and Long Ridge open space preserves and Upper Stevens Creek County Park surround Skyline Ridge Preserve. From its highest point, a 2,493-foot knoll, one can see south and west to the nearby forests of Castle Rock and Portola Redwoods state parks and Pescadero Creek County Park.

This high ground was for centuries a workplace for Ohlone people processing the rich acorn harvests from four varieties of oaks; bedrock-grinding stones have been found here. Other plants used by the natives were found in abundance and were harvested on the way back from summer camps on the coast as they returned to winter camps along the foothills of today's Santa Clara and San Mateo counties' bayside. Early American settlers built ranch houses and raised cattle, hogs, horses, and hay along the crest of the Skyline ridge as early as the 1850's. In 1868 William Page built a road across the northwest corner of the preserve to link his lumber mill in present-day Portola Redwoods State Park with the embarcadero in Palo Alto.

California Governor James "Sunny Jim" Rolph used the farmhouse at Skyline Ranch as an occasional summer capital in the 1930s. Today a chestnut orchard and a Christmas tree farm occupy many acres on the east and south side of the preserve.

In addition to 10 miles of trails, there are two small lakes, horse trailer parking and a nature center operated by volunteer docents. There are also picnic areas, an observation deck, miles of trails for hikers, bicyclists, equestrians, and the physically limited.

Rules: Open dawn to dusk. No dogs.

Maps: MROSD brochure Skyline Ridge OSP, USGS topo Mindego Hill.

Down Historic Old Page Mill Road

The only reason to take this dead-end 2.5 miles down and 2.5 miles back is to fully appreciate the difficulties the early settlers had traveling this country. The trail follows a good part of the early logging route to Page's mill down on Lambert Creek. The trail drops some 650 feet as it twists and turns and the hiker will have to climb back that same amount of elevation.

Start from north entrance at the corner of Skyline Boulevard and Alpine Road and walk 400 feet down Alpine Road to the trail entrance on the left. Take this multi-use trail that passes west of Alpine Pond, to its intersection with paved Old Page Mill

Road. Turn right here, heading downhill (northwest) under tall old firs and past some sculptured sandstone outcrops. As the trail reaches a clearing there are wide views southeast over a succession of forested ridges.

At this clearing, the unpaved road swings left, winding around the forested east side of the canyon of seasonal Lambert Creek. On the way the trail crosses Lambert Creek tributaries cascading over sandstone boulders on the steep mountainside. About a mile downhill the road goes through some chaparral on a south-facing slope. Blooming at road's edge in summer are yellow bush poppies, *Dendromecon rigida,* and magenta tinted chaparral-peas, *Pickeringia montana.*

The trail re-enters the forest dominated by tall Douglas firs, *Pseudotsuga menziesii,* and twists through more switchbacks to reach a washed-out bridge over the creek near the preserve boundary. Stop here and retrace your steps.

The return trip back up the mountain is the time to consider the traveler of 135 years ago, hauling lumber up this road. The lumber team was usually made up of six to eight mules harnessed in pairs, pulling two wagons, one loaded with 4,000 board feet of lumber and a trailing wagon with 2,000 board feet. It was a day's trip to the top and then another day down Page Mill Road to the embarcadero. Today's hiker retraces the same route to the chaparral area, then continues uphill on Old Page Mill Road. When one reaches the junction with trails circling Alpine Pond. Either continue on this old road to reach the ranger office on the site of the former ranch buildings, or take the trail around the pond's east side to enjoy its blue waters rimmed with reeds. Nearby is a bedrock mortar used by Indians to grind acorns. Follow the path through the underpass to the parking area.

Alpine Pond Loop

This is an easy nearly level stroll around the pond on a path that leads to the Daniels Nature Center and to observation points from which to enjoy birds, fish, frogs, and insects. Start from the north entrance at the corner of Skyline Boulevard and Alpine Road, hikers and wheelchair users take the trail through the underpass. About 100 feet inside the preserve take the trail to the right and follow it through the meadow. At breaks in the lake's border growth on the left are several places where visitors can get close to the water and look for fish, frogs and water insects

Redwing blackbirds, barn swallows and marsh wrens live around the shore, and wildlife tracks can often be found in the mud at lakeside. After 0.3-mile around the pond one reaches the Daniels Nature Center, and on weekdays one can relax on the deck while viewing the pond. Take a closer look at the aquatic life from the floating observation platform built over the pond or from the deck of the nature center. A northern harrier hawk can be observed watching the lakeshore for unsuspecting frogs; and occasionally a belted kingfisher or a great blue heron can be seen.

Horseshoe Lake Shore Loop

This is a short climb of less than a half-hour, dropping some 115 feet to picnic sites on Horseshoe Lake's shore. Start from the preserve's entrance on Skyline Boulevard three quarters of a mile southeast of Alpine Road. Pick up the trail heading downhill into a valley surmounted on the west by the steep flanks of the preserve's summit. As the trails descend through this upper watershed of East Lambert Creek, the U-shaped lake can be seen wrapped around a tree-topped knoll.

The trail leads to the south end of the lake across the earthen dam on a farm road, then along the lake's marshy southeast rim. In the quiet of early morning or late on a summer day, you may catch sight of the some of the wildlife that inhabit the woods and meadows of this preserve, deer, raccoons and foxes. Birds can be seen swooping down on the lake for insects most any time. Continuing around the lake, the trail passes through a copse of buckeyes, *Aesculus californica,* festooned with moss nurtured by the fogs that hang in this vale so often. Just before reaching the equestrian parking area, a footpath curves south. Take this path to reach a grove of canyon oaks, *Quercus chrysolepis,* on a knoll high above the lake, a nice, shady place to enjoy a picnic.

After refreshments, follow the trail north around the other arm of the lake, making a gentle descent to the main trail from the parking area.

Bay Area Ridge Trail

This six-mile trip takes a bit more than three hours and gives a complete view of the preserve. Bicyclists and equestrians take the high road over the preserve's central knoll; hikers go around its southwest face on a lower alignment. Then, all can continue to the southeast end of the preserve on a multi-use trail. On the first segment after Horseshoe Lake, hikers may take a slightly longer, woodsy trail up and over a high ridge before rejoining bicyclists and equestrians on the rest of the route to the southeast end of the preserve.

Starting from the preserve's north parking area, hikers can choose either the underpass trail to the east side of Alpine Pond or the bicyclist/equestrian route from the trail entrance 400 feet south along Alpine Road. Both routes converge on Old Page Mill Road beyond Alpine Pond. From there, bicyclists and equestrians go uphill (east) past former ranch buildings and take the old farm road to the left. They continue on it over the top of the preserve's summit and down to Horseshoe Lake (an elevation gain of 200 feet and loss of 400 feet in 1.4 miles.)

Hikers turn south beyond the pond on a foot trail through a mature canyon-oak forest. Following an easy path uphill, this trail crosses terraces, and passes the low shed where former owners slaughtered hogs raised on this site. Then, as the trail gradually climbs the grasslands above the canyon of Lambert Creek, the views extend to miles and miles of forested ridges and rolling grasslands. The coast is visible on clear days.

Continue around the central knoll's steep sides into heads of little ravines and out onto its rugged, imposing brow. The trail passes through stretches of dense chaparral and then into little oak and madrone woods. Around the southernmost point of the ridge, turn northeast and descend quickly to intersect the graveled farm road, the bicyclist/equestrian route to Horseshoe Lake.

From here, hikers, equestrians and bicyclists follow the same Bay Area Ridge Trail route across the dam and uphill around the east side of Horseshoe Lake. At the first trail junction, take either the multi-use former farm road straight ahead (east) or the

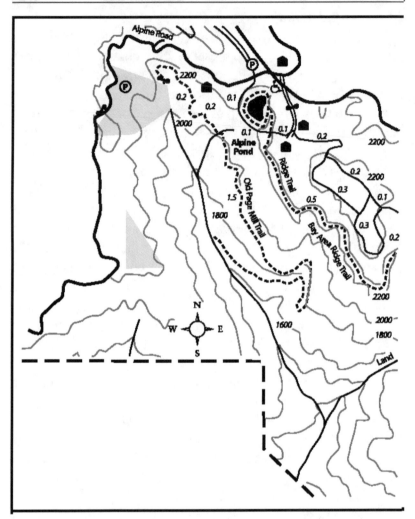

hikers-only trail right (south). The wide, multi-use trail goes into the forest and proceeds 0.3 mile southeast under a high canopy of evergreen branches. The 0.6-mile, hikers-only route ascends on many switchbacks along the west side of a steep-sided ridge to reach a small plateau shaded by mature Douglas firs. Almost immediately the hikers' trail drops down the east side of the ridge, twists a bit and shortly rejoins the multi-use route.

From this junction the graveled farm road winds around small knolls, crosses gullies and passes the Christmas tree farm. The path leaves the farm road and follows a section of the old

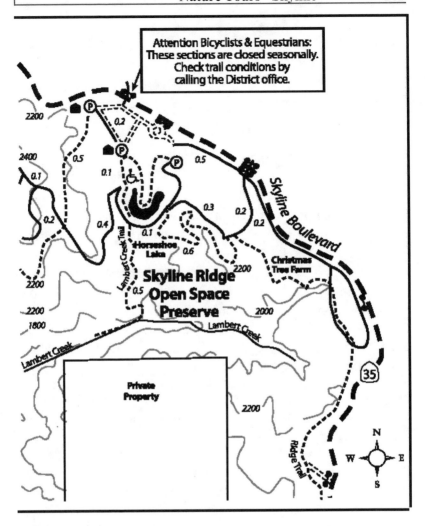

Summit Road through cool oak woodland. After a half-mile, turn right onto a beautiful trail that crosses the fern-clad banks of a tributary of Lambert Creek. Gradually one climbs to a walnut and chestnut orchard on a little knoll overlooking the southeast end of the preserve.

PART VIII
WALKING TOURS

Half Moon Bay
City of Half Moon Bay – Tel. 650-726-8270

Getting There: From the intersection of Highways One and 92, go north to the first traffic signal (Main Street), turn right to the second four way stop sign. Turn left and go one block to Johnston Street.

Our walking tour will begin at Mill and Johnston Streets where the flow of the local history began. It was here that the first town was developed on the San Francisco Peninsula. The seed was planted in 1841 when Candelario Miramontes, a sergeant from the San Francisco Presidio, was granted some 4,418 acres of land between two creeks – Pilarcitos to the north and Purisima to the south. The land previously had been used to graze the vast herds of cattle and sheep belonging to Mission Dolores near the presidio. Not long after Mexico had won its independence from Spain, the mission lands were being split up. The government in far-off Mexico City contributed so little to the Californios that soldiers at the Presidio had not been paid for six years.

1. MIRAMONTES brought his wife and 13 children and 30 cattle and horses to his new land grant. He built an adobe house for his family about where the office building stands here at 745 Mill St. He farmed some five acres on the southwest side of the creek, calling his place Rancho San Benito and the new village was initially called San Benito (after St. Benedict). His son, Bernardo Miramontes, built another adobe just to the west across the street with one side about even with the sidewalk on Calle de Molino, or Mill Street. Mill Street got its name because it ended east at the town's first mill for grinding grain. Nothing remains of the old mill. Calle Real or King Street ran north and

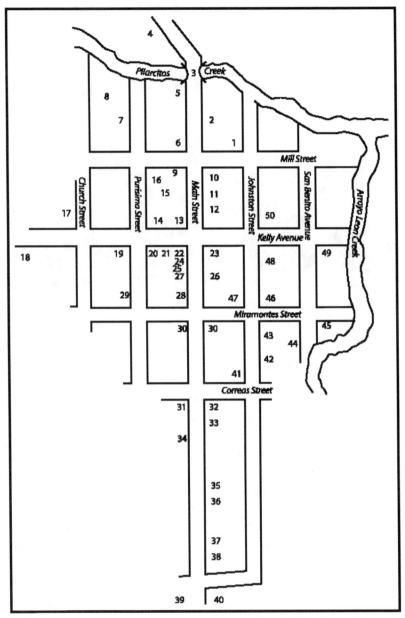

south where Main Street is now, connecting with the trails used to move the cattle herds back and forth to Mission Dolores and San Francisco Presidio. Walk down to Main and turn right.

2. ONE OF THE EARLY COMBINATIONS of general store and saloon was on the right, about where the Half Moon Bay Feed & Fuel Store is now located, Henry C. Bidwell, who

Henry Bidwell's saloon and store once sat on this site.

had a store in Pescadero, opened a saloon and store here in the late 1850's. The feed and fuel store owned by Carl Hoffman is a "must see" for anyone seeking the flavor of the Coastside's rural ambience.

     3. A WOODEN BRIDGE ACROSS PILARCITOS CREEK was built on about the same alignment as the present day Main Street bridge. As you go across the bridge spanning Arroyo de los Pilarcitos, be aware that this structure was buiilt in 1900 using reinforced concrete, one of the first ever, using discarded steel cable from San Francisco's California Street cable car line as reinforcement bars. At the four way stop sign, cross Main Street and continue along Main to the open area beyond the riparian foliage. About 100 yards to the west, another key pioneer, Tiburcio Vasquez, a former overseer at Mission Dolores. built his adobe home.

     Vasquez, whose namesake nephew was to become an infamous outlaw, had been granted 4,436 acres two years earlier. In 1846, the year Candelario Miramontes died, Vasquez moved to his property and built his home on the west side of the creek.

     On the rare occasions when either Vasquez or the Miramontes family traveled to the presidio, they had to negotiate a steep trail across the top of San Pedro Mountain. There was another trail that followed the course of Pilarcitos Creek back into the mountains and through a gap leading to the mission; it had been used to drive cattle to and from the mission and could only be traveled initially on horseback. It was 1853 before Vasquez drove a brand new $400 wagon across the mountains from the bay side of the peninsula and what is today San Mateo. He was the first to make the trip over nearly the same path that today's Highway 92 follows. Later road builders just cut deeper into the hillsides to widen the trail to a usable roadway.

Vasquez had a church built on one corner of what is now the town cemetery. He also had an adobe built for the priest which was located about where that two-story office bulding now houses the real estate office.

4. PABLO VASQUEZ, his son, built a house of red-wood in 1869 at what is known today as 270 Main St. Pablo Vasquez is remembered as the last of the local Californio dons, renowned for his appearance at festivals and parades mounted on a striking palomino. His Greek Revival style house had an

*Estanislao Zaballa would not recognize his
store and saloon now that everything is so upscale.*

*The Debenedetti Building is here because
JosephDebenedetti walked from San Francisco to sell goods
to Coastside farmers in the 1860's and became
a Half Moon Bay success story.*

annex added on the north wing in 1892.

5. BACK ACOSS THE BRIDGE, you will see on the right the modern Zaballa House complex. This was the site of one of the village's first stores and saloons. Estanislao Zaballa, who married the oldest Miramontes daughter, surveyed the first town layout, and opened his store, saloon and a stable out back in the 1850's. Bidwell opened his store and saloon across the street seven years later. The Miramontes family had been selling off bits and pieces of their land since California had become the 31st state in the United States of America. William and James Johnston bought nearly half of the rancho in 1853 and begun a large farming operation south of the village.

James Denniston farmed the most fertile part of Palomares' rancho to the north, and built a pier at Pillar Point where produce and lumber could be loaded aboard small schooners for shipment to San Francisco. Denniston and a partner also bought land at the end of what is now Kelly Avenue and built a flour mill to grind grains being raised by area farmers. The town was called Spanishtown, dropping the San Benito name, well into the 1870's. As more and more English-speaking business people moved in, it was more often referred to as Half Moon Bay.

6. SAN BENITO HOUSE was built in 1905 by Emmanuelle Danieri with its unusual second story bay window. James Mosconi ran the hotel that sits at the corner of Main and Mill Streets. The original second story verandas were eliminated in a renovation. Turn right on Mill Street and go one block to the corner of Purisima.

7. **A FARM HOUSE IN THE VILLAGE** can be seen across at 340 Purisima St. Martin Carty built his house and barn in 1873 and 1874 after acquiring the land 10 years earlier from the Miramontes family.

8. BEHIND THE CARTY HOUSE, Jose de los Santos Miramontes had his adobe home and farmed the land along the creek before the village began growing. Go across Mill and turn east past Sushi Main Street to the corner.

9. EUROPEAN IMMIGRANTS played significant roles in the growth of the village. At the southwest corner of Mill and Main is the two-story Debenedetti Building. In the late 1860's and early 1870's, Joseph Debenedetti came to Half Moon Bay, walking all the way from San Francisco with his goods in a backpack to sell door to door. The next year he and his brother-in-law rented a building and opened a general store on Main Street. After marrying a local girl, Teresa Scarpa, he built a residence on Main Street in about the center of this block next to the store, and opened another store in Pescadero. Through the years, the store building expanded. The second story was added after the 1906 earthquake caused severe damage, making major renovations necessary.

10. ACROSS AT 415-421 MAIN ST., Manuel Francis, son of Portuguese immigrants and a county supervisor, built the commercial building with living quarters upstairs in 1922 for $10,280. The Mission Revival style uses ceramic tile for roofing and frontage decoration.

11. ANOTHER ITALIAN IMMIGRANT, Angelo Boitano, operated a general store at 429-431 Main St. that lasted from the 1880's through three generations of his family. His brother Emelio later ran the store. In the 1870's, the building was used as a saloon, a post office and restaurant.

By the end of the 1870's, the village had grown to a population of 600 people, the third largest on the peninsula. Kathryn Gualtieri's excellent town history reports that in 1877 the commercial district contained four blacksmith shops, six general stores, a hotel, a bakery, several saloons and restaurants, two butcher shops, a millinery and dressmaking shop, a livery stable, a harness shop, a barber shop, a drug store, a tin shop, three fruit stores, a shoe shop, two wagon-making shops and two fast freight lines.

12. ANTONE QUILLA BUILT the two-story store building at 435 Main St. after fire destroyed the 1860's structure that had successively housed a hotel and a general store. Antone's building erected in 1903 has seen duty as quarters for two bars and a soda fountain before its present occupants.

13. THE CUNHA STORE at the northwest corner of Kelly and Main streets was known locally for years as the Index Corner, because the Index Saloon occupied the space. Lively political rallies and dances were held upstairs. The corner started as a paint store in 1872, but that burned down. The present structure was built by Joseph Debenedetti in 1900. William Cuhna, part of the extensive Cunha family that arrived here from the Azores in the 1870's, changed it to a grocery store in the 1930's. Today the store is run by Bev Cuhna Ashcroft, a grand lady considered by many the unofficial mayor of Half Moon Bay. Turn right on Kelly Ave.

Kelly Avenue was named for Charles E. Kelly, one of the hustlers of early Half Moon Bay who was elected county assessor in 1857 and 1858, and county treasurer in 1859 and 1860.

14. ART NOUVEAU CAME TO TOWN in 1928 with construction of the new front at 645 Kelly Ave. by Ben Cuhna with Manuel Phillips Dutra as the contractor. The new stucco front was erected by Cuhna over a 1913 wood frame building. A.P. "Mac" Dutra was a later owner of the building that houses a funeral home. Continue to the corner of Purisima and turn right.

15. A PLOW FACTORY was located in the vacant lot in the middle of the block. It was set up by Robert I. Knapp to build a special invention that made it easier for farmers to plow on sandy hillsides endemic to the coast. The factory ended up here after two earlier moves, one caused by a fire that threatened

*Ben Cuhna's dream home was the envy
of all his neighbors when he built it in 1908.*

to engulf the entire village.

16. AN ITALIANTE FALSE FRONT HOUSE sits at 415 Purisima St. It was built about 1898 by Louis de Martini, but was known locally as the Giannini House after the family that occupied the place for years. Continue to Mill Street and turn left to the end of the street.

17. OUR LADY OF THE PILLAR CATHOLIC CHURCH, which fills the property along Church Street at Kelly, is the town's third Catholic church. The first was built by Tiburcio Vasquez at the corner of the town cemetery just east of Main Street on Highwway 92. Vasquez' grave, originally beneath the church floor, marks one corner of the first church site. Another church replaced the old one in 1883. The present church was built in 1954 and the stained glass windows including the large round one above the entrance, donated by Joseph Debenedetti, were moved from the razed chapel to the new church. The Bell Monument in the church garden features the bronze bell made in 1867 in Troy, N.Y., and rung for the first time in 1868 at the original church. Continue on Church to Kelly and turn right past the school across the street.

18. BEN CUHNA BUILT HIS OWN home at 520 Kelly

Ave. in 1908. A local contractor who constructed many buildings on the coast, he spared no expense, using scalloped shingles
and topping the Eastlake-style mansion with a polygonal tower.
The Alves family bought the house in 1923 and operated a dairy
at the rear of the property, where potters now create more mal-
leable artistry from clay. The Half Moon Bay Chamber of Commerce now occupies the old mansion. Go back east on Kelly to
Purisima.

19. A BUSY AND HISTORICAL CORNER at the
southeast quadrant of the intersection, there were two red brick
buildings, the first dating from 1866, that housed a general store
and a Wells Fargo Express office with a social hall upstairs. The
buildings also were where the Levy Brothers opened their first
store that grew into a chain of peninsula department stores. All of
the original buildings fell apart in the 1906 earthquake. The
present structure was erected after the quake.

20. OCCIDENTAL HOTEL occupied the corner across
Purisima from the 1870's until fire destroyed it in 1894. It was
rebuilt and operated until after World War II. It was razed and a
post office building operated here from 1962 until just before the
21st century when new, more modern quarters were furnished.

21. NEXT DOOR at 650 Kelly Ave. was the Occidental
Hotel Annex that contained living quarters for the hotel owner,
Andrew Gilcrest. A walkway linked the two parts of the hotel.
Shops were located on the ground floor. The building was erected
to match the larger neighboring building all the way to its hipped
roof and formed brackets beneath the eaves. The annex was built
in 1913.

22. HALF MOON BAY'S VERY OWN PLAZA at
Kelly and Main has a bell tower housing a bell that had been
used at the Half Moon Bay Grammer School from 1906 until
1938 when the school was demolished. Angelo Bergano donated
the bell to the city for the tower. The bell is cast iron number 30
made by the National Bell Foundary in Cincinnati, OH.

23. ACROSS MAIN STREET is the third and final location of the Bank of Half Moon Bay. The building then housed
the Bank of Italy that became the Bank of America (now swal-
lowed by a North Carolina conglomerate). It now houses Half
Moon Bay City Hall. Remain on the west side of Main and turn

The house at 546 Purisima St. was built in 1869 for one of the town's first doctors.

south. In the original village, the main thoroughfare ended here and the street jogged west a block over to Purisima and headed south again. In the middle of today's Main Street, Asuncion Luis Gomez built his home and the village's first school, and Next to where today's plaza is located, Estevan Vidal ran a bakery.

24. THE HALF MOON BAY BAKERY was opened by Nat Castiglione at 501 Main St. in 1926. Using brick ovens, he became famous for his Italian breads. The heady odors of great baked goods still waft from there.

25. THE INDEPENDENT ORDER OF ODD FEL-LOWS Building at 522-526 Main St. was built in 1895 and for years served as a major gathering place for public events such as medicine shows and chautauqua variety shows. The upstairs is still used by the local IOOF chapter for meetings.

26. THE OLDEST PLACE HOUSING BUSINESSES continuously is across the street at 527 Main St. Originally built in 1873 for Angelo Boitano's saloon and general merchandise store, the second floor was family living quarters.

27. BUILT AS A HOME IT BECAME A DENTIST'S OFFICE, the house at at 538 Main once more is quarters for another dentist. Built in 1906 for John W. Gilcrest, son of an Irish immigrant who ran the Occidental Hotel stables, he rented it to a dentist named Hooper. Note the leaded glass in the front bay window and matched in the dormer window.

28. THE GIORGETTI BUILDING at the northwest corner of Main and Miramontes is dedicated to Federico and Maria Giorgetti and their son, Leo, and all the other pioneer Italian families who contributed so greatly to Half Moon Bay's proud history. Go right (west) on Miramontes and to Purisima.

29. IN THE DAYS WHEN DOCTORS MADE house calls, the small home at 546 Purisima St. was big enough for his office and living quarters. Dr. Albert Milliken lived and worked there from 1869 to 1889 when the house was sold to a stage driver and his family. Return east on Miramontes to Main Street.

30. ROBERT I. KNAPP'S SIDEHILL PLOWS started at this corner, both the southeast and southwest corners of the intersection. Where "Half to Have It, the Main Street Exchange" is now located, Knapp started one of the village's most success-ful early enterprises. A wheelwright from New York State, he went into partnership in 1870 with an Irishman named Pete Quinlan, who had just opened a blacksmith shop at the corner. While repairing wagon wheels and other farm equipment. Knapp discovered that farmers were having trouble using ordinary plows on the sandy coastside hills. He invented one that with only a minor adjustment could be used in either direction to plow on hillsides. By 1879, by showing them at county fairs around the state, he soon had so much business he had to move to larger quarters across the street. The building later caught fire and the volunteer fire department prevented its spreading and saved the downtown. A strong temperance advocate, Knapp formed the Good Templars Association to try keeping people out of saloons; he ran for governor twice on the Prohibition Party ticket. He also owned the town's private water company. Continue south on Main Street past Correas.

31. CHARLIE'S COUGH CURE concocter, Dr.

Charles Morgan, the local pharmacist, had the house at 700 Main St. built in 1907. Among the house's unique features is the fireplace made of small round stones.

32. ANOTHER CONTRACTOR'S DREAM HOME was built in 1912 across the street at 703 Main St. Manuel J. Bernardo, Jr., was the builder who used his skills to create a house with four bay windows, a hip roof and a gabled front porch. There may have been some sibling rivalry involved in his attention to many of the more time-consuming details.

33. HIS BROTHER, Frank Bernardo, had already set the standard in 1906 when he bought the Joseph Debendetti House, mounted it on logs and rolled the two-story structure three blocks to its present location next door at 711 Main St. He added the annex and the front porch.

34. ANOTHER CARPENTER, Antonio Marsh, built the house at 724 Main St. in 1907 for himself and his family. His unique artistry extended to specially shaped shingles over the bay window. Carpenters seemed to have proliferated at this end of Main Street where lots had been platted in the town's first subdivision beyond the town center.

Before the land was subdivided, the area to the west of here was farmed by members of the Miramontes family. Two of the brothers had adobe houses for their families and raised crops south and west of what is now Purisima and was then called Calle Condada (County Road).

35. JOSE C. HELHENA was also a carpenter and built the Victorian-style house at 731 Main St. on the east side of the thoroughfare. Large overhanging bay windows were featured.

36. THE I.D.E.S. HALL at 735 Main St. was built in 1928 for the Imandade do Divino Espirato Santo Society to replace one built in 1911. The hall and the Capella in front play key roles in the annual Chamarita Festival, the fete for the Holy Spirit celebrated for centuries by people from the Azores and Portugal. The festival is held on Pentecostal Sunday each year.

37. THE STICK-STYLE VICTORIAN at 775 Main St. was built in 1895 by Charles Mills, a local contractor, for his family. Mills used rounded shingles and scroll-sawed brackets on the fascia.

38. GEORGE F. GILCREST, a local school principal,

*This was the way the Metzgar House at 940 Main St. looked
in 1877, the main home of a gentleman farmer
and attorney, and his family*

had the house at 779 Main St. built in 1899. Turned trim at the
corners and carved trim at the gables are featured. Gilcrest sold
the home in 1904 to Alvin Hatch, son of a pioneer sawmill operator and later a county supervisor. Cross Main Street and go to:

  39. THE METZGAR HOUSE at 940 Main St., which
was built sometime in the 1870's for William Metzgar, a pioneer
farmer who came to the coast in 1854. He was also a practicing
attorney. Go back on Main Street to the next intersection and
turn right.

  40. HARDLY RECOGNIZABLE: where the European
style bistro, Cetrella, operates at 845 Main St., is the renovated
old farmer's cooperative packing shed. This was where Delores
Mullen, the late doyenne of Half Moon Bay, worked and influ-
enced social and political affairs for years. Turn right and then
left for the long stroll past newer houses on Johnston Street to
Correas.

  41. THE HOLLYWOOD COURTS, at 642 Johnston
St. were built in 1925 in the early days of motor inns. Built dur-

ing the short-lived oil boom on the coast, the small motor court was home to roustabouts and oil riggers for a time. It has been converted to facilities for vacationers on longer term stayovers.

42. THE OLD SCHOOLHOUSE built in 1858 by pioneer farmer, James Johnston, is the core of the house at 611 Johnston St. The structure was moved from Johnston's farm to its present site in 1865 where it was used as a school for some years, then as a meeting place for various groups before being converted to residential use and renovated often.

43. THE JOSEPH M. FRANCIS HOUSE at 607 Johnston St. was built in 1913. Francis and his brother, Manuel, were owners of a general merchandise store on Main Street. He was also a county supervisor. The house is known as a craftsman, popular in that period. Turn right on Miramontes to San Benito.

44. ONE OF THE OLDER HOUSES in town, the one at 608 San Benito St. was built in 1871 for James L. Anderson, who had bought the town lot for $350. The property was sold a year later for $650 to Pete Quinlan, Knapp's blacksmith partner who broke with his teetotaler partner and went into the saloon business.

45. ORIGINALLY A TWO-ROOM COTTAGE built in 1872 for J.L. Janssen, a wheelwright, the house at 806 Miramontes St. has seen many changes over the decades. This includes its expansion and fireplace made of river stones and broken boulders. Look to the east down Miramontes Street, one has to imagine the village's one and only brewery that was operated for a number of years next to Leon Creek. A private residence since has been built on the site. Go back to the corner of Miramontes and Johnston streets and turn north to the chapel on the northeast corner.

46. A CHURCH IN CONTINUAL USE since it was built, the Methodist Episcopal Church is the first building in the village to be designed by an architect. Now surrounded with a vast array of buildings in the same style, the church at the corner was first erected and opened for religious services in November of 1872. Designed by San Francisco architect Charles Geddes in the Gothic Revival style, it is one of only three original Peninsula churches still standing today.

The Methodist Episcopal Church, built in 1872
is one of only three original churches
still in use in San Mateo County.

47. ONE OF THE FIRST VILLAGE SMITHIES, Joseph E. Denny had the house at 727 Miramontes St. built in 1873. Major changes were made in the house beginning in 1886 when G. Touri bought the house from Denny.   It has seen many renovations since then.

48. THE VILLAGE JAIL,   built in 1911, obviously was built to meet a very low demand for incarceration. If more than two drunks were tossed in the two-cell hoosegow overnight, accommodations were a bit crowded. The jail is now used as a museum by the Spanishtown Historical Society. Turn right on Kelly Street to the corner of San Benito.

49. KNOWN AS THE BAKERY or the August Bailey

House, the complex at 505 San Benito St. was begun in 1892 with the Queen Anne Victorian house with its beehive shingling and colored glass borders around the windows. Bailey built the two-story structure at the rear for a bakery and the brick ovens are still there.

50. LAST IS THE MOST IMPORTANT so far as the National Register of Historical Places is concerned. The house at 751 Kelly Ave. is the only building in town in the register. It was built in 1865 by Williams Adams Simmons who doubled as a carpenter and an undertaker (and probably saved a few gold pieces by making his own coffins, one suspects). The building was renovated in 1993 with the original design kept intact.

A much too cozy a place to sleep off a bender,
the Half Moon Bay jail had only two tiny
cells. It now serves as a museum.

Pescadero Walkabout

Looking north on Stage Road, Pescadero.

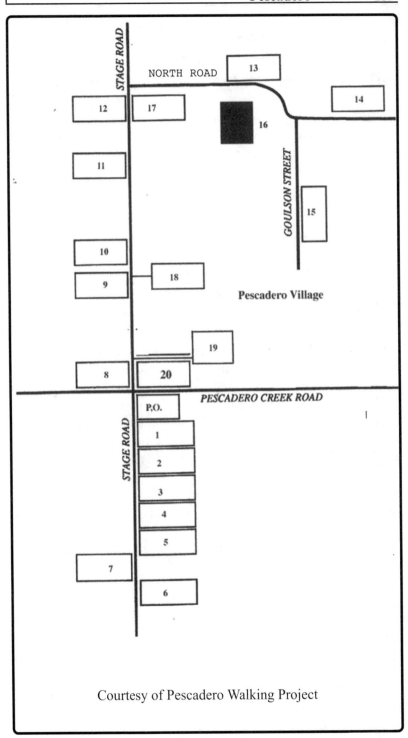

Courtesy of Pescadero Walking Project

Pescadero Walkabout

GETTING THERE: Take Highway One south to Pescadero Creek Road and turn left 2 miles to the town.

PLEASE NOTE: The Pescadero Walking History Project provides a more detailed annual walkabout as a fund raiser. For more details, call 650-879-0737.

We will start the tour at the southeast corner of Stage Road and Pescadero Creek Road with a general overview and historical summary. First of all, in modern usage, the town's name is Spanish for fishmonger. But when the area was given its name in the Mexican land grant, Rancho El Pescadero, made to Juan Jose Gonzales in 1833, it meant fishing place. Its proximity to the ocean and Pigeon Point where a whaling station was operated may account for the name never being changed or Anglicized as was done with many early names. Immigrants from Italy, Portugal and the Azores Islands (some of whom worked at whaling in the late 19th century) as well as people from the northeastern United States settled the town following the Gold Rush. First on the scene following annexation of California by the United States was Alexander Moore who built a house about a mile south of town in 1863 and started farming the rich bottomland he bought from Gonzales. His brother, Thomas, built a house of his own later that year right down Stage Road on the left, which you will see in a few minutes.

Pescadero was the fourth largest town south of San Francisco in 1868 when the boundary line for San Mateo County was pushed to a line 10 miles south of here from Tunitas Creek, the former southerly boundary. Some 400 residents provided services to surrounding farms and two large hotels, the Swanton House and Pescadero Hotel, were popular vacation spots for people who journeyed down to look for agates and other wonders on Pebble Beach west of town. Loggers were harvesting redwoods east of town. There was a creamery and a cheese factory and four mills to grind grains. The town even had telegraph service by 1869.

As you look to the north up Stage Road, one can see that most of the present commercial buildings are of more recent vintage. A disastrous fire in 1921 wiped out the original business structures on the northwest side of Stage Road. This was followed five years later by a fire that virtually swept away the business across the street. In 1927, the venerable Swanton House and all its cottages burned down. As a result, most of the older buildings remaining in town are private homes and churches.

Before beginning the walkabout, keep in mind that most of the buildings you will see are private residences and are not open to the public. Please respect their privacy. Public buildings do, of course, welcome you.

1. SOUTH ON STAGE ROAD: Walk south past the post office. The first building on the left, now occupied by the Native Sons of the Golden West, was built in 1890 for the Methodist Episcopal Church. Originally, there was a 70-foot louvered bell tower with a spire mounted atop it, but this was torn down in the 1940's. This Gothic Revival built entirely of choice redwood was used as a church until 1915 when the congregation became so small they could not afford to keep it open, and it was sold. It has since seen duty as a cultural center, a cultural school for Japanese-American children and now as a meeting place for the Pebble Beach chapter of the Native Sons. The village now owns half interest in the building and is expected to see expanded use as a community center.

2. THE TWO-STORY SHIPLAP-SIDED structure was built in 1878 for the local chapter of the International Order of Odd Fellows. The street façade was made more elaborate in 1890 with addition of the balustraded balcony and the decorative wooden brackets under the eaves. It has been used as a private residence for many years. The present owner sells unusual handmade toys from the garage in the rear, a modern addition.

3. ONE OF THE MOST ORNATE houses in town is next, the Woodhams House built in the late 1890's by Alfred Woodhams for his bride as they moved to town to open a butcher shop. Subsequent generations of the family lived there for the next 100 years.

4. THE THOMAS MOORE HOUSE at 80 Stage Road may be the oldest building in town. Believed to have been built in 1863, the year Moore was married, it would have been constructed shortly after the house of his brother, Alexander, which was burned by vandals in 1975. Another house you will see at the other end of the street is practically a carbon copy of this one and may have been built just after the Moore home. Designed along the Greek Revival lines, many of its motifs are repeated in other local houses of the period.

5. ITS PROVENANCE LOST, the house at 70 Stage Road is not named. Estimates are that it was built in the 1890's. Its builder used the device of scoring the redwood planks to give them the appearance of stone, a technique used in finishing the Pescadero Community Church at the other end of the street.

6. A KEY PART OF THE COMMUNITY for generations – the I.D.E.S. Hall is next at the end of Stage Road. This is where the Chamarita Festival, the fete of the Holy Spirit is held on the sixth week after Easter each year. The festival features a parade, a dance and a food fest that celebrates a rite dating back to the 15th century in Portugal. The festival has been observed here since the 1860's. The exact date of this building is not known, but an 1878 drawing of Pescadero shows the building on the other side of the street. Cross the street and head back north on Stage Road.

7. THE HOUSE ON TURKEY LANE is now Rosehenge. As late as 1919, this end of the street was called Turkey Lane and this house on the left was simply called The House on Turkey Lane. But the owner since 1989, whose vast experimental garden features roses of many varieties, gave it the new name suggested by a friend. The exact age of the house is unknown. The two-story portion is original, but the one-story, a more recent renovation, shares many of the interior features of other houses in town built in the 1860's and could have been built any time between then and 1878, it is believed. In the spring, the aroma from more than 100 rose bushes fills the air.

As you walk back toward the business center, note the large barn about a quarter of a mile down the road. It now houses a seasonal produce stand run by the Muzzi family who sell artichokes, strawberries and other items from Level Lea Farm spread out behind the barn. Built in the 1860's, it is the oldest standing barn in the village. If your tour is in the season, you may want to make a stop there on your way out of town.

8. LOS AMIGOS MARKET & TAQUERIA is ahead just across the intersection on the left with its gas pumps in front. In the 1860's, Mrs. Charles Swanton, wife of one of the two blacksmiths in town opened a hotel at this corner. Trees were planted all along the Pescadero Creek Road frontage. The business was so successful that cabins were added, extending for some 200 feet behind the two-story hotel. The Swanton House, as it was called, escaped the 1921 fire, but was destroyed by another fire in 1926, leaving only the old magnolia tree as the only remnant of that era.

9. THE BANK BUILDING is a 20th century creation, built in 1923 for the First National Bank of Pescadero as part of the village revival after the 1921 fire that wiped out most of the businesses on this side of the street.

THE VILLAGE'S UNSOLVED MURDER MYSTERY: On this block next to the old Swanton House was the home of the area's richest man, Loren Coburn. Coburn made a fortune by gaining control of the 17,753-acre Rancho Punto de Año Nuevo for $30,000 in the 1850's. He failed in his first attempt to make a quick profit by selling some 20 acres at the point to the federal government for a lighthouse for $40,000. But he made a lot of money leasing and selling land to the Steele brothers and other area dairymen. He moved to town and built a house here on Stage Road. He angered people in the area by trying to prevent people from visiting Pebble Beach, where he built an ill-fated hotel. His personal life was filled with troubles; his first wife died of cancer and his only son suffered brain damage from a bout with typhoid fever. As he neared his 90's, one of his many relatives tried to have him declared incapable of handling his affairs and a court battle raged for months over control of his fortune. Shortly after he died in 1918 at the age of 92, his second wife was found beaten and hacked to death in the house here.

A man who claimed to have seen two men leaving the scene of the murder later changed his story and no one was ever prosecuted. Local legend holds that the wavering witness was seen driving a new car not long after the investigation was dropped. And after a lengthy review, the Coastside Comet reported in July, 1920, the judge granted one of Coburn's main partners control over most of the $600,000 estate. The incapacitated Coburn son was left with a $50,000 trust fund for his care.

Just a quiet little farm town was Pescadero in those days.

10. MUZZI'S MARKET is next, another 20th century construction, run by the younger generation of the family, Vince and Joe Muzzi, Jr., and his wife Veronica, and features home-made pastries and sandwiches as well as produce from the family farm. The mural on the front was originally painted by the noted artist Al Krebs and restored in recent years by local artist Christ Dutsch.

11. NORM'S MARKET & ARCANGELI BAKERY is another fine market, bakery and butcher shop: Norm's Market. It is run by Norm Benedetti. His grandfather, Sante Arcangeli, started the market across the street in 1929. Now Norm has modernized with many local specialty items of honey, jams, baked goods, sandwiches and a full butcher shop.

12. THE OLDEST SURVIVING PROTESTANT church in the county sits alongside Pescadero Creek resting on its original foundation and without major renovation – the Pescadero Community Church built in 1867. The original church had only a square bell tower, but in 1889 a steeple was added.

*Three generations of the Goulson family worked
the forge here, carrying on a 200-year family tradition.*

The redwood exterior has been scored to look like stone. Cross the bridge and turn right on North Road.

13. ONE OF THE TOWN'S BLACKSMITHS was housed for years in the building on the left. John Goulson, whose family had been blacksmiths in England for two centuries, opened a smithy here in 1868 that was later run by his son Alfred and then his grandson Douglas.

14. ST. ANTHONY'S CHURCH: Past several houses of more recent vintage, is St. Anthony's Church, which was built in 1869. This Classic Revival structure suffered a temporary shakeup in the 1906 earthquake, which rocked it off its foundation. It was set back on the foundation with only minor repairs needed. As you will see, the spire is octagonal and cut by four dormers with louver-filled arches and a small cross at each apex.

15. BACK DOWN NORTH ROAD TO GOULSON: Halfway down the block on the left is the Bartlett V. Weeks House built in 1872 by one of the three local branches of the Weeks family originally from Kennebunkport, Maine. Unlike many of the houses of the period, it was built without shutters and has the main entrance around the side of the ell extension. The house is now occupied by the third generation of the Weeks family.

16. RETURN TO NORTH ROAD, and turn left. The large metal front building on the left was once Pescadero's own Dodge auto dealership. Turn left on Stage Road.

17. THE JAMES MC CORMICK HOUSE on the left is set back from the road among the trees. It is almost a duplicate of the Thomas W. Moore House seen at the other end of Stage Road. The window arrangement is one of the few differences, using four panes instead of six as in the Moore house. The redwood siding is scored to give it the appearance of stone, just as was done at the church across the street. This house was believed to have been built at about the same time as the church in 1867. The conifer in the front yard is a monkey tree, *Arucania aracauna,* brought from Chile.

Speaking of trees, Pescadero's proximity to the woods evidently inspired 17 of its local citizens to organize the Pebble Beach Grove of the Order of Druids in January of 1886. Since their rites were held secretly in the woods, no public notice was taken of them from that date on. Another intriguing Pescadero mystery: the disappeared Druids.

St. Anthony's Catholic Church was built in 1869.

The old unpainted building housing the antique store is a 20th century structure, having been built after the 1926 fire that destroyed most of the business district on this side of the street.

18. THE STAGE ROAD SHOPS set back away from Stage Road escaped the fire. In the late 1800's, it housed another blacksmith shop, but now holds three shops run by local businesswomen, and the Pescadero Creekside Barn, a unique bed and breakfast with room for two guests.

19. ANOTHER PESCADERO TRADITION is Duarte's Tavern. Frank Duarte, an immigrant from the Azores, brought a barrel of whiskey from Santa Cruz in 1894 and started the bar. Prohibition shut down the business a couple of decades later. When the fire of 1926 destroyed the building, all that was saved was the old bar itself. The business was reopened in 1934 along with a sandwich shop run by Emma Duarte whose homemade pies became famous. Their son, Ron, entered the business in the 1950's. A huge garden for their fresh produce was started in back of the place. He added artichoke soup, crab cioppino and other delicacies to the menu, creating long waiting lines of customers on weekends. Bon appetite! It's a fine way to refresh oneself after the walkabout.

Pillar Point Harbor
&
Princeton By The Sea
Jurisdiction: San Mateo County Harbor
District — Tel. 650-726-4723
San Mateo County – Tel. 650-363-4161

Seabirds know Pillar Point Harbor is a working boat harbor
and patiently await their turn at fish scraps.

Getting There: Take Highway One to Capistrano Road. Turn left at signal. Then take next left after a short half block, then a right and then another right into parking lot. Park at the rear of the parking lot.

This walkabout is for people enamored of the sea and all the things associated with marine and maritime life. Set aside at least three hours for a leisurely stroll that will include boat watching, bird watching, and a brief communing with nature in what is left of the Pillar Point slough. And if you are lucky, there may be some hot dog surfers taking on the big rollers at Mavericks. They are always fun to watch. Add another hour if you should succumb to the lure of eating, drinking and shopping at some of the colorful spots on the route.

The harbor itself has undergone a series of changes in the past 200 years or so. Before the Spanish arrived, of course, this was prime hunting and fishing grounds for the Ohlone natives who occupied the country for several millennia. Proof of this was discovered when a farmer uncovered a native midden or trash heap while draining a portion of the marsh; archeologists found artifacts of all kinds in the midden, evidence of centuries of use by native peoples. During Spanish and Mexican occupation, the uplands were first a grazing land for Mission Dolores cattle herds and then part of Rancho Corral de Tierra del Norte granted in 1839 to Guerrero Palomares, the prefect of Mission Dolores in San Francisco.

Twenty years later, part of the land was in the hands of James G. Denniston, a state assemblyman who was farming the flatland portions of the Palomares property. Denniston built a deep-water landing for schooners at Pillar Point, and it was for many years the key shipping point for north coast lumber, hay and produce being sent to San Francisco.

The harbor was one of the main stops on the short-lived – 1905-1920 – San Francisco & Ocean Shore Railroad that was one of the first big attempts to develop the coast. The station serving the harbor was in the building now occupied by the Moon Bay Restaurant just east of the Princeton-Highway One intersection traffic signal. The railroad promotion brought visitors from San Francisco through a tunnel, and around on the route now occupied by Highway One. Lots were sold for as low as $400 each for a planned new city to be called El Granada overlooking the harbor. Some 1,727 lots were sold for as total of $976,779, but few people built houses on them in early years before the speculative bubble burst. Now individual houses built on those lots in the past 30 years are selling for nearly as much as was raised by the promoters from the entire original land sale.

The harbor's history as a "safe port" for boats caught in serious storms offshore has been a mixed one. Sitting as it does behind 450-foot high Pillar Point is ideal for some nine months of the year when seasonal winds come from the northwest. But during the winter months when winds shift to the west and south, it was a death trap for boats until an outer breakwater was constructed after World War II. Even the first breakwater proved an inadequate barrier when really serious storms hit the coast, so an inner breakwater was constructed. Since the inner breakwater was constructed, the harbor has become much more secure for the fleet of fishing and pleasure craft that fill the piers and anchorages.

There are also excellent facilities for trailerable boats to put into the water and a large parking lot for the boat trailers.

For visiting fisher people lacking their own boats, there are two excellent places with boats available: Captain John's (650-728-3377) and Huck Finn Sportfishing (650-726-7133), both of which can provide fishing licenses, bait, snacks and a variety of boats.

Walkabout

Wandering about the harbor offers an excess of great choices. There is a bar: The Harbor Bar (650-728-5566); a popular restaurant Ketch Joanne's (650-728-3747); two fish markets – Princeton Sea Food (650-726-2722) and Ship To Shore Fish Market (650-726-8506), both with restaurants, too. And the sportsfishing places also have gifts for sale.

If one prefers to wander and take a close look at the life of fishermen (there are a few women, too), walk out on the big pier, keeping a wary eye on truck traffic going to and fro. The boats leave the dock early in the mornings, so chances are that

Nothing goes to waste at the fish cleaning table.

one is more apt to see those returning to unload the day's catch.

The other choice is to walk to the northern edge of the parking lot and out on the fishing pier, where anglers cast for perch and rockfish. The sights, depending upon the time of day, can include terns and pelicans diving for their food. Terns work alone and in pairs, screeching signals at each other. Pelicans more often are in groups and their dives are always accompanied by greedy sea gulls waiting to grab at any catch that happens to slip out of the pelican's pouch. To the south of the fishing pier are finger piers filled with pleasure boats, a mixture of sailing and motor craft.

A FEW STEPS UP TO CAPISTRANO ROAD: Retracing one's steps from the pier, continue past the restrooms and up the short stairway to Capistrano Road. At the top of the stairs and across the road is the Pillar Point Inn (650-712-9277), its egg-shell blue paint weathering nicely in the salt air. To the left, the first stop is Barbara's Fish Trap (650-728-7049), its gaudy bright colors a lure to seafood lovers, especially the chowder, for generations. Farther along the sidewalk, the sea wall and harbor are on the left with views all the way to the point. Across the street on the right is the Half Moon Bay Brewing Co. (650-728-2337) in a building that has grown like topsy in the past two decades. Starting out as an old house converted into a café, it expanded through several lives and owners before reaching its present state, a very polished exterior and friendly interior; voted best new restaurant on the coast in 2001, it will undoubtedly have a long run.

Beyond the Brewing Company parking lot on the east side of Capistrano is the start of the funky side of the harbor life. Sylvia's Curiosity Shop (650-728-9118) is in an old off-white stucco building and one has to enter just to satisfy one's curiosity. The clapboard-sided building next door is smaller and even funkier, housing As You Like It, another curious array for sale. The larger building to the north with the banner Old Princeton Landing (650-728-9103) across the front houses a surf board shop and Maverick's Roadhouse Café (650-7728-1233).

Opposite across the intersection with Prospect Road is Mezza Luna (650-728-8108), a fine Italian restaurant in the old Princeton Inn built in 1908 and nearly a century of colorful history unconnected with its present occupants and owners. Once a bordello and a hotel, like many large Coastside buildings during the years of Prohibition (1919-1933), the old inn was said to be a haven and hangout for bootleggers. Many Coastside people found banning consumption of liquor unpopular, and were said to have ignored the frequent midnight runs of small boats to ships offshore and returns to handy interim storage points like the inn. Frank Miramontes, a later member of the first family to have settled on the coast and a service station operator during the period, reportedly testified during the trial of an accused bootlegger that "I just sell gasoline and have no interest in what they do to burn it up." His was the community attitude. One raid reported Sept. 17, 1920 in the Coast Side Comet newspaper told of five hotels from Half Moon Bay to Rockaway Beach (including the one in Princeton by the Sea) being raided by prohibition agents who seized "enough liquor to fill two five-ton trucks," but none of those arrested were named and the weekly newspaper never bothered to report what criminal penalties, if any, were ever

*Tools of the crab fishing trade, these traps are a common
sight in the byways of Princeton by the Sea.*

imposed.

PROSPECT TAKES YOU WEST: Next, go west on
Prospect Street, a short block with towering Monterey cypress
trees on the left. On the right behind Mezza Luna is a produce
stand that sells farm-fresh goods on summer weekends. At
Broadway, turn left a short half-block and then right on Princeton
Drive.

On the left is a large wood frame building where the
Harbor House has its meeting facilities. More tall cypress border
the narrow road on the left here. On the right is Coastal Lifestyles
Fitness Center (650-728-1031), completely equipped to keep your
heart pumping at the prescribed level. Tucked amongst the
cypress on the left is a dock storage facility. Next door is the
Harbor House (650-728-1572), a small seaside inn. Next door is
Andy Koral's boat restoration yard (650-728-2548). Across the
street, a more polished building houses Teknova (650-728-8011),
an industrial enterprise next door to a maker of custom patio
furniture. A boat storage yard is next to the west.

On the harbor side of Princeton Drive is the start of an

amazing array of boat projects in various stages of progress and neglect. There is a mixture of fiberglass, wood and cement craft propped up on stanchions. Weekends, the owners of some can be seen working to make their boats seaworthy. Beyond the storage yard is the active part of the boatyard, which has a crane to lift boats out of the harbor and return them to the water as well. Across from the boat yard are a series of storage yards, some of which contain trucks, trailers and other paraphernalia as well as boats. One particularly sleek wooden sailboat has sat neglected on its stanchions for more than a decade, seemingly abandoned and forgotten. Occasionally someone replaces the worn plastic tarp that only partially protects the deteriorating craft.

On the harbor side again, the Princeton Boat Storage and Fresh Fish House has a large operation next door to the Half Moon Bay Yacht Club's boat storage yard at the corner of Vassar Street. On past Vassar are a series of warehouses, a small one followed by a larger one and then the huge fish processing plant and the pier where fishing boats unload their catches. The large warehouse on the right houses their packing boxes. Beyond the packing house is a small industrial office building that contains the offices of Coastside Associates (650-7228-7157), a construction firm, and Acoustical Interiors (650-728-9441), a building materials business.

TO BEACH OR NOT TO BEACH: Princeton Drive dead-ends at West Point Drive. Here one has the choice of going left to the beach and out to the small marsh -- all that is left of a much larger fresh water slough that once extended back to where the county airport is now located. Or one can go right and loop around for the return trek.

If the beach and marsh are the choice, take a left and go down to the harbor's beach. Turn west on the beach and once more, there is a view of the harbor activities as well as a view back to the foothills of the Santa Cruz Mountain range to the east. At middle to low tide, it is a pleasant stroll all the way to the point where the ocean view is of the surf offshore at Mavericks. This is where the expert surfers test their nerve and skills on

Binoculars are critical gear for any walkabout,
but especially around marshlands frequented by birds.

mountainous waves. A return back to the east and one can take a
little side trip to the marsh, which is a feeding ground for many
resident birds the year-round, and in the spring and fall a resting
place for all manner of water fowl migrating to and from their
winter and summer territories. There is a road that circles the
marsh to the west, but its narrow travel lanes and careless drivers
make it too hazardous for foot traffic. It is advisable to return to
the beach and retrace the steps to West Point Drive. The view
from the beach is much more pleasant anyway.

WEST ON WEST POINT: Go west on West Point Drive
past three private residences on the left to Harvard Street. Turn
right on Harvard. The three blocks back to Broadway are a
colorful mixture of industrial, storage and a few small private
residences tucked in here and there. In the off-season, one is apt
to pass piles of crab pots and other fishing gear stored alongside
the road. There is a mixture of enterprises with off-beat names
like Two Dreamers (650-726-4999) and the more descriptive
Mavericks Surfboards (650-728-1237). And Exclusive Fresh
(650-728-7321) at the corner of Airport Street sells fresh fish
exclusively. Just past a medium-sized storage building is the

Bombay Boat and Bike Club's storage yard "for members only."

Just past two sizeable private homes, one reaches Broadway once more and it is just a short right then a left on Prospect. As one strolls back along the sea wall, the seats at the Half Moon Bay Brewery and Barbara's Fish Trap beckon. Who will best ease one's pleasantly tired body is a decision you will have to make. We have tried both and both are tops.

PART IX
THE KIDS WILL LOVE IT (AND SO WILL YOU)

Año Nuevo State Reserve

Jurisdiction: California State Parks – Tel. 650-879-2033

Reservations: 800-444-4445

Web Site: http://www.parks.ca.gov/parksindex/

Getting There: Take Highway One south for 28 miles to main entrance on right.

Here is nature in the raw, a stretch of coast where marine mammals live as they have for centuries providing an ideal natural history learning experience for young and old alike.

It happens 28 miles south of Half Moon Bay on a low, rocky, windswept point that juts out into the Pacific Ocean. The Spanish maritime explorer Sebastian Vizcaino anchored off the point on January 3, 1603. His diarist and chaplain of the expedition, Father Antonio de la Ascension, named it Punta de Año Nuevo (New Year's Point) for the day on which they sighted it.

Today, the point has changed somewhat from the way Vizcaino saw it from his passing ship. Elephant seals, sea lions, and other marine mammals still come ashore to rest, mate, and give birth in the sand dunes or on the beaches and offshore islands. Some four centuries of pounding by the Pacific surf has severed a part of the point from the mainland mass and created an offshore island that did not exist in Vizcaino's day.

On shore is a unique and unforgettable natural spectacle that draws hundreds of thousands of people each year. Año Nuevo

Hiking off into the reserve to see the seals and other wildlife at the point.

State Reserve is the site of the largest mainland breeding colony in the world for the northern elephant seal. The males battle for mates on the beaches and the females give birth to their pups on the dunes. The interpretive program run by the California State Parks has attracted increasing interest every winter for two decades. The wide interest means that anyone hoping to see the seals during the winter breeding season must make reservations early. During the breeding season, which is December through March, daily access to the reserve is available only on guided walks. Most of the adult seals are gone by early March, leaving behind the weaned pups that remain through April. They return to Año Nuevo's beaches during the spring and summer months to molt and can be observed during this time through a permit system. Advance reservations are always recommended for people planning to take the walks.

Rules - Regulations
• **No pets.** Pets are not allowed in the reserve and cannot be left inside parked vehicles in the parking lot. Kennels are not available.

• **Keep your distance.** Elephant seals are dangerous wild animals. Never get within 25 feet of an elephant seal, and make sure your children don't either.

• **No collecting.** Shells, rocks, wood, plants or animals; all features of this reserve are protected by law.

• **No smoking or fires.** Smoking is not permitted in buildings or on guided walks. Fires of all types are prohibited.

Facilities

A Visitor Center features natural history exhibits and a bookstore offering educational items such as books, postcards and posters. Restrooms, drinking water and picnic tables are available near the Visitor Center only. Food and beverages are not sold at the reserve.

Geology

The hardy rock here is known as the Monterey Formation. It started out as sedimentary clay and silt laid down beneath the sea some 12 or 13 million years ago. Since then, it has been gradually transformed by time, temperature, pressure and the addition of silica from the skeletal remains of one-celled sea creatures, until today it is a thinly layered, light-gray to whitish mudstone. It was raised off the sea bed by tectonic action as the Pacific plate collided with the continental plates. The Monterey Formation underlies much of the reserve.

The Monterey Formation material that forms the point today has been lifted above sea level and is being shoved northward at about two to three inches per year along the San Gregorio Fault Zone, which cuts northward through the back of the reserve and goes back out to sea at the mouth of San Gregorio Creek. Several small thrust faults associated with the major fault zone can be seen in the cliff face along the south shore of the Año Nuevo reserve.

The westerly portion of the marine terrace is covered by sand dunes that are migrating from north to south, driven by the prevailing northwesterly winds. This 300-to-350-acre dune field is one of the few remaining active dune fields on the California coast, most of the others having been disrupted or destroyed by human activity. While the Año Nuevo dunes are not threatened by development, they are changing character as a result of decreased sand availability and adjacent agricultural activity.

History

For centuries before Vizcaino named the point, the area was occupied by one branch or another of the Ohlone natives. Some 176 years after Vizcaino's voyage, a group of Spaniards led by Captain Gaspar de Portolá stopped at the point during their search for Monterey Bay (which they missed due to misinformation on a Vizcaino chart). Some 200 members of the Quroste clan of the Ohlones spent summers and falls at the point. The Qurostes had a huge structure large enough for all the clan to use for meetings, and individual pyramid-shaped huts of split wood for sleeping, Portolá's expedition discovered. This point was a major tool manufacturing center for the Qurostes, who collected chert from the beach for use in making spear points, knives, scrapers, arrow points and other utilitarian items. The products from this high quality beach rock was also used to trade with other clans and tribes; examples have been found at many archeological sites in the coast ranges and Central Valley. It appears that some of the trade was for obsidian spear points from the eastern Sierra, which were found at Año Nuevo. During the summer and fall months, the village on the point was a center the natives used to hunt, fish, and gather abalone and other shellfish from the sea.

Some 22 years after the Portolá expedition passed by here, Mission Santa Cruz was founded 25 miles to the south and this area became a grazing ground for cattle from the mission. Hundreds of Ohlones, including the Quroste, were baptized and brought into the mission ostensibly to help them become civilized. But many contracted various European diseases, lost contact with their native culture and died in great numbers.

After the missions were secularized, this territory became part of a private rancho; Governor Juan Bautista Alvarado officially granted the area in 1842 to his uncle, Don Jose Simeon de Nepomuceno Castro, a prominent resident of Monterey. In 1851, Castro's heirs sold the 17,753-acre rancho to Isaac Graham, a Tennessean who 14 years earlier had helped oust an unpopular governor imposed from Mexico City. Loren Coburn and his brother-in-law, Jeremiah Clarke, a San Francisco attorney, bought the rancho for $30,000. In 1861, the Steele brothers leased a portion of the rancho and developed a very successful dairy operation that continued for 80 years. The old barns and other historic buildings at Año Nuevo are relics of the Steele Brothers Dairy.

Lost on the Rocks

As ship traffic increased along the California coast during the 1800s, so did the shipwrecks. The often foggy, rock-strewn shoreline claimed 48 victims from four ships that were lost on the rocks between Año Nuevo and Pigeon Point during the 1850's and 1860's. Although the federal government had approved money for a lighthouse, it took 15 years to get one built. Part of the delay was due to Coburn and Clarke delaying the sale of land, asking $40,000 for the nine-acre island and another 19.5 acres of shoreline. A fog whistle was finally installed on the island in 1872 and the lighthouse was erected at Pigeon Point. A five-story light tower was finally added at Año Nuevo Island in 1890. An automatic buoy replaced the station in 1948.

After World War II, new irrigation technology brought intensive row-crop farming to the Año Nuevo area. Windbreaks of Monterey cypress were planted (some of which still survive), irrigation ponds were built, and straight rows of Brussels sprouts were planted in the area just east of the point. Only after the area was purchased by the State of California in 1971 was re-colonizing of native plants begun and the scars of farming and sand mining slowly erased.

Birds

Bird life at Año Nuevo is extraordinarily varied and fascinating in every season. In the spring, mallards, pintails, wigeons and both Green-winged and Cinnamon Teals can be seen on or near the fresh water pond within the reserve. Migrating waves of

The old barn is the Visitor Center at the point.

warblers, vireos, thrushes, orioles and other land birds also pass through the area in the spring. Red-winged Blackbirds nest near the pond along with the Marsh Wren. Several species of hummingbirds are most noticeable in springtime, when they carry out their spectacular courtship rituals.

Swifts and swallows can often be seen hunting insects above the upland brush fields. Quail, meadowlarks, sparrows, finches and other seed-eaters live right in the brush. Towhees, bushtits and wrentits can be found in both the chaparral and dune areas. Several kinds of hawks and falcons, including Northern Harriers, Black-shouldered Kites, Red-tailed Hawks and American Kestrels are often seen hovering above the fields.

Flocks of varied species migrate through the area each spring, most of them on their way to nesting areas in Canada and Alaska. Brown Pelicans move north from their winter range in Mexico each spring and can be seen along the California coast throughout the rest of the year.

Elephant Seals

The large colony of northern elephant seals that assembles here each winter is the hottest attraction for human visitors to Año Nuevo State Reserve. Named for their large size and pendulous noses on the males, these large animals spend most of their lives at sea, coming ashore only to molt, give birth, and mate.

The northern elephant seals once inhabited the Pacific Ocean by the hundreds of thousands until being slaughtered wholesale in the 1800s for the oil rendered from their blubber. By 1892, only 50 to 100 individuals were left in the only remaining colony on the Guadalupe Island off the coast of Baja California. In 1922, the Mexican government gave protected status to elephant seals, and the U. S. government followed suit a few years later. Since then, elephant seals continued to multiply exponentially, and extended their breeding range as far north as Point Reyes. Today, there are approximately 160,000 northern elephant seals.

The first elephant seals on Año Nuevo Island were sighted in 1955, and the first pup was born there in 1961. In 1978, there were 872 births. Males began to haul on the mainland in 1965. A pup born in January 1975 was the first known mainland birth of a northern elephant seal at Año Nuevo. During the 1994-95 breeding season, approximately 2,000 pups were born on the mainland.

The elephant seal breeding season begins at Año Nuevo in December, when the first males arrive and engage in violent battles to establish dominance. From 14-to-16-feet long and weighing up to 2.5 tons, these huge bulls fight to the bitter end for a firm rung on the breeding ladder. The successful bulls do much of the breeding.

In late December, the females begin to arrive and form "harems" on the beaches. Much smaller than the males, they av-

Watching warily for any intruders into his harem,
the bull elephant seal is always ready
to fight off challengers.

erage 10 to 12 feet in length and weigh 1,200 to 2,000 pounds. Three to six days after she arrives, the female gives birth to the pup that was conceived the previous year. Normally, only one pup is born to each female, and she nurses for 25 to 28 days.

Ordinarily, a mother nurses her own pup, although if they are separated another female may adopt the youngster. Feeding on its mother's rich milk (55% fat), the pup grows from approximately 75 pounds at birth to 250-350 pounds in less than a month. Some resourceful pups nurse from two or three females. They can weigh 600 pounds and are aptly called "super weaners".

Females come into season and mate about 24 days after giving birth. However, the fertilized egg does not implant in the wall of her uterus for about four months a rare phenomenon called "delayed implantation." The pups could not survive if born at sea. Adult females may mate several times before returning to the ocean, abruptly weaning their pups by desertion. By mid-March, most of the adult seals are gone, leaving the pups behind.

When the weaned pups are four to six weeks old, their original coat of black fur molts and is replaced by a shiny new silver coat. Soon afterward, they begin learning to swim in the shallow offshore waters or ponds formed by rainwater. Very curious and rather awkward and somewhat afraid of the water at first, they learn quickly, spend more and more time swimming about. During the last three weeks of April, they go to sea one by one and disperse northwestward. They feed off the coast of northern Washington and Vancouver Island in British Columbia and do not appear on land again until September.

Pinnipeds such as elephant seals, like other mammals, must replace old skin and hair. Most animals shed hairs the year-around, but pinnipeds do it all at once. The molting process is so abrupt in the elephant seal that it is called a catastrophic molt. During the spring and summer months, the elephants seals return to Año Nuevo for their annual molts pretty much on a regular, schedule: from April to May, females and juveniles; May to June, sub-adult males; and from July to August, adult males.

Females give birth for the first time at an average age of three to four years and have an average life expectancy of about 20 years. Males have a life expectancy of 14 years. Males are mature at five years and don't reach high rank until the age of eight with prime breeding years between 9 and 12.

Other Marine Life

A combination of the moderate climate and nature's enriching natural fertilizer from the elephant seals and other pinnipeds make intertidal life at Año Nuevo among the most luxuriant in the world. Air and sea temperatures vary far less from winter to summer than is true in other parts of the world. As a result, tide pools along the rocky shoreline teem with life. More than 300 species of invertebrates have been recorded at Año Nuevo, including an unusual number of rare species.

In addition to the northern elephant seal, harbor seals, a much smaller and quite wary and elusive mammal, frequent the point. Two kinds of sea lions are also present: Steller and California. The tawny brown or yellowish Steller sea lions, which mate on the rocks around the offshore island from mid-August, are most often seen on the rocky outer portions of the island. Dark brown California sea lions do not breed at Año Nuevo, but hundreds of them, mostly males, visit the island in September and October, when they use it as a resting place on their annual feeding migration northward from rookeries in Mexico. The loud and incessant bark of the males can be heard for miles. The forlorn, almost human wail of a female who has lost her pup stands out in sharp contrast from the cacophony of the males.

Harbor seals live on the offshore island all year and breed there in April and May. They can often be seen bobbing in the surf just off the reserve's beaches, with only their heads out of the water. They can also be seen occasionally on offshore rocks where the mottled pattern of their coats stands out.

Sea otters occasionally can be seen offshore diving for food or floating on their backs. Like the elephant seal, this animal is returning from near-extinction to reoccupy its former range. Sea otter mothers and pups returned to Año Nuevo in the early 1980s, the first sea otters to enter this immediate area in more than a century.

Throughout the spring months, the telltale 10-to-15-foot spouts of the gray whale are sometimes visible as they pass the during their annual migration between their breeding grounds off Baja California and their summer feeding grounds off Alaska.

Visitors must obtain a hiking permit to enter the Wildlife

*That's too close! Demanding a bit more
privacy, this Año Nuevo denizen roars a warning.*

*Pelicans and their gull companions also
feel secure on the wide, sparsely visited reserve beaches.*

Protection Area. Permits are issued on a first come, first served basis, 8:30 a.m. to 3:30 p.m. April through September, and 8:30 a.m. to 3 p.m., October and November.

Visitors must leave the area by 6 p.m. daily. The Wildlife Protection Area of the Reserve will be closed except for official guided walks from December 15 - March 31. These closures and the guided walk programs allow natural development of the elephant seal herd.

Camping Reservations

Camping Reservations can be made online or by phone. For more information on family, group, or environmental camping, see the California State Parks web site listed on Page 177.

Burleigh H. Murray Ranch

Jurisdiction: California State Parks – Tel. 650-726-8819
Web Site: http://parks.ca.gov/park

Go south from Half Moon Bay, just over a mile from the intersection of Highways One and 92. Turn east off Highway One on Higgins-Purisima Road. Proceed just over 1.5 miles to the park. A small graveled parking area is just outside the park gate.

This 1,121-acre park provides an opportunity to view Coastside ranching and dairy farming as it was practiced from the mid-1800's into the 20th century.

Originally a part of a Mexican land grant, the park is named for Burleigh H. Murray, who was born on the ranch July 19, 1865. His grandfather, Robert Mills came to California from Vermont in 1852 following the lure of the gold rush. After working in the mines at Auburn in Placer County, he worked in San Francisco as a glazier. His work included windows in the Ralston mansion in Belmont. He took his earnings and acquired 1,000 acres that had been the upper part of the 4,424-acre Rancho Arroyo de los Pilarcitos granted in 1841 to Candelario Miramontes, a San Francisco Presidio soldier. Mills settled at the present Murray ranch with some sheep and cattle and began a successful dairy farm in 1862.

When Mills died in 1897, the ranch went to his wife, Miranda Murray, who left it to her son, Burleigh C, Murray. It then passed to his son Burleigh H. Murray, who died in 1937. Another generation of the family ran the dairy for several years. It was donated to the state for a park in 1979.

The Mills Barn and surrounding out buildings are maintained in what the park service calls "a condition of arrested decay." Mills Barn hugs the hill beside Mills Creek. This historic structure dates back to the late 1800's and is a good representation of an English Lake Country Bank Barn. "Arrested decay" means the state has not allocated any money to restore the structure; its walls are all supported by a series of exterior props.

Rules: No dogs. Open from 8 a.m. to sunset.

Acquired by the State of California in 1983, this historic ranch sits in a pristine valley that harbors groves of mature eucalyptus, and a rich assortment of wildlife. With the addition of Rancho Raymundo at the eastern boundary, the park property extends from Higgins Purissima Road in the west to Skyline Boulevard in the east.

Facilities and Activities

The trails are open to hikers, cyclists and equestrians. Portable restrooms are located about one-third of the way up the trail and a second one about two-thirds of the way. Picnic tables are located in two strategic spots, one in the shade of a eucalyptus tree about three-quarters of a mile from the entrance and the other opposite the barn.

Hiking Trail

The current trail consists of the old ranch road winding its way alongside Mill Creek for about 1.5 miles rising slowly some 600 feet in elevation. The trail is high above Mill Creek and its rich riparian mix of trees and shrubs. Spaced a few yards apart are several groves of eucalyptus. A few of the larger ones appear to have been the original plantings back in the late 1800's when the State of California promoted a program aimed at their proliferation in an attempt to bring hardwoods to the area. Most of the trees are younger. The road continues up to a 1930's bungalow that serves as a park residence.

At this point the trail veers off the road and turns to cross the creek allowing the visitor to look back in time while viewing the Mills Barn and the few surrounding out buildings.

Originally 200 feet in length and capable of housing 100 dairy cows the Milk Barn is unique; the only building of its type remaining in California. The foundation of the barn and other buildings including an un-reinforced arched stone bridge, rely on Italian masonry techniques dating back to Roman times.

Continuing on the road beyond the barn, the valley and the path narrows between steep, chaparral-covered hills. The walking is good for an additional mile above the barn past the wooden tanks supplying water for the park residence, then the trail fades away into the dense growth of stinging nettles, *Urtica holsericea;* poison oak, *Toxicodendron diversilobum;* and coyote brush, *Baccharis pilularis ssp. consanguinea.*

Fitzgerald Marine Reserve

Jurisdiction: San Mateo County – Tel. (650) 728-3584

Getting There:
Take Highway One to Moss Beach. Turn west on California Street, go to the end of the street and turn right to the parking lot.

This a nature wonderland for all ages, but particularly fascinating to the young because it offers a chance to get an intimate look at a variety of seaweed, crabs, sponges, sea anemones, mollusks, starfish and fish that make their homes in the intertidal zone, that area between low and high tide. The marine reserve extends along the coast for three miles from north of California Avenue south to Pillar Point, and out into the ocean for 1,000 feet. The reserve is one continuous stretch of rocks made up of what geologists call the Monterey Formation, a form of stone that was raised off the sea floor some 12 to 13 million years ago by tectonic action of expanding Pacific plates banging against the continental shelf. Weathering of the stone creates pools and other hiding places for the smaller marine creatures

Rules: No tidepool animals, shells or rocks may be taken, but fishing is permitted with a fishing license for various fish and eels. No dogs allowed.

The reserve was established in 1969 at the urging of then San Mateo County Supervisor James V. Fitzgerald, who scuba dived off the rocks with his brother as a teenager. It is open from sunrise to sunset and docent trips are offered under the auspices of San Mateo County's Coyote Point Museum.

If one visits the reserve when no docent is available, it would be advisable to go equipped with a pocket guide to explain the wildlife being seen. The National Audubon Society has a guide entitled *Familiar Seashore Creatures* available at local book stores; its full color photographs are invaluable in identifying the marine creatures. Another handy reference is *Guidebook to Pacific Intertidal Life* by Ron Russo and Pam Olhausen.

The reserve is a popular destination for classroom field trips. On one trip, the sixth grade students from Oakland's Bret Harte Middle School found, photographed and wrote reports on hermit crabs, kelp crab, mossy chiton, rocky prickleback, bat starfish, ochre stars, California mussels, brown turban snails, tidepool sculpin, purple sea urchins and a giant green anemone

When the tide is low, the sandy beach is accessible for strolls along the water, but be warned that high tides almost obliterate the beach. To avoid becoming stranded, check the tide tables posted at the visitor center or those published daily in local newspapers.

Lintt Trout Farm

11751 San Mateo Road   Telephone 650-720-0845

Getting There: Take Highway 92 east from Highway One past the flower farms. Just about 100 yards beyond the last sharp curve, the entrance is on the right.

Here's an easy way to take the kids fishing. One of the last in a grand tradition of natural fun things for the kids, here a youngster can dangle a line and bait and be certain pull out a fat trout.

Pescadero Marsh

Jurisdiction: California State Parks
Web Site: http://parks.ca.gov/park

Getting There: Go south on Highway One 18 miles to the entrance just 0.1 mile north of Pescadero Creek Road. Turn right into parking lot.

This 500-acre marsh preserve, the only sizable marsh

between Bolinas Lagoon in Marin County and Elkhom Slough in Monterey County, is an estuarine haven for year-round resident birds and those who stop over on annual migrations north and south. The rich waters of the estuary provide food for egrets, herons and kingfishers most of the year, winter feeding and breeding grounds for buffleheads and ruddy ducks and grebes. This estuary fed by both the Butano Creek and Pescadero Creek can be observed alone or join nature walks guided by rangers.

In prehistoric times, the estuary and delta of the two creeks extended well inland past present day Pescadero. During the winter rainy season, the flowing creeks and their tributaries ran freely into the ocean. In the dry summer and fall seasons, the Pacific surf created a sand bar that blocked the diminished water flow, damming it into an ever-changing, ever-twisting course where marine life was nurtured, algae, worm and fish that fed thousands of birds. And each wet winter, the rush of the water broke through the sand bar and released the young fish to the ocean in cycles that recurred down the ages.

In the early years of this century, the cycle was broken for good. European farmers who had settled in Pescadero drained much of the original marsh and used the area for agriculture. The remaining marshy area was used as a hunting club. Migrating birds were the targets, as well as ducks and Asian pheasants raised specifically for hunting. In the 1960s members of the Sequoia Audubon Society raised money to buy part of the land from the Nunziatti family who owned the marsh. During the early 1970s the state parks acquired this nucleus and continued acquisition until today the state owns 90 per cent of the original marshland. Conservation easements on farming lands to the east were negotiated. A marsh restoration effort is ongoing, managed by the state, and the Sequoia Aubudon Society has been commemorated with a trail named for it, which the society still maintains.

Rules: Open 8 a.m. to sunset. Trails are for hikers only. Hunting and dogs not allowed in preserve; dogs on beach, leashed only. Boats not allowed in sloughs during nesting season, March through August.

Sequoia Audubon Trail

Set aside an hour and a half for this two-and-a-half mile round trip on a trail dedicated to the Audubon Society.

Start from the parking lot south of the creek on the west side of the highway, where there are a restrooms and the meeting place for the nature walks. Cross the highway bridge on a safe sidewalk on the west side, then go left down to the beach and under the bridge to reach the trail.

Turn right at the junction where a signboard has information about spawning steelhead and advisories to boaters. The path goes straight ahead on the Sequoia Audubon Trail. On the right, a track leads to a beach on Pescadero Creek itself. This estuary with calm waters and small beach would be a pleasant place to swim on a hot day, avoiding the dangerous cold undertow of the ocean beach itself. The main Sequoia Audubon Trail soon reaches another junction, where on the left there is a bridge over a slough and a viewing platform. The water level in this area of the marsh is being managed by manipulating dikes and tidal gates; state scientists want to keep water in the slough, marsh and pond for longer periods of time. Here one can often see snowy egrets and blue herons feeding.

The trail follows along a levee next to the slough, several hundred feet north of the main Pescadero Creek. Past a huge, sprawling eucalyptus there is bench near the creek where one can view the marsh extending to the south. After about a mile, the hiker go back to the viewing platform and bridge that was passed earlier. Then take the right hand trail going northwest where one will see bushes of twinberry, *Lonicera involucrate,* that has reddish-yellow flowers in spring and black, edible berries in fall. Shortly, the path leads to another viewing bench, where one turns left (south) to return to the signboard, goes under the bridge and on back to the parking area.

North Pond Trail

This is a shorter trip; one mile long and requiring little more than three-quarters of an hour to explore the quieter east side of the marsh. Take along a bird book and binoculars and perhaps a camera to get the most out of this little trek.

Reaching the North Pond Trail is a bit hazardous, because one must cross Highway One, which carries fast and dangerous traffic, especially on weekends. The trail goes around the north and east sides of North Pond, reaching a small slough on the south side. Rising higher on the North Pond Trail, there is a splendid view of the entire marsh, the two tributary creeks, the pond with its resident and migrating birds and the ocean to the west. As you reach the viewing area, try to imagine what the people of the Portolá Expedition must have felt in October of 1769 when they came this way going north. Here one can get an impression of what the Coastside looked like before the Europeans arrived (by blotting out the hum of cars on the highway, of course). The Spaniards and their native retinue had to detour to the east around wetlands such as this, because they could not wade across such an expanse of marsh. And returning south a month, the rains had the streams running over their banks. The only use they found for such hazardous places was to try and catch a few birds to eat. But they had no reed boats to maneuver through the estuary the way the native Ohlones did. The Pescadero Marsh is a special place, thanks to the foresighted members of the Audubon Society for their restoration work.

On this trip, the hiker must return the way one came.

Pigeon Point Light Station
State Historic Park

Jurisdiction: California State Parks Tel: 650-879-2120

Getting There: Take Highway One for 20 miles south of Half Moon Bay.

The 110-foot Pigeon Point Lighthouse, one of the tallest lighthouses in America, has been a safeguard for mariners since 1872. It took 20 years after a brand new schooner, the 172-foot Carrier Pigeon (the point's namesake), went aground on offshore rocks beyond the point to get work started. This was due partially to a greedy landowner and partially bureaucratic sloth. Its five-wick lard oil lamp, and first-order Fresnel lens, comprised of 1,008 prisms, was first lit at sunset, November 15, 1872. The lens stands 16 feet tall, 6 feet in diameter, and weighs 8,000 pounds. It sits in a lantern room constructed at the Lighthouse

Service's general depot in New York before being shipped around Cape Horn. A 24-inch Aero Beacon long ago replaced the original Fresnel lens; the lighthouse is still an active U.S. Coast Guard aid to navigation.

     Getting a lighthouse built at Pigeon Point was a slow and agonizing process that dragged on for two decades despite shipwrecks resulting in considerable loss of life on the rocks to the south of the point. Agitation for a lighthouse centered first on Año Nuevo Island to the south due to an analysis by the Army Corps of Engineers. Loss of the Carrier Pigeon schooner on the rocks had not involved any loss of life. But on January 17, 1865, the Sir John Franklin went on the rocks at the point now named after the doomed ship; 12 of the 20-man crew drowned. On Sept. 22 in the next year, the British bark, Coya, enroute from Australia to San Francisco went on the rocks just south of Pigeon Point, drowning all 26 of the crew and passengers. Another ship, the Hellespont, also bound for San Francisco from Australia, went aground and broke up, drowning 11 of the 17-man crew. Part of the delay was due to prolonged negotiations with Loren Coburn for land to build a light at Año Nuevo Island. There was also an argument over whether to build there or at Pigeon Point. Pigeon Point advocates won and the light went on some 20 years after sinking of the Carrier Piegon. While a fog signal was erected that same year at Año Nuevo, it was another 10 years before a full-fledged lighthouse was built there.

     Originally, the point was a favorite fishing spot for the Ohlone natives, who summered on the coast for centuries. With the arrival of Europeans in the late 1770's, the area was turned into grazing land for Mission Santa Cruz and then became a part of the 1839 Mexican land grant, Rancho Butano.

     A Portuguese company operated a whaling station at Pigeon Point from 1862 through 1895, using small sailing vessels that pursued passing gray and humpback whales and attacked them with exploding harpoons, then dragged them to shore for butchering. There were four Portuguese families and a company of 17 men at the station at one time. The largest whale taken here was in June of 1877. It was 200 feet long and was so large whalers anchored it offshore until additional boats could be found to tow the behemoth ashore. Pigeon Point Anchorage and Wharf,

*Pigeon Point, where whalers, shippers
and Ohlones met the sea's whimsical moods for centuries.*

which shipped lumber from here, was in operation in 1869-70. Although the company name included "wharf," the actual means of loading was to rig a pulley operation from an onshore tower to the mast of the ship offshore. Load after load was run out to the ship in this manner. All traces of the whaling operation, which was just south of the point, and the shipping paraphernalia are all gone now.

The lighthouse is open for visitors. For those energetic enough and able to climb 144 steps to the top of the tower – equal to climbing 10 flights of stairs – there are guides who pause at intervals during the climb. Nonetheless, the climb is not recommended for people with cardio-vascular problems, vertigo, claustrophobia, or infirmities of the lower limbs. The areas surrounding Pigeon Point Light Station are rich with life. Marine mammals such as seals and whales can be seen regularly from shore as they pass by beyond the surf. The intertidal zone along this part of the coast, particularly in the rocky reefs that flank the light station, contains a diverse and a numerous variety of plant and animal life. From the boardwalk behind the fog signal building, one can watch for gray whales on their annual migration between January and April. One can also walk through the tide pool area, 100 yards north of Pigeon Point.

Hostel

      There are also hostel facilities that are especially popular with bicyclists touring the coast on Highway One. The lighthouse keeper's housing is restored and operated as a hostel by Hostels International American Youth Hostels. There are 52 beds, four private rooms, kitchen and a meeting room. Reservations are available by calling 650-879-0633.

      Prices range from $13 to $15 a night. Access hours are 7:30-10 a.m. and 4:30-11p.m.

Point Montara
Fog Signal and Light Station
Jurisdiction: California State Parks Tel: 650-728-7177

Getting There: Take Highway One and as one passes through Moss Beach, look for the hostel signs on the left. Address P.O. Box 737 Montara, CA 94037

      The Point Montara Fog Signal and Light Station, established in 1875, is a handy place from which to explore the nearby Fitzgerald Marine Reserve and other beaches close by, and watch passing whales during the November to April migratory season.

      The Fitzgerald Marine Reserve is one of the richest intertidal areas on the California coast. Extensive shale reefs are home for a wide variety of marine life, such as giant green anemones, limpets, purple sea urchins, crabs and snails.

      The turn-of-the-century structures at the lighthouse have been preserved and restored by Hostelling International - American Youth Hostels and California State Parks, in cooperation with the U.S. Coast Guard.

Hostel

      There are 45 beds and four private room available at rates of $14 to $16 per night per person. Reservations can be made by calling 650-728-7177. Access hours are from 7:30-

Point Montara Light Station draws young and old.

10 a.m. and 4:30-11 p.m.

For more information about the Hostel at Point Montara,
go to http://www.hiayh.org/ushostel/california/montara.htm

The Sanchez Adobe

**Jurisdiction: San Mateo Historical Association – Tel.
(650) 359-1426**

Getting There:
**Take Highway One to southern Pacifica and turn east
onto Linda Mar Boulevard. Proceed about 1 mile to
the Adobe on the right at 1000 Linda Mar Blvd., just
past the Adobe Street traffic signal.**

This is a living history site that dates back to the
establishment of the California Missions by the Franciscan order,
specifically Mission Dolores in San Francisco. In order to provide
food crops for the mission, an *asistencia,* or support farm was

established on the west bank of San Pedro Creek in 1786. A large adobe structure was built to house the farm's overseers quarters, a granary and tool room. Farming was done on the wide bench along the creek. Cattle and sheep grazed on the surrounding hillsides.

After the missions were secularized and their land taken over by the Mexican government in 1834, the support farm building crumbled from disuse and lack of care. In 1839, the son of the owner of Rancho Buri Buri, Don Francisco Sanchez, who was himself a former alcalde (a combination mayor and judicial officer) of San Francisco Presidio, was granted 8,926 acres that included the San Pedro Valley, which abutted his father's rancho. Using the foundation and some of the material from the old farm structure, Sanchez spent four years from 1842 building a handsome two-story adobe home that was 22 feet wide and 64 feet long and contained six large rooms. After Sanchez' death in 1862, his widow sold off most of the ranch property, but kept the house until the 1890's when it was sold to a former Confederate general named Edward Kirkpatrick. Kirkpatrick expanded the house by attaching a wooden addition, making it a 20-room mansion and surrounded it with formal gardens. When Kirkpatrick sold the property in 1908, it became Hotel San Pedro, a popular stop on the short-lived Ocean Shore Railroad line. In subsequent years, the Adobe was used as a roadhouse during Prohibition and packing and storage shed. It was a restaurant until the end of the 1930's

Eventually it fell into disrepair until being purchased by the County of San Mateo. Funds were allocated for restoration, which was completed in 1953. After passage of Proposition 13 limited the amount of tax funds to the county, the San Mateo County Historical Association agreed to take over the historical landmark's operation.

The adobe now houses a remarkable collection of artifacts from the early period including saddles and farm tools as well as household furnishings and clothing. All six rooms of the original adobe are furnished and opened for viewing.

Special programs are often held at the Sanchez Adobe to educate visitors and students about its colorful past. Demonstrations such as brick making and corn grinding are

This is the Sanchez Adobe as it is today,
a well-kept museum reflecting its colorful past.

scheduled. It is a popular school field trip destination. There are picnic, water and restroom facilities available on the seven-acre site. Admission is free. The Sanchez Adobe is open to the public Tuesday, Wednesday and Thursday from 10 a.m. to 4 p.m., and on Saturdays and Sundays from 1:00 p.m. to 5:00 p.m. The Store is closed on all holidays. No pets are allowed on the premises.

School programs and group tours are available through reservations.

Beach rides, ponies and horses are for rent by the hour.

Ponies rides for the little tots are taken in an enclosed and supervised oval track. Horses may be rented individually for riding on the trail above Half Moon Bay beaches, or by joining a guided tour of the beaches on horseback.

Waddell Beach – Windsurfers Playground

Jurisdiction: California State Parks

Getting There: Take Highway One 29.5 miles south of Half Moon Bay.

This is where the hot dog windsurfers come to take advantage of nearly constant northwest winds and rolling surf. It is known worldwide as one of THE SPOTS for windsurfing. The steady strong northwest winds and good surf provide ideal conditions for this demanding sport. Launching from the tops of incoming waves the best windsurfers can complete full loops and continue on their way. Para-surfing, sometimes called kite-surfing, a variation that uses a small parachute extended on a long line to power the surf board, has also come into popular use here. With the strong winds and occasionally heavy surf, Waddell Beach is not recommended for novice wind surfers.

Regular surfers, boogie boarders, and surf fishermen also find it an ideal spot to pursue their activities. And the beach is a great place for camera buffs who want some good action shots, or for people who like to just sit and marvel at the athleticism of others.

When you get bored with all the action at the beach, there is a ideal place for bird watching on the inland side of Highway One in the Theodore J. Hoover Natural Preserve. Hoover, brother of former president Hoover, was a recent owner of the property logged for years by William Waddell. Waddell farmed and logged along the creek that bears his name.

To get his produce and lumber to market, Waddell built a railroad along the bottom of the cliffs overlooking the beach. It ran to a site south of the point. He then constructed a pier in the lee of the point from which lumber was loaded aboard ships. All traces of the pier and railroad have disappeared.

*Montara Beach, just one of the many vast Coastside
sweeps of sand and sea that beckon to visitors.*

PART X

BEACHES & PICNIC SPOTS

The San Mateo County Coastside beaches come in all shapes and sizes. Some experience a variety of weather conditions ranging from extended visits from the sun (including one clothing optional site) to downright chilly winds. Extensive piles of driftwood and other marine detritus decorate some. Others are pristine stretches of sand that extend for miles.

In addition to outfitting yourself with good walking shoes and other comfortable clothing, one can add to enjoyment of the seashore with a handy guide to help you understand what you are seeing. The best is one of the National Audubon Society Nature Guides, *Pacific Coast* by the McConnaugheys, Evelyn and Bayard. They have done one of the most complete guides with full color plates of birds, mammals, fish, seaweeds, sea shells and all the assorted life you are likely to encounter. The guide also contains lots of background material with maps of the creatures' ranges and habitats, too.

The Ocean: Always use caution when you are in or near the ocean. The ocean water is very cold year round. Swimming can be dangerous. Even a short swim can cause cramps or hypothermia (a life threatening condition which occurs when your body temperature drops below normal). In addition, strong rip currents can pull even the most experienced swimmers off shore.

State Beaches of Half Moon Bay

Of all the myriad attractions of the Coastside, the beaches of Half Moon Bay are among the most exciting. Set off by a broad greensward along much of the area, they sweep from Pillar Point Harbor in the north all the way south to Miramontes Point. Best of all, there are 10 access points along this eight-mile stretch of sand, most for day use only and one with camping facilities. You choose between walking, biking or riding a horse within sight and sound of the sea. Surf fishermen and surfers also make good use of the beaches

A large share of the silicon strand is linked by a three-mile, paved trail along the cliff-top overlooking the California

State beaches section. The trail crosses two major Coastside streams and several smaller creeks. At all state beaches there is a $1 fee for day-use at convenient parking areas if the entrance gate is occupied by a ranger. If not, parking is free. A seasonal parking permit is available for $35 and for camping facilities. The city beaches are all free.

A FEW WORDS OF CAUTION: use common sense walking on the beach. Parts of the strand are so narrow that at high tide, a heavy wave can pull one out to sea. Also be aware that between May 1 and Oct. 31, there is a quarantine on mussels, because of toxins in their systems during this period. Eating mussels taken during this period can cause death.

We will begin our review at the the southerly edge of Pillar Point Harbor, using the names of their access roads to identify them first. All streets head toward the ocean from Highway One.

Coronado Street/ Surfers Corner

Opposite Coronado is a small parking area off Highway One hardly big enough for the number of vehicles that crowd in when the surf's up. This is where the beginning surfers come in droves. Unless you are a hard core surfer. Skip this one. Someday, state and local authorities will awaken to the need and expand the parking area and unclog the traffic jam created here weekends and holidays.

Miramar Drive/Miramar Beach

This is another beach with limited parking. It is also one of the narrower portions of the beach where caution must be used at high tide. In stormy weather, the wave action is so spectacular it draws people to the Miramar Inn to catch the action as saltwater sprays the restaurant's picture windows.

Naples Beach

The beach broadens a bit here, but parking is limited.

Young Avenue/Dunes Beach

This is the start of the California Beaches at Half Moon Bay and is open from 8 a.m. to dusk daily. Facilities include restrooms and a badly potholed parking lot. The Park Service must feel guilty about charging to park here, because the entry booth is the one most apt to be empty, which results in no charge. Daytime use only from 8 a.m. to dusk daily.

Venice Boulevard/Venice Beach

Four-tenths of a mile on this washboard dirt road takes you to large parking lot with clean restrooms and an outdoor shower. The paved trail reaches in both directions from here to Dunes Beach in the north and Francis Beach in the south. The gate is almost always open to take your fees here. Day use only from 8 a.m. to dusk daily.

Kelly Avenue/Francis Beach

Six-tenths of a mile from Highway One through four boulevard stops, you reach this park that has overnight camping and day use facilities. There are 58 camping spots available on a first come, first served basis at a charge of $12 a night each. Day use is $1 a day for each car. Restrooms and showers available.

Wildlife — Snowy Plovers — At Francis State Beach, plovers are protected in these fenced areas along the bluffs just north of the campground. The fences were erected in 1995 to keep the plover nesting areas free from human and animal activity to allow for successful breeding.

Once numbering in the thousands, it is estimated that only 1,200-1,600 western snowy plovers survive along the coast. The western snowy plover is listed under the Federal Endangered Species Act as a threatened species because of loss of nesting habitat due to human development, invasion of European beach grass and predation by ravens, foxes, domestic dogs and cats.

The western snowy plover is six inches long, and has light black, brown and white feathers with dark patches on either side of the neck, behind the eyes, and on the forehead. They can be hard to spot. Watch for them as they scurry down to the water's edge for food. When resting, they choose depressions in the sand, such as footprints, where they are camouflaged and out of the wind.

Plovers feed and nest on the beach just above high tide lines, where human activity is the greatest. The coastal population breeds along the Pacific coast from southern Washington to southern Baja California, Mexico, with the majority of birds breeding along the California coast. Nesting season runs from mid-March through mid-September. Plovers usually lay three eggs. Both eggs and nests are well camouflaged and extremely hard to see even at close range. Mothers incubate the nests during the day and fathers at night. Chicks leave the nest within hours of hatching but cannot fly for a month.

The Half Moon Bay Ranger Station sponsors a Plover Watch Volunteer program. Volunteers are identified by maroon jackets and baseball caps. They are on the beach during nesting season to spot nests and help build enclosures. Volunteers use radios to alert the rangers to any serious situations. Volunteers are also available to educate the public about the snowy plover.

For information on how to become a volunteer or other questions, contact Half Moon Bay State Beach rangers.

Because of the presence of the Visitor Center and camping facilities, Francis Beach is often the jumping-off point for hikes along the beach. The trail to the beach begins around the park maintenance area between the sand dunes. Another leads off to the right to a creek-crossing for horses. Walkers will continue on the main trail. At the metal bridge spanning Pilarcitos Creek, there is a bronze plaque honoring John Hernandez, a local resident, who helped ramrod this Coastside Trail into being. Continuing north you will pass fields of yellow lupine in season as wells as low-growing coyote bush, bright orange poppies, and yellow mustard and oxalis. Soon you reach Venice Beach where there are ample parking and restrooms.

Dunes are lower, and views from the trail expand where creeks flow into the Pacific. Many paths lead out to the bluffs or down to the beach.

The trail passes through the meadows at Sea Horse Ranch, then crosses a metal bridge over Frenchman's Creek to reach Sweetwood Park, a grassy meadow protected by a semicircle of wind-sculpted Monterey cypresses and Monterey pines. Picnic tables, barbecues and restrooms are set among the trees. The narrow path along the high north bank of Frenchmans Creek leads to a few benches and a bluff-top trail where the view often mixes sailboats and fishing boats and further offshore tankers and other ocean transports.

You can choose between one of the narrow trails along the cliffs or the wide Coastside Trail all the way to the east end of the meadow to Dunes Beach, where there are restroom facilities. Continuing on this trail one reaches Roosevelt Beach, (accessible from Highway One via Mirada Road) where you find high dunes, partially planted with dune grass, and a well-defined trail to the beach. The Coastside Trail officially ends emerge at the outflow of Arroyo en Medio, a good three-mile jaunt that can take from an hour to two hours depending on how much one stops to enjoy the sights.

Poplar Avenue/Poplar Beach

A large free parking area maintained by the City of Half Moon Bay is reached at the end of this paved city street, which intersects with Highway One. On the way to and from the park, you will stop at Railroad Avenue, where the short-lived Coastal Railway system ran from 1907 to 1920. The only remnant of the enterprise is a building just to the south of Poplar on Railroad Avenue. It has unusually wide eaves and roof overhang and is painted yellow. That was the railway station, converted to a private home years ago. The large parking lot at the end of Poplar has an area set aside for horse trailers and this cliff top park is a popular area for equestrians. Trails run north and south. Open from 8 a.m. to dusk daily.

Redondo Beach Road/Redondo Beach

Go down this narrow, paved city street for nearly a mile to a dirt parking area used mainly by surf fishermen who trek down the cliff to do their casting. It is also the southern end of the Poplar Beach trail. Open 8 a.m. to dusk daily and maintained by the City of Half Moon Bay.

Miramontes Point Road/Miramontes Beach

The opening of the posh Ritz Carlton just around the corner turned this formerly scrabble-sided, slip-slide route to the beach into a high class access complete with paved and curbed parking, sophisticated signage and golf course views as you descend on the trail to the beach. Now reached from the signalized intersection with Highway One along a wide paved street bordered by flowers.

The deluxe 261-room Ritz Carlton sits on the bluff above Miramontes Beach; public access to an adjoining beach can be reached through grounds north of the hotel.

Cowell Beach

Just a half mile south of the Half Moon Bay city limits on the west side of Highway One is the entrance to this unique access made possible by the Peninsula Open Space Trust's land purchase. A small, unpaved parking area with a restroom is the entrance of a half mile path to the beach. There is a promontory with interpretive signage and another restroom. One can view seals lolling on the beach to the south of the promontory, an area off-limits to human visitors. To the north, a stairway leads down to the beach. Tucked up against the tall cliffs, it is one of the more protected of the coast's beaches. The land was part of a ranch that once belonged to an early Coastside restaurateur, Kurt Doebbel, who built a grand 17-room mansion three miles south in the village of Purissima, now only an empty grove of giant cypress. Henry Cowell, a banker and lumberman, foreclosed on a mortgage he held on the ranch in 1890 and thus his name lives on.

NORTHERN BEACHES
PACIFICA

Sharp Park Beach

This is the northernmost of the public beaches. Farther south are the Pacifica State Beaches, all managed by the City of Pacifica. The Coastal Trail follows the shore with only a few detours back to sidewalks along Highway One.

The trail runs for a mile along Pacifica's Sharp Park district. From north of Paloma Avenue to Clarendon Road, a wide, paved half-mile trail parallels a sturdy sea wall buttressed with huge boulders. After passing the Pacifica pier, a generous landscaped border of lawn separates Beach Boulevard and parking bays from the trail. Picnic tables and barbecues are spotted about, benches, and tall, square columns topped with attractive light fixtures invite visitors and residents to enjoy this beach and open space.

Beyond Clarendon Road, the trail rises to the top of huge, imbedded boulders topped with loose earth to protect the Sharp Park Golf Course from winter storm erosion. This public course built around Laguna Salada and several other lagoons extends back to Highway 1 then east toward the Golden Gate National Recreation Area lands on Sweeney Ridge. The elevated trail continues past the golf course to the north side of Mori Point, where it follows Mori Point Road out to Highway One, then continues on a paved sidewalk on the west and then to the east side of the highway.

Rockaway Beach

Around the point south of a deserted limestone quarry is the Rockaway Beach section of Pacifica, where public beaches are accessible north and south from Rockaway Beach Avenue. The area is reached from a signalized intersection with Highway One. At the mouth of small streams at each end of this beach are little coves nestled between two rocky points. North of the boulevard is a good parking lot. A short section of paved ocean front trail is fenced with nautical rope. At the south end are changing rooms, a few benches, a tended lawn and parking. A fence surrounds the ridge south of Rockaway and there are no sidewalks along the highway that carries heavy traffic daily.

The Golden Gate National Recreation Area in cooperation with the National Oceanic and Atmospheric Administration, the Pacifica Chamber of Commerce, and the City of Pacifica opened a joint Visitor Information Center in Pacifica. It is located at 225 Rockaway Beach Ave., Suite 1. Maritime displays, maps, trail guides and nature books and tourist information are offered at the center, which is open daily.

San Pedro Beach

Just south of this rocky point is a wide, 1.5-mile-long sandy beach that draws surfers by the dozens. The beach can be reached while southbound on Highway One just south of the Crespi Drive traffic signal; northbound, take a left just past the Linda Mar Boulevard signal. There are generous parking areas and restrooms. While this is a favorite surfing beach, there are also picnic tables and room for children to search for shells and make sand castles. The upthrust at Pedro Point and Devil's Slide prevent any access south from the Pacifica State Beaches to Gray Whale Cove.

NORTHERN BEACHES
MONTARA - PILLAR POINT

Gray Whale Cove State Beach

This beach just south of Devil's Slide on Highway One is run by a private concessionaire who charges an admission fee. The chief attraction is that this is a clothing optional beach, the only one within 50 miles. A small dirt parking area is located on the east side of the highway. Use extreme caution when turning into the parking area when southbound on Highway One. Crossing the highway to the beach entrance is also dangerous and should be done with caution due to heavy highway traffic and limited lines of sight around the curves. The beach is reached by a steep trail from the entrance.

*San Pedro Beach is popular with surfers
and waders alike.*

Montara State Beach

This mile-long, broad beach of golden sand and rolling surf is just north of Montara on Highway One at the outfall of Martini Creek. This is where the Portolá Expedition camped for three days in October of 1769 waiting for the rains to subside so they could climb San Pedro Mountain, a week before they discovered San Francisco Bay. There is a small, unpaved parking area on the west side of the highway. Steps lead down the side of a ravine to the beach where Martini Creek drops into the sea. The land drops steeply into the ocean here and currents continually strew bits of sea plants and creatures onto the shore, tossed there by a combination of deep upwelling and surface wave action. Parking is also available at the south end of the beach, where there is a public restroom. Until 5 p.m. daily, you can park beside the restaurant there.

Pillar Point Harbor

There is a small stretch of beach inside the harbor breakwater that is popular for its cozy ambience. It is reached most easily from Highway One at the Princeton signal. A turn into the harbor itself will bring one to a large parking area. Since this is also access to a boat ramp used by sports fishermen, one must use caution when walking through this area to the beach to the south of the ramp. Pillar Point was designated as a "safe haven" harbor for boats in trouble offshore, but the southern exposure required protection to be built by the Army Corps of Engineers and managed by San Mateo County Harbor District. When the harbor was completed in 1961, it quickly was discovered that the great outer circle of the breakwater was insufficient to deflect the strong winter storms. After the addition of an interior breakwater in 1982, the anchorage was safe and is now filled with local fishing vessels and pleasure craft, adding to the fun of beach picnics here.

On Gray Whale Cove Beach clothing is optional.

SOUTHERN BEACHES
SAN GREGORIO-AÑO NUEVO

Año Nuevo State Reserve and Coastal Access

Best known for its northern elephant seal rookery, this state park has miles of beaches that are more remote and isolated than the rest on the San Mateo County Coast. The reserve also contains extremely varied natural features as well as a fascinating human history. The point was named by Spanish explorer Sebastian Vizcaino on Jan. 3, 1603 while sailing the coast looking for safe harbors. When the Portolá Expedition passed through in October of 1769, they found the largest Ohlone Village seen on this coast. Though only a summer encampment, it had a large wooden meeting hall able to accommodate the 200 natives summering there and was surrounded by small one and two person wooden sleeping shelters.

The land was later used for grazing cattle from Mission Santa Cruz until the missions were disbanded. In 1841, the land became part of Rancho de Punto de Año Nuevo granted in 1841 to Simeon Castro. William Waddell, who owned land to the south along the creek that now has his name, had a wharf at Point Año Nuevo in 1860. Waddell had a saw mill on the creek in 1862 and logged redwoods in the area and shipped the lumber to San Francisco. After the property was broken into smaller pieces that included the Cascade Ranch and the Steele Brother s Dairy, the State of California purchased Año Nuevo Island and a strip of adjacent mainland in 1958 to create the reserve. It has now been expanded to include over 4,000 acres of coastal mountains, bluffs, dunes and beaches. The section of the reserve where the elephant seals breed is restricted to public access by guided tours (from December 1 to March 31) or by permit (from April 1 to November 30). Park rangers and docents are in the reserve to assist visitors in the restricted area. No access is allowed to Año Nuevo Island where a lighthouse once stood.

Lands on the northeast side of Highway 1 that are part of Año Nuevo State Reserve only are now being developed for public use. Some of the old farm roads are used for ranger patrol, but these roads are gated to prevent public vehicle access. But there are five access points to Año Nuevo Beaches in addition to the main entrance near the San Mateo/Santa Cruz County line.

1. Gazos Creek

The northernmost coastal access in Año Nuevo Reserve is at Gazos Creek just 1.5 miles south of Pigeon Point on Highway One The parking area at Gazos Creek has restrooms and steps down to the beach. The signs state the rules very directly: NO VEHICLES, DOGS, FIRES OR CAMPING.

In the spring and early summer, one can enjoy a walk south along the beach, looking for seaside daisies, *Erigeron glaucous,* beach primrose, *Oenothera cheiranthofolia,* and other pink and yellow blossoms. While parking and beach access trails here are used mainly by fishermen, other visitors too will find this an adventurous way to experience the quieter, more remote parts of the coast. But one should not attempt to walk south on the beach itself except at low tide, because of the narrow strands.

2. Franklin Point

South of Gazos Creek, there is a small parking area and gate on the south side of Highway One opposite a large stand of eucalyptus trees. This trail is marked by a unique wooden sculpture called "The Fist" because of its shape. There actually are two small pullouts here, not far apart. The terrain here is very different from that of the grasslands farther south. Sand dunes here are interspersed with marshlands, all covered with dense vegetation of dune grass and other plants nutured by the damp air. The trail to the beach is not very well defined, and goes through some wet areas. Stay on the trail, as the undergrowth is susceptible to damage. It is about half-mile hike from the highway to the dunes near Franklin Point. There one can see to the north a long sandy beach stretching all the way to Gazos Creek, the north end of Año Nuevo State Reserve. Much of this beach is covered at high tide, but at low tide it is perhaps one of the least-visited beaches on the San Mateo County Coast, at least by humans. Sea-turtle tracks and hatchlings have been reported on this stretch. It is important to make sure that these beaches remain protected as there are fewer and fewer remote areas for these giant creatures.

3. & 4. Whitehouse Creek

Just another mile drive south on Highway One, you will find two roadside parking areas here, one on the south, one on the north side of Whitehouse Creek. There is evidence of early settlement here, but no buildings remain, only Monterey pine and eucalyptus trees and non-native gorse bushes. The south side trail crosses fields to join the Cascade Creek Trail and reaches the coastal bluffs beside the steep gulch of Whitehouse Creek.

The north-side trail wanders through the grasslands, all easy walking and inspires one to enjoy the fresh sea breezes and sunshine. Coming here on a foggy day could prove tricky or worse because the trails are too indistinct and the bluffs appear too suddenly. Sea otters can be seen resting in the kelp beds off the rocky shore. Water runoff erosion and storm surfs have carved out a rocky "sea stack" just beyond the cliff still wearing a grassy thatch on top, an isolated remnant of the coastal prairie.

5. Cascade Creek Trail

Another half-mile south on Highway One and still six miles north of the park's main entrance is a small parking lot on the south side of the highway. This is the entry to a trail that crosses about a mile of grassland toward the southwest, with views of Año Nuevo Island at the end of the curving coast. Native bunch-grass and prostrate coyote brush is the main flora. There are signs of a controlled burn, performed in the winter to rid the area of invasive, prickly gorse bushes. The Ohlones used controlled burns to clear area around their camps, the Portolá Expedition observed, so this ecological tool has been in use here for hundreds if not thousands of years. A row of eucalyptus and cypress trees remains from a windbreak planted years ago to shelter agricultural fields. Note a marshy area at the delta of Cascade Creek, where a dam once stood to impound water for irrigation in the summer. This marsh is now a bird habitat. Here you are at the northern border of the closed area of Año Nuevo Reserve. One may travel anywhere you want on the reserve to the north, but not to the south, which is reserved for sea mammal breeding grounds. A trail along the bluff goes north to the next beach access points at Whitehouse Creek, less than a half mile north.

Bean Hollow Beach

At Bean Hollow State Beach, there is a small parking lot, restrooms and picnic tables. This beach is the outfall for Arroyo de los Frijoles (Spanish for canyon of the beans), A series of small lakes extend upstream that had once been proposed as a park to be connected to Butano State Park a few miles inland. A reservoir and a small body of water called Lake Lucerne is just across Highway One to the east, but is off limits to the public.

Pebble Beach to Bean Hollow

South of Pescadero Creek about two miles is this beach that has long been popular because of the unusual shiny pebbles — agates, opals, jaspers, and carnelians — that people once collected. In the 19th century when Pescadero had all-to-brief fame as a summer resort, visitors from the Bayside would stay at hotels in the little town of Pescadero and collect pebbles from the beach. The hotels are gone now and collecting pretty pebbles is no longer permitted. Exploring the tidepools is okay as long as one does not disturb the sea creatures hiding there. It's better to take along one of the National Audubon Society guides so you and the kids can better understand what's living there. There's a little pocket-sized guide called *Familiar Seashore Creatures* that's just perfect for this job. Everything's in full color with plenty of explanatory notes.

There is a parking lot with restrooms, and steps leading down to the small beach. Somewhat sheltered by the rocky points at each end, this beach is protected enough to splash in the water, with little of the undertow problems found at most coastal beaches. If you get restless and want to take a walk on the cliffs overlooking the beach, stroll the mile down to Bean Hollow and the mile back. You can get there and back easily in an hour, or stretch it to two hours if you want to stop and smell the sea breezes or maybe spot a migrating whale offshore.

Pescadero State Beach

Near the town of Pescadero is Pescadero Beach and Marsh. Take Highway One 17 miles south from Half Moon Bay and the beach parking lot is on the right at the Pescadero Road intersection. Pescadero State Beach's two miles of sandy beach, dunes and rocky outcroppings lie on the west, or ocean, side of Highway One.

Pomponio State Beach

Pomponio State Beach is only about 1.5 miles south of La Honda Road alongside Highway One, and is linked to San Gregorio Beach by a long continuous strand. Before considering a walk between the two beaches, check to make certain the surf is calm. Also make sure the tide is low and will not be rising in the meantime. The walk could be fun. There is a good parking area, restrooms and picnic tables. There's also a small pool behind the sand bar where children can safely splash around. Because of its remoteness, this beach is one that usually has room when all the rest are filled to overflow.

San Gregorio State Beach

This beach is just south of the intersection of La Honda Road with Highway One, at the point where San Gregorio Creek runs into the ocean. (open 8 a.m. to sunset) San Gregorio has a large parking lot, with a self-service fee structure (called an "iron ranger") and restrooms. This large beach, with a cave under the cliff at its north side, tempts the visitor to walk south for long distances. Swimming here is not advisable, due to the strong undertow, which has been known to pull people out to sea. This is one of the better driftwood beaches. After a good storm is the best time for driftwood browsing and gathering other interesting marine detritus. In the parking area is a historic marker noting that Captain Gaspar de Portolá and his party of Spanish explorers camped here for three days in October, 1769. The diaries kept by the expedition's navigator, Miguel Constansó show they camped in the valley to the southeast of the beach and had to rest and recuperate from scurvy and other digestive problems.

MORE PICNIC SITES

Memorial Park of San Mateo County

Family picnic sites are located at the east end of the park. They are filled on a first come, first served basis. Four reservable group picnic areas accommodating 50 to 300 people (Huckleberry Flat Areas 1 - 4) are found in the eastern part of the park.

*Picnicking in the redwoods
is a treat to nature's creativity with light,
shadows and refreshing breezes.*

The sites have water, tables and barbecue pits. The areas are available by reservation. Call 650-363-0212.

Getting There: Take Highway One to Highway 84 (La Honda Rd); go east to Pescadero Road and turn right (southeast) on Pescadero Rd, go past Sam McDonald Park and go about 4 miles to park entrance on left.

Portola Redwoods State Park

Picnic tables and barbecue rings are located near all three parking lots in the park. Obtain park map at Visitor Center for $1. Parking Fee is charged.

Getting There: Take Skyline (Highway 35) south to Alpine Road; turn right (west) to entrance road, turn left and follow signs to Visitor Center.

Sam McDonald County Park

A few picnic tables are spotted among the towering redwoods along Pescadero Creek.

Getting There: Take Highway One south to La Honda Road (Highway 84). Turn left (east) to Pescadero Creek Road. At fork with Alpine Road, take left fork and follow to the Heritage Grove.

San Pedro Valley County Park

There are many picnic sites in this park. A $4 parking fee is charged.

Getting There: Take Highway One to Linda Mar Boulevard. Turn east to end of street, make a right turn to park entrance.

*The Pumpkin Festival brings contests of all
sorts, including a scramble to the top
of a make-believe mountain.*

PART XI
FUN
TIME
ON THE COAST

The Great Pumpkin arrives
annually for the Half Moon Bay Festival.

THE HALF MOON BAY PUMPKIN FESTIVAL
The Most Festive of All the Coastside Fetes

This is the grandest of all grand happenings on the coast. On the third weekend of October the Great Pumpkin comes to Main Street, Half Moon Bay, along with several thousand people from the Bayside of the hill for the annual Arts and Pumpkin Festival.   This is the time when the coast erupts with orange stripes and the kids dash into the fields to pick their own jack-o-lantern candidates. The arts and crafts are artful and entertaining, and so is wonderful linguica, pickled Brussels sprouts, Welsh pasties, and all things pumpkin: ice cream, soup, bread, pies,

And there are scarecrows and stuff!

And more pumpkins!

cheesecakes and cookies. The lead-off event is weighing the biggest pumpkin (it passed the half ton mark in 2001). There is a competition for the newest recipe for using pumpkin – the strangest so far was a Pumpkin Caesar Salad. Other competitions include the Great Pumpkin parade (held Saturday at noon), a 10-kilometer pumpkin run, a pumpkin climb and a masquerade ball at the I.D.E.S. Hall on Saturday evening. Proceeds from the festival support several local charities. For more information, call 650-726-9652.

YEAR-LONG FESTIVALS
Flower Market

Held monthly, this is to show off one of America's premier flower growing areas. Everyone admires the rows and rows of white and lavender stock, fields of heather, and hillsides covered in white and yellow marguerites that decorate the coast. So, once a month the local flower growers and wholesalers sell directly to the public at the Flower Market.

The Flower Market is held the third Saturday of each month throughout the year from 10 a.m. to 4 p.m.; the market is held outdoors at Kelly Avenue and Main Street from May through September. The rest of the year, the market is held in La Piazza, 604 Main St., in Half Moon Bay.

SPRING
Chamarita

Chamarita, or the Holy Spirit Festival, is a traditional Azores-Portuguese celebration, one of the many cultural treats the Portuguese population has introduced to this area soon after their settlement here late in the 19th century.

A church service, which opens with a blast of fireworks, begins the festival. The festival itself, which dates from 1296 in Portugal and from the 15th century in the Azores, features a parade with colorful marching bands, Portuguese flags, silver-and-leather clad equestrian groups, and queens with white lace ball gowns. After the procession, a special beef-based soup called *sopa do Espirito Santo* and a sweet bread called *massa sovada* is served. Queen Isabel of Aragon is said to have initiated this part of the ceremony, honoring the Holy Spirit by feeding the poor. A dance (Chamarita is Portuguese for dance) is held as part of the celebration.

In Half Moon Bay, they parade down Main Street to the Catholic Church and return one hour later to the I.D.E.S. (Imperios

Dos Santos Espirito Santo) Hall on south Main Street, where a small chapel (*Imperio*) is maintained for the ceremony. The Half Moon Bay Chamarita Festival is held the seventh Sunday after Easter; call 650-726-5202 for more information.

Pescadero has its own version of the festival a week earlier on the sixth Sunday after Easter. Call 650-726-5701 for additional information on the Pescadero Chamarita.

Spring Fest and Auction

This festival is held in March at the Pacifica Community Center to benefit the Pacifica Co-op Nursery School. An auction of hundreds of items, from weekend travel packages to handmade dollhouses, benefit the nursery school. For more information, call 650-355-4465.

Artichoke Golf Classic

This golf tournament sponsored by the Half Moon Bay Chamber of Commerce is held at the Half Moon Bay Golf Links in May. For information, call 650-726-8380.

Pacific Coast Dream Machines

The "dream machines" range from old cars to planes, engines, tractors, and all kinds of mechanical marvels. All are on display along with food, games, and entertainment. This event is held at the Half Moon Bay Airport in April to benefit the Coastside Adult Day Health Care Center. A nominal entrance fee is charged. For information on entries and dates, call 650-726-2328.

SUMMER

La Honda Country Fair and Music Festival

Some countrified, knee-slapping music and maybe some jazz, plus local arts and crafts, and lots of fun are offered annually – usually the second weekend in July – among the redwoods. La Honda Gardens in the middle of the village is the location of this music and crafts fair. Call 650-747-0965 for information.

Fourth of July

The Coastside is the coolest of the cool places to spend the Fourth of July. While inlanders are sweltering in the 90's and 100's, Coastsiders and their guests are relaxing in their usual upper 60's to low 70's. Things start with the annual parade down Main Street in Half Moon Bay at 11 a.m. In the evening, community-sponsored fireworks ignite over the breakwater at Pillar Point, and brilliantly light up the entire harbor area. Call 650-726-8380

*One of two golf courses at the end of Miramontes
Point Road in Half Moon Bay.*

for more information.

In Pacifica, the Fourth of July Fiesta is held at Frontierland Park at Yosemite Drive and Oddstad Boulevard from 11 a.m. to 5 p.m. The event also includes food, concessions, entertainers, bands and games. Call 650-738-7380 for more information.

Tours des Fleurs

Coastside nurseries open their doors to the public in July at this popular event sponsored by the Half Moon Bay Chamber of Commerce. One can learn all the inside scoop about the vast Coastside horticultural industry, and tour the area at the same time. Call 650-726-8380 for more information.

Half Moon Bay Charity Golf Classic

This annual golf tournament draws sports celebrities and famous entertainers to benefit Seton Coastside Medical Center. It is held at the Half Moon Bay Golf Links in July. Call 650-991-6448 for more information.

Pacifica Antique and Collectibles Street Fair

Over 100 dealers of antiques, collectibles, and memorabilia set up shop along Palmetto Avenue in Pacifica for a one-day event in July. A Lions' Club fundraiser. Call 650-355-4122 for more information.

*Many of the Dream Machines celebrate
the Coast's extensive agricultural heritage.*

Pescadero Arts and Fun Faire

This is on the third weekend of August, a music, food, and crafts festival that benefits the South Coast Children's Services. Call 650-879-0848 for information.

A Taste of Pacifica

A food, wine tasting, art, and music happening is held at Rockaway Beach in August. Call 650-355-4122 for information.

FALL

King's Mountain Art Festival

For original art and very different kinds of craft items, come to this art festival at the King's Mountain Community Center on Skyline Boulevard in Woodside. The art is displayed in a redwood grove, a perfect backdrop. This well-organized event offers shuttle buses to the festival from parking spots along Skyline. It is usually held Labor Day weekend. Call 650-851-2710 for information.

Harbor Day

This annual event is held at Pillar Point Harbor towards the end of September and is sponsored by the Half Moon Bay Fishermen's Marketing Association. A seafood barbecue, arts and crafts booths, entertainment and environmental education presentations are all part of the festivities. Call 650-728-0209 for information.

Pacifica Coast Fog Fest

You can almost count on the sun shining brightly at Fog Fest time in Pacifica; the town has never even won the "Foggiest City Contest." This tongue-in-cheek festival begins with the popular "Discover Pacifica" parade on Saturday morning. During the two-day event there is a human fog calling contest, "fog dogs" offered for the adventurous, and lots of arts and crafts booths, food concessions, a classic car show, wine and beer gardens, and musical entertainers from reggae to rock. The Fog Fest is held in late September on Palmetto Avenue in Pacifica. Call 650-355-4122 for informatiom.

Chili Cookoff

At Pillar Point Harbor in October, town folk and restaurateurs try to outdo each other with the most unusual and delicious chilies. The alligator chili and other esoteric recipes may require a special category in the competition. A panel of expert tasters turn this into a real down-home event, featuring championship-level savory chilis plus well-known and local bands. Proceeds benefit the Coastside Opportunity Center. Call 650-726-9071 for information.

WINTER

Stage Road Winter Faire

The best time to celebrate the holidays in Pescadero is on the first weekend in December. Go to Stage Road for arts and crafts, festive music, and lots of homemade baked goods. Proceeds support the South Coast Children's Services. Call 650-879-0013 for information.

Harbor Lights Ceremony

Your neighbors may be great with the Christmas tree lights, but wait until you see how the boat owners liven up the harbor at Pillar Point. An imaginative display of red, green, and white lights use masts and spars in all kinds of shapes. Their reflections off the water, the camaraderie of the boat owners, and the good humored judging of the "best" decorated boat, makes this an entertaining, and free holiday event. Held around the middle of December at Pillar Point Harbor. Call 650-726-4723 for information.

DRAMA, MUSIC & TALENT

This Side of the Hill Players

An amateur theater group that has been performing top-notch plays since 1985. They are always among the best. Performances are at the Mel Mello Center for the Arts, 1167 Main Street in Half Moon Bay. Call 650-569-3266 for tickets and information.

Pacifica Spindrift Players

An excellent amateur theater group presents a variety of plays throughout the year. They perform at the Oddstad Theater, 1050 Crespi Drive, Pacifica. For ticket information, call 650-359-8002.

Bach Dancing and Dynamite Society

The setting is the Douglas Beach House at Miramar Beach. The time is late Sunday afternoons (sometimes every week, sometimes not). The music may be Bach, Cuban style jazz, something from the swing era, a Flamenco guitarist or a piano recital. Or it may even be the San Francisco Comedy Semi-Finals. It is always dynamite entertainment. To look at the latest schedule go to www.bachddsoc.org on the Internet or call 650-726-4143.

REGULAR WEEKEND GIGS

Apple Jacks

Local bands play rock and country music on the weekends in this historic bar. At 1 Entrada Way at La Honda Road, La Honda. Call 650-747-0331.

Cameron's Inn

Entertainment varies from local folk singers to comedians to karaoke to better-known bands. Audience participation is encouraged. Located at 1410 South Highway One, Half Moon Bay. Call 650-726-5705 for the latest schedule, or check their website: www.cameronsinn.com.

La Di Da

Live blues, folk, rock, and contemporary bands play on Saturdays and Sundays from 11 a.m. to 1 p.m. in this colorful coffee house. 500 Purisima, Half Moon Bay. Call 650-726-1663.

Merry Prankster Cafe

Bluegrass, country, folk, and other bands play on occasional Saturday evenings and Sunday afternoons. 8865 La Honda Road, La Honda. Call 650-747-0660.

Mezza Luna

Music, a large bar with a dance floor, fireplace, and stage; a great getaway, at 459 Prospect Way, Princeton-By-The-Sea. Call 650-728-8108.

Nick's

A variety of dance music at Rockaway Beach, Pacifica. Call 650-359-3900.

Old Princeton Landing

Rock and blues bands are usually featured. Famous musicians have been known to show up for a jam session here, 460 Capistrano Road, Princeton-By-The-Sea. Call 650-728-9103.

San Gregorio General Store

Here it's bluegrass, rock and Irish music around the old bar, Stage Road and Highway 84, San Gregorio. Call 650-726-0565.

EATERIES

Inexp.=Inexpensive. Below $10 Main Course
Mod.=Moderate. $10-$15
Exp.=Expensive. $15-$25

HALF MOON BAY

Bangkok House

Thai food is served in a tasteful decorated dining room with leaded glass windows, and a fireplace. Serves curries, satays, prawn and vegetable soup, and other Thai dishes both mild and fiery. Open Tuesday through Sunday for lunch and dinner. 225 S. Highway One in Shoreline Station. 650-726-5247. Mod.

Caddy's Restaurant

On the 18th tee at the Half Moon Bay Golf Links, contemporary cuisine for breakfast and lunch, lighter fare for evenings. 2000 Fairway Dr. 650-726-6384. Mod.

Cameron's Restaurant and Inn

A basket of fish and chips or a burger and fries – voted by locals as best burger on the coast — choose one of 25 beers on tap, 60 bottled, or a shake from the full soda fountain. For fun, there's darts. Entertainment some nights. The double decker bus outside is for smokers. Open daily for lunch and dinner. 1410 S. Highway One. 650-726-5705. Inexp.

Casey's Café

Summertime hours: Open 11a.m. to 9 p.m. Monday-Saturday, Sunday brunch, 9 a.m. to 5 p.m. 328 Main St. 650-560-4880. Inexp.

Cetrella

A European style bistro, brand new in 2001, Mediterranean coastal cuisine. Open for dinner daily, Sunday brunch 10:30 a.m. to 2:30 p.m. 845 Main St. 650-726-4090. Exp.

Chateau des Fleurs

French specialties include classical rabbit sautéed in red wine and duck paté with Grand Marnier, also chicken, steaks, veal, lamb and seafood prepared in lighter sauces. Casual coastside clothes. Open daily for lunch and dinner. 523 Church St. 650-712-8837. Mod.

China Kitchen

A full menu to eat in or take out. 80 N. Highway One. 650-712-6511. Inexp.

Happy Cooker Restaurant

Another favorite of the locals for breakfast and lunch. Good solid food. In the Strawflower Center at 50 N. Highway One. 650-726-2260. Inexp.

The Happy Taco

Tacos, tortas, chorizo, ricas, carnitas and more. 184 San Mateo Road. 650-726-5480. Inexp.

It's Italia Pizzeria

Pizzas (voted best on coast by locals) include artichoke hearts, caramelized onions, shitake mushrooms, Italian sausage, Mozzarella. Open daily for lunch and dinner. Located at 40 Stone Pine Center, off Main Street. 650-726-4444. Inexp.

Joe's on the Coast

At one time, a cousin of the Joe's Italian Restaurants in Westlake in Daly City and Woodlake in San Mateo. Italian and American dishes served daily for breakfast, lunch and dinner. 2380 S. Highway One. 650-560-9260. Mod.

Main Street Grill

Another popular hangout for the locals. Lunch and dinners served. 435 Main St. 650-726-5300. Inexp.

McDonald's

The franchise arches. At entrance to Strawflower Shopping Center. 100 N. Highway One. 650-726-1222. Inexp.

Original Johnny's

Steve and Ilva Evan carry on the quality set by his father, Johnny, in 1967. A local favorite for breakfast and lunch. Voted best home cooking on the coast. Open 7 a.m. to 3 p.m. Tuesday through Saturdays. 547 Main St. 650-726-6266. Inexp.

Papa George's Restaurant

American menu. 2320 S. Highway One. 650-726-9417. Mod.

Pasta Moon

Try homemade Italian sausage with rosemary and chicken breast, fettucine with smoked salmon, or linguine with prawns in a saffron cream sauce. These and many other Italian dishes. Open daily for lunch and dinner. 315 Main St. 650-726-5125. Mod..

Ritz Carlton Half Moon Bay
The Conservatory

Five distinct food and beverage servings throughout the day. One Miramontes Point Road. 650-712-7050. Exp.

Ritz Carlton Half Moon Bay
Navio

Specializes in coastal cuisine and seafood. Serves breakfast, lunch and dinner daily plus Saturday and Sunday brunch. One Miramontes Point Road. 650-712-7050. Exp.

Round Table Pizza

In the Strawflower Shopping Center at 50 N. Highway One. 650-726-5207. Mod.

Sam's Coffee Shop

Behind the Olympia Service Station at 210 Highway 92. 650-726-3167. Inexp.

San Benito House

California country inn fare is highlighted by homemade breads and soups – voted best on coast — and salads with ever-changing entrees. The attached Garden Deli specializes in huge sandwiches. Open Thursday to Saturday for dinner and for Sunday brunch. The deli is open daily for lunch. 356 Main Street. 650-726-3425. Mod.

Segunda Vez

Mexican Food. 20 Stone Pine Road. 650-712-4455. Mod.

Señor Coca's

Serves Mexican food with standard south of the border dinner specials. Open daily for lunch and dinner. 211 Highway 92. 650-726-3737. Mod.

Siam Restaurant

Thai dishes include satays, jumbo prawns stuffed with ground shrimp, peanut salad, and chicken coconut milk soup. Open daily for lunch and dinner. 108 N. Highway One. 650-712-0583. Inexp.

Souper Dooper

The name says it all. Several kinds of steaming bowls of homemade soups, including excellent clam chowder and minestrone are offered here. Burgers, sandwiches, salads, including home-style potato salad. Open daily from 11:30 a.m. to 6 p.m. 328 Main St. in Zaballa Square. 650-560-4880. Inexp.

Spanishtown Mexican Restaurant

Good combination plates are favorites, but also more unusual fish, rabbit, and goat preparations are offered. Portions are large. Fruity sangrias and Mexican beer and soft drinks. Open daily for lunch and dinner. 515 Church Street. 650-726-7357. Inexp.

Subway

Franchise sandwiches. In Strawflower Shopping Center at 80 N. Highway One. 650-712-0330. Inexp.

Sushi Main Street

One of the busiest restaurants in town and voted best Asian food on coast by locals. Japanese food is the focus; has an Asian inn ambiance. Specialty is sushi of all kinds; a full range of other Japanese items also served. Open daily for lunch and dinner. 696 Mill St. 650-726-6336. Mod.

Taqueria La Mexicana
Mexican Food. 250 S. Highway One. 726-1746. Inexp.

Three Amigos
Voted the best Mexican café on the coast, best burritos – the giant "wet" burritos are the reason, and voted best late-night meal on the coast. Open daily from 10 a.m. to 10 p.m. 200 S. Highway One. 650-726-6080. Inexp.

Two Fools Cafe and Market
All-American dishes like meat loaf with garlic mashed potatoes, or a top notch vegetarian meal are here. Open daily for lunch and dinner, closed Mondays for dinner. 408 Main St. 650-712-1222. Inexp.

MID-COAST
Anchorage
Perched on the edge of Pillar Point Harbor, the best maritime view of the bay is combined with fish dishes from sand dabs to sushi and bouillabaisse. Eat indoors in the chowder house atmosphere or outdoors on the veranda. Open daily for lunch and dinner; Sunday brunch. 4210 N. Highway One, El Granada. 650-726-2822. Exp.

Barbara's Fish Trap
One of the coast's most enduring traditions, this funky cafe offers a good variety of fresh fish, mostly grilled or fried in a casual atmosphere. Chowder's superb. Outdoor seating is also available. Open daily for lunch and dinner. No credit cards. 281 Capistrano Road, Princeton. 650-728-7049. Mod.

Cafe Gibraltar
Mediterranean dishes here include a mixed antipasti platter with homemade flatbread; entrees such as clams sautéed with Spanish chorizo; or try wild mushroom risotto. Outside seating adjoins the cafe. Open Wednesdays through Mondays. Corner of 7th and Highway One, Montara. 650-728-9030. Mod.

Chart House

Located on a bluff overlooking the ocean, rocky cliffs, and Montara State Beach. America cuisine is offered: fresh fish, grilled chicken and steaks, and a loaded salad bar. Open daily for dinner. 8150 Highway One, Montara. 650-728-7366. Exp.

Demi Lune

Italian-American décor with red table cloths, pleasant settings, and attentive service highlight the appetizers, pastas, meats and special seafood preparations such as pistachio encrusted halibut and moist battered sole. Open for dinner Wednesday through Sunday and for weekend brunch. 3048 N. Highway One, Miramar. 650-726-8114. Mod.

El Gran Amigo Taqueria

2448 Highway One, Moss Beach. 650-728-3815. Inexp.

Half Moon Bay Brewing Co.

Overlooking harbor, voted best new restaurant on coast in 2001. From fish and chips to new cusine, the food is great and their bartender, Glenn Mannina, voted best on coast. 390 Capistrano Road, Princeton. 650-728-2337. Mod.

Harbor Pizza, Lunch Saturday & Sunday, 11 a.m.-10:30 p.m., Dinner Monday-Friday 3:30 p.m.-10:30 p.m. 65 Alhambra Ave., El Granada. 650-726-3501. Inexp.

Highway One Diner

Bring back the '50's with harbor view, hamburgers, hotdogs, fried chicken with mashed potatoes and gravy. Open daily except Mondays for breakfast, lunch and dinner. 4230 Highway One next to The Anchorage, El Granada. 650-726-4991. Mod.

Ketch Joanne and Harbor Bar

A fishermen's hangout just steps away from their boats. A maritime theme and the potbelly stove beckon. Occasionl live entertainment in the bar; open daily for breakfast, lunch, and dinner. Pillar Point Harbor, Princeton. 650-728-3747. Mod.

Maverick's Roadhouse Café

Funky. 460 Capistrano Road., Princeton. 650-728-1233. Inexp.

Mezza Luna

Echoes of Tuscany: fresh bread, pizza and desserts match excellent pastas, sauces (locals voted best Italian food on coast). Lightly battered calamari one of the best anywhere. Wine list voted best on coast. Live entertainment weekends. Open daily for lunch and dinner. 459 Prospect Way, Princeton. 650-728-8108. Mod.

Miramar Beach Inn

Once a Prohibition roadhouse of ill repute, broad picture windows now overlook the spectacular surf show. New cuisine menu offers several seafood and steak specialties and dishes featuring artichokes. Open daily for lunch and dinner and Sundays for brunch. 131 Mirada Road, Miramar. 650-726-9053..Exp.

Moon Bay Restaurant

Chinese food opposite Princeton traffic signal. 1015 N. Highway One, Princeton. 650-726-2888. Mod.

Moss Beach Distillery

Voted most romantic and best business lunch spot on the coast, this cliff-hugging former speakeasy has a long-rumored blue lady ghost to spice the new cuisine that focuses on fish (locals voted best fish on coast) meat and pasta. There is also a downstairs bar and light food area with outdoor deck chairs and blankets for snuggling. Open daily for lunch and dinner. Beach Way and Ocean Boulevard, Moss Beach. 650-728-5595. Mod.

Pizzeria del Sol

Breakfast, fish and chips, prawns, calamari and pizza Free delivery. 2350 Carlos St., Moss Beach. 650-728-5151. Mod.

Princeton Seafood Company Market and Restaurant

The clam chowder here is a local Clam Chowder Cook-off winner and many fish entrees have been longtime favorites of locals. Open daily for lunch and dinner. Pillar Point Harbor, Princeton. 650-726-2722. Mod.

Three Zero Café

This airport café (voted favorite breakfast spot on the coast by the locals) has been an early morning "must" for years. Open daily 6 a.m. to 3 p.m. At the entrance to Half Moon Bay Airport, N. Highway One. 650-728-1411. Inexp.

Twinberry Café & Bakery

102 Sevilla Ave., El Granada. 650-726-9775. Inexp.

SOUTH COAST
Alice's Restaurant
Long a popular a stop for motorcyclists, hikers, and lovers of the outdoors, Alice's is in a wooden cabin with a spacious deck for outside seating and views of the towering redwoods. Sandwiches and breakfasts are simple but ample, good, and reasonably priced. Open for breakfast and lunch daily. Located on Skyline at La Honda Road. 650-851-0303. Inexp.
Duarte's
A great mixture of locals and out-of-towners find this a popular destination eatery for the pies and seafoods. Specialties are lightly battered calamari (one of the best on the coast), crab cioppino and abalone. Homemade pies (the strawberry rhubarb is famous) and artichoke soups are delicious. Open daily for breakfast, lunch, and dinner. Get there early on weekends or you may wait for a table. 202 Stage Road, Pescadero. 650-879-0464. Inexp.

PACIFICA
Café D' Capo
90 Eureka Square. 650-359-5448. Mod.
El Gran de Oro Pizzeria
1710 Frncisco Blvd. 650-355-8417. Inexp.
Guerrero's Taqueria
164 Reina del Mar. 650-355-2833. Inexp.
Invitation House
The Korean and Japanese menu is extensive, so you may want your waiter to guide you. Open daily for lunch and dinner. 270 Rockaway Beach Ave. 650-738-8588. Mod.
Kentucky Fried Chicken
4408 Pacific Coast Highway at Rockaway. 650-355-0920. Inexp.
Moonraker Restaurant
All of the seating faces picture windows overlooking the Pacific. At night, spotlights play on the crashing waves below. New American light cuisine. Open for dinner daily. 105 Rockaway Beach. 650-359-0303. Exp.

Mr. Azteca Mexican Food
761 Hickey Blvd. 738-0873. Inexp.

Mr. Lee's Chinese Food
A wide array of fish dishes is offered as well as a daily dim sum menu for lunch only. Open daily for lunch and dinner; food to go available. 5560 Highway One in the lighthouse-shaped building at the entrance to Pedro Point. 650-359-9085. Mod.

Nick's Seashore Restaurant
A local favorite for years with wave-level views where one settles into the tufted banquettes and tries the scalone or other specialties. Lounge and large banquet space for group meals available. Open daily for breakfast, lunch, and dinner and frequently has nightly entertainment. 100 Rockaway Beach. 650-359-3900. Mod.

Pacifica Thai Cuisine
18960 Francisco Blvd. 650-355-1678. Inexp.

Palm City Chinese Restaurant
In the Linda Mar Shopping Center. 659-738-1899. Mod.

Ristorante Mare
Serving authentic Northern Italian cuisine, including minestrone, roasted meats, and a variety of pastas in an inn-like setting. Open daily except Mondays for dinner. Lunches on Fridays only. 404 San Pedro Ave. 650-355-5980. Mod.

Rock'n Robs
This is an old fashion diner serving ample hamburgers and milkshakes in frosty goblets surrounded by '50's memorabilia. Open daily for lunch and dinner. Located at Rockaway Beach, 450 Dondee Way. 650-359-FOOD. Inexp.

Round Table Pizza
Linda Mar Shopping Center. 650-736-1010. Mod.

Tams Cuisine of China
Served in an upscale atmosphere are a variety of Chinese dishes. Slightly spicy orange-flavored prawns are good, as are many of the vegetable dishes. Open daily for lunch and dinner. 494 Manor Plaza. 650-359-7575. Mod.

Taqueria Los Toros
Mexican Food. 1357 Linda Mar Center. 650-738-1633. Inexp.

Taqueria El Toro Loco
Mexican and Peruvian, corner of Francisco Boulevard and Paloma
Road. 650-355-5548. Inexp.
Vallemar Station
2125 Pacific Coast Highway. 650-359-7411. Mod.

SNACK TIME...Where the Goodies Are

HALF MOON BAY
Café Salet
Strawflower Shopping Center. 650-726-3332.
Cunha Country Store
This store out of the past has wooden floors and savory deli smells;
luncheon meats, sandwiches, fresh local produce, and a selection
of groceries. Open daily from 8 a.m. to 8 p.m. Main Street and
Kelly Avenue. 650-726-4071.
Half Moon Bay Bakery
Fresh and savory French bread has been a favoriote here since
1927, snacks and other goodies, too. 514 Main St. 650-726-1841.
Half Moon Bay Coffee Company
A combination coffee house, breakfast and lunch bar always a
busy place.   Indoor and outdoor seating available. Open daily
from 6 a.m. to 9 p.m. At the corner of Main Street and Stone Pine
Road. 650-726-3664.
Healing Moon
Here you will find fresh and organic deli lunches, hot soups, and
fresh sandwiches. Has an enclosed back garden. Open daily from
10 a.m. to 6 p.m. 523 Main St. 650-726-7881.
La-Di-Da
A really neat place with painted furniture and artwork to enhance
good coffee, desserts, and lunches. Weekend entertainment. Open
daily until 7 p.m. on weekdays and 6 p.m. on weekends. 500C
Purisima. 650-726-0306.
M. Coffee's
Fresh-brewed coffee, cappuccino, or espresso. Coffee beans and
light snacks are also available. Picnic supplies, too. Open daily

from 7 a.m. to 6 p.m., weekends 9 a.m. to 6 p.m. 522 Main St. 650-726-6241.

Moonside Bakery and Cafe

German pastries and breads, wood-burning oven-cooked pizza, sandwiches and salads, expresso and other coffee drinks are served. Open daily from 7 a.m. to 6 p.m., closed Tuesdays. 604 Main St. inside the mall or on the sidewalk. 650-726-9070.

The Rotisserie Market

Slowly rotating pork, chicken, lamb and beef form the centerpiece of this take-out snack shop. Salads and other tempting side dishes, too. Open daily for lunch and dinner. 315 Main St. 650-712-7400.

Sunshine Donuts

Strawflower Shopping Center. 650-726-1161.

MID-COAST

A Coastal Affair

Coffee and snacks, 8455 Pacific Coast Highway. 650-728-5229.

Creekside Smoke House

Smoked albacore, salmon, trout, sturgeon and other fish are prepared and sold here. Salmon jerky and seafood salads, too. Open daily except Mondays from 10 a.m. to 6 p.m. Closed September, January and February. 280 Avenue Alhambra, El Granada. 650-712-8862.

El Granada Hardware Store

Coffee, sandwiches and light snacks while you shop for hardware items; use their copy machine, send a fax, or get the local scuttlebutt from the proprietor. Open daily. 85 Avenue Portola, El Granada. 650-726-5009.

SOUTH COAST

Kings Mountain Country Store

Wine, homemade salads and sandwiches, gift items while touring the Skyline. Don't miss their history-wall. Snack on their deck. 13100 Skyline Blvd., Woodside. 650-851-3852.

Norm's Market

Artichoke bread draws a heavy weekend crowd plus other hot

out-of-the-oven breads, and cheeses, wines, and other picnic and deli items. 287 Stage Road, Pescadero. 650-879-0147.

San Gregorio General Store

Fresh sandwiches, cold drinks, coffee, wine and beer provide the excuse to stop and spend an hour or so roaming through the books, records, hats, toys, memorabilia. Open daily. San Gregorio and Stage Roads, San Gregorio. 650-726-0565.

Skywood Trading Post and Deli

Another Skylonda stop for deli sandwiches and other fresh foods inside. Outside tables. Open daily. Skyline at Highway 84 in Woodside. 650-851-0914.

PACIFICA

Beach Cafe and Deli

Vegetarian items and salads are the specialties here. Just north of Rockaway Beach at 4430 Coast Highway. Open daily from 9 a.m. to 5 p.m. 650-355-4532.

Mazzetti's Bakery

Specialties at this family-owned and operated landmark are honey raisin bran muffins, Italian rum cake, pastries, and focaccia bread. Great coffee, too. Open daily from 5 a.m. to 6 p.m. 101 Manor Dr. 650-355-1007.

El Grano de Oro

El Grano de Oro brings a Latin touch with fresh-from-the-oven tortillas, stacked and ready to go. Open daily except Sundays. 1710 Francisco Blvd. 650-355-8417.

!!!GOING SHOPPING!!!

ANTIQUES

Antiques and Collectibles, 215 Rockaway Beach Ave. Pacifica. 650-738-1934.

Coastside Consignments, 2027 Palmetto Dr., Pacifica. 650-738-1078.
Country Roads Antique Store, Stage Road, Pescadero, 650-879-0452.

Debbie's Attic, 1925 Palmetto Dr., Pacifica. 650-355-1875.
Half Moon Bay Antiques, 516 Main St., HMB. 650-712-1911.
Half to Have It, Main Street Exchange, 601Main St., HMB. 650-712-5995.
Spanishtown Art & Craft Center, east of Main on Highway 92, HMB. 650-726-9971.
Vintage Collection, 356 Main St., HMB. 650-712-0366.

ART GALLERIES
Coastal Arts League Museum and Sales, 300 Main St., HMB. 650-726-6335.
Coastal Gallery, Alleyway at 424 Main St., HMB. 650-726-3859.
Court Yard Gallery, 643 Main St., HMB. 650-712-7742.
Dunn Mehler Gallery, 337 Mirada Rd., HMB. 650-726-7667.
Galleria Luna, 300 Main St., HMB. 650-726-8932.
Garden Gallery, 604 Main St., HMB. 650-712-1949.
Lessa's Studio, 501 San Mateo Rd., HMB. 650-726-7353.
Mirren Gallery, 510 Kelly Ave., HMB. 650-712-1320.
Old Alves Dairy Barn, Kelly Avenue, HMB. a studio for local artisans.
Peggy Eriksen Art and Framing, 524 Main St., HMB. 650-726-1598.
Sanchez Art Center, 1220 Linda Mar Blvd., Pacifica, Weekends Only. 650-355-1894.
Spanishtown Art & Craft Center, east of Main on Highway 92, HMB. 650-726-9971.
Spring Mountain Gallery, 225 S. Highway One, HMB. 650-726-3025.

AUTO SERVICES
Bob's Car Wash, 240 Main St., HMB. 650-726-0538.
HMB Auto Repair, 149 Main St., HMB. 650-726-0711.
Phil's Tire & Auto Center, 422 Purisima St., HMB. 650-726-5153.

BEAUTY
Hacienda Salon, 519 Main St., HMB. 650-726-0134.
Hairmasters, 225 S. Highway One, HMB. 650-726-3733.
Hair Works at Harmonies, 245 Main St., HMB. 650-712-8201.
Half Moon Bay Beauty Salon, 409 Main St., HMB. 650-726-2038.

Isis Salon & Spa, 40 Stone Pine Center, HMB. 650-726-4787.
Main Street Hair Design, 840 Main St., HMB. 650-726-4433.
Nail Elegance, La Piazza Center, HMB. 650-726-8152.
Paul Strom Hair, Skin & Body Care, 450 Dondee Wy., Pacifica.
650-355-5553.

BIKES
A Bicyclery, Highway 92 and Main Street, HMB. 650-726-6000.
The Bike Works, Stone Pine Center., HMB. 650-726-6708.

BOOKS
Bay Book & Video, Strawflower Center, HMB. 650-726-3488.
Coastside Books, 432 Main St., HMB. 650-726-5889.
Floreys, 2316 Palmetto, Pacifica. 650-355-8811.
Lulu's Publications, 1007 Crespi Dr., Pacifica. 650-738-8597.
Moon News, Stone Pine Center, HMB. 650-726-8610.
Ocean Books, 416 Main St., HMB 650-726-2665.
Pacifica Book Co.,Eureka Square off Oceana, Pacifica. 650-738-9000.
San Gregorio Store, Stage and San Gregorio Roads. 650-726-0565.

CANDY
Simply Delicious, Strawflower Center, HMB, 650-560-9081.

CATERING & PARTY RENTALS
A Festive Affair, 112 N. Highway One, HMB. 650-726-3262.
Sample This Catering, 328 Main St., #101, HMB. 650-560-4880.

CHRISTMAS TREES
Bob's Trees, 4 miles south of HMB on Highway One.
Cozzolino's,1200 Highway 92, HMB, 650-726-4383.
Four C's Trees, Highway 92 next door to Obester's.
Lemos Farms, Highway 92 next to BFI entryway.
Pastorino, 12511 Highway 92, HMB. 650-726-6440.
Rancho Siempre Verde, Highway One 4 miles south of
Pigeon Point.
Repetto's, Highway 92, HMB. 650-726-6414.
Santa's Trees, Highway 92 at Pilarcitos Creek Bridge.

CLOTHING, *Children*
P. Cottontail, 527 Main St., HMB. 650-726-0200.

CLOTHING, *Men & Women*
The Buffalo Shirt Co., 315 Main St., HMB. 650-726-3194.

CLOTHING, *Women*
Calico Barn, boutique. 521 Main St., HMB. 650-726-9646.
The Charmed Rose, 414 Main St., HMB. 650-712-1622.
Damsel In A Dress, 417 Main St., HMB. 650-726-4327.
Lady Bug, Lady Bug, Strawflower Center, HMB. 650-726-1726.
Unique Clothing, 407 Main St., HMB. 650-726-6062.

Neat old things make for great browsing
here and elsewhere on the coast.

COMPUTERS & ELECTRONICS
Radio Shack, Albertson's Shopping Center, HMB. 650-726-9128.

CRAFTS
Old Alves Dairy Barn, Kelly Avenue, HMB.
Pescadero II, 508 Main St., HMB. 650-726-7864.
Relatively Crafty, Manor Plaza, off Manor Drive, Pacifica. 650-355-5903.
San Gregorio General Store, Stage and San Gregorio Roads. 650-726-0565
Spanishtown Art & Craft Center, east of Main on Highway 92, HMB. 650-726-9971.

FEED & FUEL
Half Moon Bay Feed and Fuel, 331 Main St., HMB. 650- 726-4814.

FISH MARKETS
Half Moon Bay Fish Market, 99 Highway 92, HMB. 650-726-2561.

FISHING CHARTERS
Capt. John's, Pillar Point Harbor. 650-726-2913.
Huck Finn's, Pillar Point Harbor. 650-726-7133.
Hull Cat, Pillar Point Harbor. 650-726-2926.
New Capt. Pete's, Pillar Point Harbor. 650-726-2926.
Queen of Hearts, Pillar Point Harbor. 510-581-2628.

FLOWERS
Cozzolinos, 12001 Highway 92, HMB. 650-726-4383.
Plum Tree Flowers, 643 Main St., HMB. 726-1075.
Repettos Greenhouse, 12331 Highway 92, HMB. 650-726-1075.
Rockaway Beach Flowers, 205 Rockaway Beach, Pacifica, 650-738-8183.

FURNITURE
Ambiance, 415 Main St., HMB. 650-560-9844.
Cottage Industries, 621 Main St., HMB. 650-712-8078.
Gallery M, creative, 328 Main St., HMB. 650-726-7167.
Pacific Patio, outdoor, HMB. 650-726-3650.

GARDEN
HMB Garden & Building Supply, 119 Main St., HMB. 650-726-6696

Half to Have It, 601 Main St., HMB. 650-712-5995.

GIFTS
Ambiance, 415 Main St., HMB. 650-560-9844.

Carousel Classics, 205 Rockaway Beach, Pacifica. 650-355-3359.

Charmed Rose, 414 Main St., HMB. 650-712-1622.

Christmas by the Cove, 205 Rockaway Beach, Pacifica. 650-355-2683.

Fengari's, 400 Main St., HMB. 650-726-2550.

Hanni's Fine Gifts, Rockaway Beach Plaza, 450 Rockaway. 650-359-4721.

Harbor Seal Co., marine theme, 406 Main St., HMB. 650-726-7418

Light and Art, blown glass, 330 Main St., HMB. 650-726-3080

LunarWind Inventions, kites, 330 Main St., HMB. 650-726-9212.

Magazzi, 420 Main St., HMB. 650-726-4021.

Nuestra Tierra, Mexican imports, 421 Main St., HMB. 650-712-9135.

Paper Crane, 315 Main St., HMB. 650-726-0722.

P. Cottontail, 527 Main St., HMB. 650-726-0200.

Pumpkin Patch Hallmark, Strawflower Center, HMB. 650-726-3693.

Quail Run, garden theme, 412 Main St., HMB. 650-726-0312.

Seascapes, maritime theme, 330 Main St., HMB. 650-712-8096.

Tokenz, 539 Main St., HMB. 650-712-8457.

GOLF & SPORTS
California Canoe & Kayak, 214 Princeton Ave., Princeton. 650-728-1803.

Coastside Surf & Skate, 530 Main St., HMB. 650-726-6422.

HMB Board Shop, 3032 N. Highway One, HMB. 650-726-1476.

HMB Sports and Golf Center, Stone Pine Center, HMB. 650-712-9900.

HEALTH& FITNESS
Cheryl Fuller, Certified Massage Therapist, HMB. 650-726-2249.
Coastal Lifestyles, 371 Princeton Ave., Princeton. 650-728-1031.
Creative Health & Wellness Center, 255 Main St., HMB. 650-726-5179.
Gymtowne Gymnastics, 850 Airport St., #2, Moss Beach. 650-563-9426.
Half Moon Bay Natural Foods, 523 Main St., HMB. 650-726-7881.
Hellerwoek & Massage, Moss Beach. 650-888-8770.

HOUSEHOLD
Coastal Comforts, bath & bedroom, 432 Main St., HMB. 650-726-3600.
Cunha's Country Store, 448 Main St., HMB, 650-726-4071.

JEWELRY
Arrigotti Fine Jewelry, 353 Main St.,HMB. 650-726-0248.
Downtown Jewelry, 300 Main St., HMB, 650-726-4040.
Main Street Goldworks, Main and Miramontes, HMB. 650-726-2546.
Tokenz, 539 Main St., HMB. 650-712-8457.

LUGGAGE
Briggs and Riley, 850 Airport Road, Moss Beach. 650-728-8000.

MUSIC
Music Hut, CD's and tapes, 329 Main St., HMB. 650-726-8742.

PET CARE
Klaws, Paws & Hooves/Klever K9, El Granada. 650-728-8070.
Pets Enjoying Tenders Service, El Granada. 650-728-2166.

PRODUCE
Bob's, Highway One, 4 miles south. of HMB
Coastways, U-Pick Olallie Berries & Kiwis, Highway One, 8 miles south of Pigeon Point.
Denniston Lane, Highway One opposite HMB Airport.
Level Lea Ranch, Pescadero Creek Road, Pescadero.
Old Barn, Highway 84, 1 mile east of San Gregorio.
Phipps Ranch, Pescadero Creek Road, 1 mile south of Pescadero.

POTTERY
Old Alves Dairy Barn, Kelly Avenue, HMB.
La Honda Pottery, 65 Cuesta Road, La Honda. 650-747-0650.
Spanishtown Art & Craft Center, east of Main on Highwy 92, HMB. 650-726-9971.

TAXIS & LIMOS
California Pacific Limousine, 650-726-2664 and 650-738-5668.
Pacifica/HMB Cab Co., 650-712-9300

TOYS
HMB Toy Store, Strawflower Center, HMB. 726-1139.
Sea Squirts, Strawflower Center, HMB. 650-726-1139.

VETERINARIANS
HMB Veterinary Hospital, 719 Main St., HMB. 650-726-9061.
Linda Mar Veterinary Hospital , 985 Linda Mar Blvd., Pacifica. 650-359-6471.

WINE TASTING & SHOPS
HMB Wine and Cheese Shop, Main and Miramontes, HMB. 650-726-1520.
Obester Winery, Highway 92, east of HMB. 650-726-9463.

A PILLOW FOR YOUR HEAD

BED & BREAKFASTS
HALF MOON BAY
Cameron's Restaurant & Inn B & B
Three rooms to let are above a popular English pub-style restaurant (the second B stands for beverage) have queen beds; two of the rooms share a bath. A double-decker London bus serves as a smoking room, and assorted British post boxes and phone booths, and volley ball courts add to the spirits. 1410 S. Highway One. 650-726-5705. Fax: 650-726-9613.

Mill Rose Inn
Six suites, each with its own fireplace; bath, robe and outside entrance. Champagne is served in the gazebo spa area. Flowers abound. A gourmet breakfast included. 615 Mill St. 650-726-8750 or (800) 900-ROSE. Fax: 650-726-3031. Website: www.millroseinn.com.

Old Thyme Inn
An herb garden surrounds this restored Queen Anne Victorian. Choose from seven bedrooms, all in the herb motif. Several rooms have fireplaces, whirlpool tubs, featherbeds. A full breakfast is served. 779 Main St. 650-726-1616 or (800) 720-4277. Fax: 650-726-6394. Website: www.oldthymeinn.com.

San Benito House
Climb a steep staircase off the 1905 saloon to 12 rooms decorated in the Old West theme. Some rooms share a bath; price includes a continental breakfast and a 10 per cent discount at the San Benito House Restaurant. 356 Main St. 650-726-3425.

Zaballa House
Estanislao Zaballa's structure, the oldest in Half Moon Bay built in the 1850's, now contains a five-bedroom bed and breakfast. Surrounding the original house is a shopping center; 18 additional inn rooms and suites are on a second floor. The rooms in the older house feature an antique look. Some rooms have fireplaces and Jacuzzi tubs. Pets welcome; some wheelchair accessible rooms. 324 Main St. 650-726-9123. Website: www.whistler.com/zaballa.

MID-COAST:

Cypress Inn

This bed and breakfast beach house has 12 rooms and almost all have fireplaces, Jacuzzi tubs, and private decks with views; decorated with native folk art and a Southwest flavor. A gourmet breakfast and afternoon wine, tea, and hors d'oeuvres are included. Wheel-chair accessible rooms available. 407 Mirada Road, Half Moon Bay. 650-726-6002 or (800) 832-3224. Fax: 650-712-0380. Website: www.cypressinn.com.

Farallone Inn

Nine rooms on a hill overlooking the ocean. Summer and winter rates. 1410 Main St., Montara. 650-728-8200.

Goose and Turrets

A few blocks off Highway One, the outside seems worn, but inside is a warm book and art-filled living room. Original art and German featherbeds adorn each of the five bedrooms, private baths. Full breakfast and afternoon tea are included. 835 George St., Montara. 650-728-5451. Fax: 650-728-0141. Website: www.montara.com/goose.

Harbor House

Located on the water's edge among Pillar Point Harbor's boatyards and storage units, the Harbor House has six rooms, most with private patios and decks. Full conference facilities are located in a building next door. 346 Princeton Ave. 650-728-1572. Fax: 650-728-8271.Website: www.harborhousebandb.com.

Landis Shores Oceanfront Inn

Ocean-front Landis Shores, located on the bluffs overlooking Miramar Beach, has eight suites, each equipped with Jacuzzi, tiled private ocean-view deck, fireplace, TV, and VCR; a full gourmet breakfast, appetizers, and evening wine are included. A small exercise room and meeting room are also available. 211 Mirada Road, Half Moon Bay. 650-726-6642.

Pacific Victorian Bed and Breakfast

Only about a block from the ocean, most of the second floor rooms have balconies and views. Full breakfasts are served in the formal dining room and evening wine and hors d'oeuvres are presented in the parlor. Four rooms with private baths. 325 Alameda Ave., Half Moon Bay. 650-712-3900. Fax: 650-712-3905.

Pillar Point Inn
Right in the harbor, 11 rooms overlooking boat basin at 380 Capistrano Road, Princeton. 650-728-7377.

SOUTH COAST
B & B at Año Nuevo
This is the ultimate hideaway, a modified log home offering one cozy guest room among the pines overlooking Año Nuevo. A separate entrance ensures privacy and the stone fireplace, country furniture, and magnificent views ensure comfort. A continental breakfast is included. The secluded property offers miles of hiking trails and picnic possibilities. Located across from Año Nuevo State Reserve off Highway One. 650-879-1252. E-mail: 104434.2262@compuserve.com.

Pescadero Creekside Barn
One cozy loft room for two people at the Pescadero Creekside Barn. Featured is a claw-foot tub, brass bed and gas fireplace. Two night minimum weekends. 248 Stage Road, Pescadero. 650-879-0868. E-mail: 103406.2326@compuserve.com.

THE USUAL CREATURE COMFORTS & MORE – HOTELS & MOTELS

HALF MOON BAY
Half Moon Bay Lodge
The Half Moon Bay Lodge overlooks a championship golf course with distant ocean views. Most of the 80 rooms have fireplaces and views. Continental breakfast is included. Has a full service meeting facility as well as concierge service, glass enclosed whirlpool spas, heated swimming pool, and fitness center. Wheelchair accessible. 2400 S. Highway One, Half Moon Bay. 650-726-9000 or (800) 368-2468. Fax: 650-726-7951. Website: www.woodsidehotels.com.

Holiday Inn Express
The 52 rooms are comfortably decorated and include continental breakfast; some are wheelchair accessible. 230 Highway One,

Half Moon Bay. 650-726-3400. Fax: 650-726-1256.

Miramar Lodge & Conference Center

Has 53 rooms with in-room fridges and microwaves, data ports, two 1,000 square feet conference rooms, complimentary breakfast. Summer rates/ winter rates. Located 2 miles from town at 2390 N. Highway One, Half Moon Bay. 650-712-1092.

Ramada Limited

This is a 27-unit Spanish-style motel near beaches and two miles to town. Continental breakfast. Wheelchair accessible rooms available. 3020 Highway One, Half Moon Bay. 650-726-9700 or (800) 350-9888. Fax: 650-726-5269. Website: www.ramada.com.

Ritz Carlton/Half Moon Bay

A golfer's dream situated at the edge of the Pacific Ocean and between two championship golf courses. Has 261 rooms and suites – 65 first and second floor rooms have patios and 75 guest rooms and suites have fireplaces – all with matchless maritime and mountain views. The posh amenities – marble baths, plush robes, Egyptian cotton sheets and feather beds – make a stay here a true pamper time. There is a fitness center equipped with all the modern workout gear, a 16,000 square foot spa with massage rooms, hydrotherapy room, facial rooms and more. Child-care services are also offered. Direct paths give access to the beach. Gourmet dining is available at gourmet prices in three restaurants plus a special private dining room for intimate dinners. One Miramontes Point Road, Half Moon Bay. 9800) 241-3333 for room reservations; 650-712-7050 for dinner reservations.

MID-COAST:

Beach House Inn & Conference Center

On the bluffs overlooking Pillar Point Harbor, the 54 suites include all the other luxuries associated with world-class accommodations. A swimming pool, hot tub and patio are screened off for privacy. All suites have private patios or balconies, most have ocean views, the best on the bay; continental breakfast is included. Four completely equipped meeting rooms are available. Wheelchair-accessible rooms available. 4100 N. Highway One, Half Moon Bay. 650-712-0220 or (800) 315-9366. Fax: 650-712-0693. Website: www.beach-house.com.

Harborview Inn
This 17 unit motel is within easy walking distance of Pillar Point Harbor. Each room is cheerfully decorated and has a bay window overlooking the harbor and ocean. Continental breakfast included. 11 Avenue Alhambra, El Granada. 650-726-2329.

Pillar Point Inn
This is a two-story coastal inn overlooking the Pillar Point's busy harbor and the ocean. Each of the 11 rooms has a fireplace, private bathroom (some even have steam baths), a European-style feather bed, and a bay window. Complimentary breakfasts and afternoon beverages; wheelchair accessible rooms available. 380 Capistrano Dr., Princeton-by-the-Sea. 650-728-7377 or 800-400-8281. Fax: 650-728-8345.

Seal Cove Inn
This lavish country inn is situated near the Fitzgerald Marine Reserve in Moss Beach. All 10 of the rooms have private fireplaces and baths; two suites have whirlpool tubs. A meeting room that includes audio visual equipment is available for up to 15 participants. 221 Cypress Ave., Moss Beach. 650-728-4114. Fax: 650-728-4116. Website: www.sealcoveinn.com.

SOUTH COAST
Costanoa at Cascade Ranch
They have a rustic lodge with 40 guest rooms plus 12 private cabins all with private fireplaces and room service. Also, there are spots for campers to pitch their own tents and for RV's, conference facilities, complete spa services, bike rentals, and a gourmet deli. This is all set on 480 acres next to the proposed Cascade Ranch State Park and across Highway One from the Point Año Nuevo Reserve. (800) 738-7477.

Estancia del Mar
Ocean-view cottages on a hill above Pigeon Point with vistas all the way to Point Año Nuevo, available by the day, week or month. 650-879-1500. Web site: http://www.a1vacations.com/edm/1/

The Lodge at Skylonda
Located deep in the redwood forests are 16 guestrooms featuring a deck or patio, soaking tubs and, of course, terry robes. Services include Swedish massage, aquatic exercises in the indoor pool, tai-chi or yoga instructions. Gourmet meals and appetizers are

served next to the massive stone fireplace. No TV's. Telephones only by request. 16350 Skyline Blvd.,Woodside. 650-851-6625 or (800) 851-2222. Fax: 650-851-5504.

PACIFICA
Best Western Lighthouse
Located at Rockaway Beach, this is a multi-storied, modern hotel with over 90 guest rooms and suites and meeting facilities. Many rooms have ocean views; some have fireplaces. The facilities also include a pool, Jacuzzi, sauna, and gym. 105 Rockaway Beach Blvd., Pacifica. 650-355-6300 or (800) 832-4777. Fax: 650-355-9217. E-mail: Ihthse@aol.com.
Days Inn
One-half block from the beach, this motor inn with a Victorian facade has 41 rooms, several with ocean views. Adjacent to several restaurants. 200 Rockaway Beach Blvd., Pacifica. 650-359-7700.

PLANNING A LONGER STAY?
Plum Tree Court
Try your own private cottage set next to a charming courtyard and private patio by the week or by the month. Choose from 6 one-bedroom cottages. Decorative tile, wood burning stoves, and overstuffed leather living room furniture right around the corner from everything. Add to this a well-stocked kitchen and your own laundry room, dishwasher, TV and VCR. Located downtown at 642 Johnston St., Half Moon Bay. 650-712-0104.

HOSTELS
MID-COAST
Montara Lighthouse Hostel
Sitting on the cliff overlooking the ocean, the hostel can accommodate 49 people and features a hot tub, bike rentals, two kitchens, and beach access. Maximum stay is three nights. Guests are expected to do chores in the morning before departure. Gates are open from 7:30 a.m. to 9:30 a.m. and 4:30 p.m. to 9:30 p.m. daily. Highway One at 16th Street, Montara. 650-728-7177. Website: www.norcalhostels.org.

SOUTH COAST
Pigeon Point Lighthouse Hostel
This 40 bed hostel has a kitchen for the culinarily inclined. Maximum stay is three nights. Reservations are recommended at least one week in advance. Call 650-879-0633 during desk hours, 7:30 a.m. to 9:30 a.m. and 4:30 p.m. to 9:30 p.m. daily. Located seven miles south of Pescadero, off Highway 1, on Pigeon Point Road. Website: www.norcalhostels.org. Inexp.

RV PARKS
HALF MOON BAY
Pelican Point RV Park
Adjacent to a championship 18-hole golf course and cliffs overlooking the ocean. Facilities include 75 full hook-up sites, cable TV, laundry room, LP gas, picnic tables, store, and disposal station. Tent camping is also permitted. 1001 Miramontes Point Road, Half Moon Bay. 650-726-9100.

MID-COAST
Pillar Point RV Park
Wedged between Highway One and Pillar Point Harbor, the park has plenty of picnic tables and barbecue pits, upgraded wheelchair accessible restrooms, and landscaping. Campers look over a sandy beach. No reservations; fees. Located at the breakwater, adjacent to Surfers' Beach at 4100 Highway One, El Granada. 650-712-9277.

PACIFICA
Pacific Park RV Resort
Located on the cliffs above the ocean, this fully equipped, modern park offers hookups for 216 RV's, heated swimming pool, arcade, LP gas, and RV supplies on the premises. There is easy access to bus service and BART, and it is near restaurants and car rentals. 700 Palmetto Ave., Pacifica. 650-355-7093. In State: 800- -992-0554. Out of State: (800) 822-1250. Fax: 650-355-7102. Website: www.miramarhotels.com/pacificpark.

CAMPING
HALF MOON BAY
Francis Beach
This state beach campground has 58 tent and RV camp sites, wheel chair accessible restrooms, weekly campfire programs, and picnic tables. No RV hookups are available; cold outdoor showers. Parking fee. Dogs on a leash are allowed. No reservations, first come, first served; for information call 650-726-8820 or (800) 4447275. West from Highway One on Kelly Avenue. Website: www.park-net.com.

Pelican Point RV Park
Tent camping. Laundry room, LP gas, picnic tables, store, and disposal station. 1001 Miramontes Point Road. 650-726-9100.

Sweetwood Group Camp
This state beach is exclusively for group rentals and can accommodate up to 50 people for tent camping or day use. The gated beach area offers stretches of sandy beach, hidden from Highway One by a grove of trees. On Highway One north of Half Moon Bay, across from Frenchmen's Creek housing development. Reservations: (800) 444-7275.

SOUTH COAST
Butano State Park
This park has 40 camp sites with tables and stoves and space for fishing, hiking, picnicking, guided nature walks, and weekend campfire programs during the summer. No showers and no RV hookups. RV's limited to 24 feet for travel trailers and 27 feet for motor homes. For reservations call 650-879-2040 or (800) 4447275. Seven miles south of Pescadero on Cloverdale Road. For additional information on the park, see Page 71.

Costanoa at Cascade Ranch
This is a combination upscale campground with 88 deluxe tent cabins equipped with down comforters for those not into roughing it, and 47 standard tent cabins, and a rustic lodge with 40 guest rooms and 12 private cabins all with private fireplaces and room service. This is all set on 480 acres next to the proposed Cascade Ranch State Park and across Highway One from the Point Año

Choose between pitching your own tent in foreground
or snuggling under a down comforter in a fancier tent shown
in back at Costanoan at Cascade Ranch.

Nuevo Reserve. Also, there are spots for campers to pitch their own tents and for RV's, conference facilities, complete spa services, bike rentals, and a gourmet deli. (800) 738-7477.

Portola Redwoods State Park

There are 52 camp sites and three hike-in group-camping areas. The park has hot showers but no RV hookups. Weekend reservations recommended. Go east on Highway 84 (La Honda Road). Take Pescadero Road to Alpine Road. Turn on Portola State Park Road. 650-948-9098 or (800) 444-7275. Website: www.park-net.com.

Sam McDonald Park

This county park offers camping for youth groups and campers with horses only. A hikers' hut, for up to 14 people, is run by the Sierra Club and can be rented by the night. Located about 1 3/4 miles from Sam McDonald Park parking lot. For reservations call 650-494-9901.

San Mateo County Memorial Park

The county's oldest public park, this campground has over 100 camp sites for families; it also offers picnic spots, visitors center, camp store, a creek swmming area, campfire programs, group areas and trails. First come, first served for families; reservations required for all youth groups. Eleven miles east of Pescadero on Pescadero Road or two miles east of La Honda Road. 650-879-0210. For more information on the park, see Page 94.

PART XII
ASSISTANCE, PRACTICAL
&
RELIGIOUS

EMERGENCY

Police, Fire or Ambulance	
Emergency Only	**911**
California Highway Patrol	
Road Conditions	**800-427-7623**
Non-Emergency	**707-551-4100**
Half Moon Bay Police	
Non-Emergency	**650-726-8288**
Half Moon Bay Fire	
Non-Emergency	**650-726-5213**
Pacifica Police	
Non-Emergency	**650-738-7314**
Pacifica Fire	
Non-Emergency	**650-738-7362**
San Mateo County Sheriff	
Non-Emergency	**650-573-2801**
Poison Control	**800-876-4766 or**
	800-972-3323
Seton Medical Center Coastside	
Emergency Room	**650-563-7107**
Peninsula Humane Society	**650-340-8200**
State Fish & Game Department	**650-688-6340**

BANKS

Bank of America

620 Main St., HMB	650-726-4475
1375 Linda Mar Center, Pacifica	650- 615-4700

First National Bank of Northern California

756 Main St., HMB	800-380-9515
210 Eureka St., Pacifica	800-380-9515
1450 Linda Mar Center, Pacifica	800-380-9515

239 Stage Rd., Pescadero   800-380-9515

Wells Fargo

132 San Mateo Road, HMB   650-726-6392

1380 Linda Mar Center, Pacifica   650-738-3725

FARM BUREAU

San Mateo County Farm Bureau

765 Main St., HMB   650-726-4485

LIBRARIES

Bookmobile   650-726-3216

Half Moon Bay Branch

620 Correas Ave.   650-726-3216

Pacifica Branch

104 Hilton Way   650-355-5196

Sanchez Branch

1111 Terra Nova Blvd., Pacifica   650-359-3397

NEWSPAPERS

Half Moon Bay Review & Pescadero Pebble

714 Kelly Ave., HMB   650-726-4424

Pacifica Tribune

59 Aura Vista, Pacifica   650-359-6666

TAXIS & LIMOS

California Pacific Limousine 650-726-2664 or 738-5668

Pacifica/HMB Cab Co.   650-712-9300

TOWING

Action Towing, Moss Beach   650-726-0428

Curly & Reds, HMB   650-726-4949

Hacks, Pacifica   650-359-1941

CHURCHES

ASSEMBLIES OF GOD

Coastside Christian Assembly   650-369-8708

225 S. Highway One, HMB

BAPTIST

Coastside Baptist Church   650-726-2013

Highway One and Seymour, HMB

Iglesia Bautista en Pacifica   650-359-1996

2070 Francisco Blvd., Pacifica

Pacifica Baptist Church   650-355-2513

2070 Francisco Blvd., Pacifica

Sea View Baptist Church   650-355-3443

1450 Perez Dr., Pacifica

BAPTIST, AMERICAN
Vista Del Mar Baptist Church   650-355-6404
    1125 Terra Nova Blvd., Pacifica

BAPTIST, CONSERVATIVE
Mariners Community Church   650-726-5959
    535 Kelly Ave., HMB

BAPTIST, INDEPENDENT FUNDAMENTAL
Westside Baptist Church   650-355-0522
    390 Inverness, Pacifica

BAPTIST, SOUTHERN
Bethany Baptist Church   650-355-3244
    1443 Adobe Dr., Pacifica

BUDDHIST
Rissho Kosei-Kai Buddhist Church   650-359-6951
    1031 Valencia Way, Pacifica

ROMAN CATHOLIC
Good Shepard Catholic Church   650-355-2593
    901 Oceana Blvd., Pacifica
Our Lady of Refuge   650-747-9555
    146 Sears Ranch Road, La Honda
Our Lady of the Pillar Church   650-726-4674
    540 Kelly Ave., HMB
St. Anthony's Mission   650-879-1831
    703 North St., Pescadero
St. Peter Catholic Church   650-359-6313
    700 Oddstad Blvd., Pacifica

CHARISMATIC
Lighthouse Christian Fellowship of Pacifica 650-355-7605

CHRISTIAN
CGCF Church   650-359-1942
    1295 Seville, Pacifica

CHRISTIAN SCIENCE
First Church of Christ Science Church   650-355-2444
    2218 Francisco Blvd., Pacifica
Reading Room   650-355-2444
    90 W. Manor Dr., Pacifica

CHURCH OF JESUS CHRIST OF LATTER DAY SAINTS
Half Moon Bay Building   650-728-9923
    475 California Ave., HMB.

Pacifica Building   650-355-9844
       730 Sharp Park Dr., Pacifica.

COMMUNITY

Half Moon Bay Community United Methodist 650-726-4621
       777 Miramontes, HMB

Mariners Community Church   650-726-5959
       535 Kelly Ave., HMB

Pacifica Community Church   650-359-3314
       1165 Seville Dr., Pacifica

Pescadero Community Church   650-879-0408
       363 Stage Road, Pescadero

EPISCOPAL

Holy Family Episcopal Church   650-726-0506
       1590 S. Highway One, HMB

St. Edmonds Episcopal Church   650-3593364
       1500 Perez Dr., Pacifica

INDEPERNDENT FUNDAMENTAL

Church in the Redwoods   650-747-0797
       8910 La Honda Road, La Honda

JEHOVAH'S WITNESSES

Half Moon Bay Congregation   650-726-6129
       611 Magnolia, Half Moon Bay

Pacifica Congregation   650-359-5494
       500 Ebken, Pacifica

LUTHERAN

Coastside Lutheran   650-726-9293
       900 N. Highway One, Half Moon Bay

Holy Cross Evangelical Lutheran Church   650-359-2710
       1165 Seville Dr., Pacifica

PRESBYTERIAN (USA)

St. Andrew Presbyterian Church   650-359-2462
       1125 Terra Nova Blvd., Pacifica

SEVENTH DAY ADVENTIST

Filipino Seventh Day Adventist Church   650-355-8864
       533 Hickey Blvd., Pacifica

Pacifica Seventh Day Adventist Church   650-355-9724

UNITED METHODIST

HMB Community United Methodist Church   650-726-4621
       777 Miramontes, HMB

Without Whom.....
our San Mateo Coast would be a different world.

The principal reason we enjoy a coastline that has no rival is because of committed and dedicated people who keep working to preserve the coast for future generations.

The assault on the coast started after the turn of the century with an attempt to run a railroad from San Francisco to Santa Cruz to open the coast to new developments and cities. The attempt failed economically, and it was not until after World War II that the coast was re-discovered by those from over the hill. In the late 1960's, as developers moved in, citizen groups were formed to bring some protection to the coast. In the early 1970's, people like **Janet Adams** and **Claire Dedrick** led the successful intiative to "Save Our Shores." Peninsula resident **Mel Lane** and others pushed the State Legislature to adopt the Coastal Act of 1976. The 1980's saw a challenge to many local plans and San Mateo County Supervisor **Fred Lyon** moved quickly to make San Mateo the first county in the state to comply with the Coastal Act.

In 1986, seeing the need for further protection, people from the **Save Our Shores** organization rallied to put Measure A on the ballot. It was the San Mateo Coastal Protection Initiative, the first citizens' initiative to qualify for a San Mateo County ballot. And it passed with 64 per cent of the vote. The initiative put coastal protection squarely in the hands of the citizens of San Mateo County.

In 1994 developers attempted to exempt a large area around Half Moon Bay from the coastal protection intitiative, but failed by an overwhelming 82 per cent majority vote against it.

One of the great environmental battles of the coast involved the attempt by the state's CalTrans to build a freeway bypass around Devil's Slide. People such as **Ollie Mayer** and **Lennie Roberts** perservered over 30 years to defeat the bypass that would have destroyed the unique open space of Montara Mountain and McNee State Park. Legal challenges in 1971 and again in 1984 were used. The **Sierra Club, Committee for Green Foothills, Save Our Shores, Committee for the Permanent Repair of Highway One,** and **Dana Deman** of Shamrock Ranch in Pacifica played key roles in blocking the bypass.

A safe, environmentally superior solution to the Devil's Slide dilemma was achieved in 1996 with the 74 per cent positive vote for Measure T, the Tunnel Initiative.

Playing critical preservation roles were enlightened public officials such as **Arlen Gregorio, Jackie Speier, Anna Eshoo, Rich Gordon**, and **Byron Sher**.

The story of the San Mateo Coast would not be complete without acknowledging the thousands of private citizens and landowners who have made gifts to land trusts and land-saving organizations. The **Peninsula Open Space Trust** has preserved some 30,000 acres of coastal land to ensure the future of working farms, protect coastal resources and provide public access. The Trust's work received generous grants from both the **David and Lucile Packard Foundation** and the **Gordon and Betty Moore Foundation** to help finance the acquisitions. The **Sempervirens Fund** has had a 100-year tradition of preserving watersheds and their redwood forests.

The Coastside long has been a battleground for conflicting interests – those who have wanted to preserve the area in its most natural state vs. those who saw it as a region to exploit. The dynamic tension of these opposing views has made the Coastside a place that is still inviting, and still at risk for being too inviting.

This book is dedicated to all those people who have worked to make the Coastside what it is today, and without whom this special place would be quite different:

Janet Adams and **Claire Dedrick**, the earliest leaders of the move to preserve the Coastside's natural beauty from over-development, whose interest in saving the beaches led to the landmark state initiative, Proposition 20.

Mel Lane, the Sunset Magazine magnate and environmentalist who led an effort that resulted in the approval in 1976 of the Coastal Protection Act.

Fred Lyon, the San Mateo County Supervisor who sponsored the San Mateo County Local Coastal Program, which made the county the first to enact the local laws in compliance with the Coastal Act.

Lennie Roberts, an environmentalist as towering as any coastal redwood, whose tireless work and unfailing vigilance have been central to a dozen major fights and hundreds of minor skirmishes over open space and Coastside development, including the San Mateo County Coastal Protection Initiative of 1986 and the battle over the Devil's Slide tunnel a decade later.

Kit Dove, another Coastside environmentalist who has played a key role in such issues as the Coastal Protection Initiative and the Devil's Slide Tunnel.

Bob Girard, Michael Kay, Dave Bomberger, Hertha Herrington and the rest of the 1986 Coastal Initiative coalition.

Chris Thollaug, April Vargas, Chuck Kozak, John Lynch, Mary Hobbs and the other leaders of the Devil's Slide tunnel campaign.

Zoe Kersteen-Tucker, under whose leadership the Committee for Green Foothills has emerged as a major protector of open space land in the coastal region.

David Iverson, founder of the **Half Moon Bay Open Space Trust** and **Half Moon Bay Neighbors Alliance,** a tireless protector of open space.

Arlen Gregorio, the former State Senator and County Supervisor, who championed Coastside protections and blocked development of a freeway connection to Montara.

Jackie Speier, who, first as a member of the county board of supervisors and then in the State Assembly and State Senate, worked diligently to pass laws preserving open space.

Anna Eshoo, a loyal friend of the Coastside, pushed for strong environmental protections both as a County Supervisor and as a member of the U.S. Congress.

Byron Sher, known as the environmental conscience of the State Senate, worked hard in Sacramento and earlier as a member of the Palo Alto Council to preserve the Coastside.

Mary Henderson, who began her own crusading environmental efforts on the San Mateo County Coastside and became one of the earliest appointees to the state Coastal Commission.

Ted Lempert spent years as a county supervisor and as a member of the State Assembly backing protection for the Coastside.

Audrey Rust and the **Peninsula Open Space Trust,** which have placed thousands of acres of Coastside lands in preserves for future generations.

Tony Look, Veri Clausen, Brian Steen and the **Sempervirens Fund,** which has upheld a century-long tradition of preserving and restoring the Coastside forests and watersheds.

Dolores Mullin, the political godmother of Half Moon Bay and the Coastside for more than half a century, two-term member of the Half Moon Bay City Council, cofounder and chair of the Half Moon Bay Art & Pumpkin Festival and chair of the Half Moon Bay Beautification Committee.

Brian and Kristin McNamara, fixtures on the Coastside for more than 30 years with Brian instrumental in making the Pumpkin Festival an annual success.

Bob Lacey, promoter, entertainment director of the Half Moon Bay Art & Pumpkin Festival, who has kept the Coastside alive with the sound of music and laughter.

Terry Pimsleur, public relations innovator and cofounder of the Half Moon Bay Art & Pumpkin Festival and the Pacifica Fog Festival.

Hal Cameron, owner of Cameron's Inn, a bed and breakfast, a tavern and a community gathering place, site of many a political event who has played a key role in the annual Pumpkin Festival.

Jim Fox, San Mateo County District Attorney, a Half Moon Bay native son and Coastside lover, who served as city attorney for Half Moon Bay for almost pro bono wages.

Quentin Kopp, now a San Mateo County Superior Court Judge who as a former State Senator helped preserve the Coastside.

Joe Simitian, Assembly member and former Palo Alto mayor and long-time Coastside preservationist, who has worked tirelessly for protection of the Coast.

Grace McCarthy, three-time mayor of Pacifica, county planning commissioner, member of the state Coastal Commission and a towering civic leader.

Jean Fassler, the first mayor of Pacifica and a member of the County Board of Supervisors.

Jeri Eaton Flinn, Clark Natwick, June Langhoff and all the **Pacifica Environmental Family** who work tirelessly as unpaid volunteers restoring and maintaining beaches, and providing schools with speakers and demonstrations of Coastside environmental issues.

Honora Sharp, whose handwritten will led to the creation of Sharp Park in Pacifica.

Penny Keating, founder of the **Beach Coalition** in Pacifica, who with her surfer husband, **Dick**, have enhanced the Coastside for years.

Ray Higgins, who in 1946 purchased the Sanchez Adobe and then sold it to San Mateo County a year later for use as a historical museum.

Nick Gust, motel owner, restaurateur and Pacifica political godfather, who dominated the town's civic and economic affairs for decades.

Bill Drake, longtime editor of the Pacifica Tribune and the voice of that community.

George Dunn, the founding editor and publisher of the Half Moon Bay Review and Pescadero Pebble.

George Bauer, who ran the newspaper for more than 30 years with distinction and personality.

Debra Godshall, the current publisher of the Review carrying on the tradition of community journalism.

Alvin Hatch, a county supervisor for more than three decades and namesake of Hatch's Wood; he last ran for board in 1960 at age 86, and was a leading voice for decades for coastal protection.

Roy W. Cloud, county superintendent of schools and historian whose efforts saved the Memorial Park redwoods in 1923, the county's first public open space, and set the pattern for future acquisitions.

John L. "Nick" Carter, Half Moon Bay's first mayor, and all the other mayors including **Deborah Ruddock** and **Toni Taylor**.

Ellis Benson, longtime principal of Half Moon Bay High School.

Henry Doelger, whose proposal to duplicate his Daly City "ticky tacky" houses on the Coastside sparked the uprising that created the area's environmental movement and antidevelopment leadership.

Mel Mello, for decades the county's Coastside agricultural inspector, Half Moon Bay City Councilman, Mayor, community leader and namesake for the community theater .

Mike McCracken, attorney and longtime defender of the rights of property owners, and yet a tireless advocate of sensible preservation of natural resources.

Don Borley, at one time the only physician on the coast and who delivered at least half the babies in the Half Moon Bay area.

Mark Smith and **Joe Gore**, owners of the 3-Zero Café at Half Moon Bay Airport, a favorite user-friendly breakfast and community gathering place.

Bob Senz, owner of the Ocean Shore Hardware Store in Half Moon Bay, where you can buy nearly anything you want in life, founder of the Pacific Coast Dream Machines annual auto show and charity fund-raiser and perhaps the town's leading philanthropist, involved in virtually every community fund-raising effort in the last 20 years.

Naomi Patridge, a catalytic figure in the development of programs and facilities for the Coastside youth and youth sports.

Jeff Clark, owner of one of the Coastside's better surf shops, said to be the first to surf Mavericks, the now-legendary big-wave break that has gained fame around the world, and namesake and director of Clark's Quiksilver/Mavericks Men Who Ride Mountain big-wave surfing contest.

Susan Alvaro, a member of the County Board of Education and coordinator of the Coastside Collaborative for Children, Youth and Families.

Steve and Ilva Evan, owners of Half Moon Bay diner Original Johnny's, (she bakes the pies herself from a recipe she got from her mother-in-law **Fiorina Evan**).

Phyllis Standaert, the face and voice of the Half Moon Bay Review from her post at the newspaper's front counter.

Elizabeth McCaughey, who wakes up the Coastside with her M.Coffee espresso bar and café in downtown Half Moon Bay.

The Duarte Family, for four generations serving artichoke soup and ollaieberry pie to hungry travelers in Pescadero.

Ted Bregy, who taught at Half Moon Bay High School and coached volleyball, basketball and swimming for 25 years.

Ted Adcock, founder of the Half Moon Bay community/senior center that bears his name and for two decades a member of the board of directors of the Coastside Adult Day Health Center. Adcock was also a major force behind the Senior Coastsiders now under the dedicated direction of **Cara Schmaljohn**,

Clara Fluharty, considered the mother of Pescadero and leader of the Pescadero Community Church Ladies Guild.

Robert McMahon, Pillar Point Harbormaster for 17 years, and his successor **Dan Temko**.

Sue Prichard, whose desire to brighten up a downtown Half Moon Bay plaza with bits of tile became a community project and an artful source of pride.

The Dutras and **the Millers** – **The Dutra family** opened the Coastside's first and only funeral home and became community leaders. **The Miller family** took over the business, merged the family names and continued the tradition of caring for the community at its time of need and caring for the community's needs.

John Barbour, who has restored the Moss Beach Distillery to its mysterious splendor, reviving the legend of the ghostly "Blue Lady" to this Prohibition-era landmark.

Mike Ferreira, Portuguese community leader, planning commissioner and council member who operates the popular Joe's On The Coast on Highway One.

The Cunha Family, grocers to the community for three generations, led in the latter day by **Bev Cunha Ashcroft**, another of Half Moon Bay's community godmothers.

Pete Douglas, who started the Bach Dynamite & Dancing Society in the 1950s and nearly a half-century later is still bringing an eclectic mix of jazz, modern, pop and classical entertainment to the Coastside.

The Muzzi Family, multi-generational mainstay farmers of Pescadero, part of whom are owners one of the town's grocery stores.

Paul Shenkman, cofounder of the restaurant Pasta Moon, who opened Cetrella in the old Half Moon Bay Growers' Association building in Half Moon Bay and brought new attention to quality dining on the Coastside.

Mark Jamplis, who breathed new life into the Miramar Beach Restaurant, a century-old Coastside establishment and one-time Prohibition speakeasy.

Carl Hoffman, owner, and **Lisa O'Neill**, manager and fixture at the Half Moon Bay Feed & Fuel, keeping alive 100 years of Coastside ranching traditions.

James V. Fitzgerald, longtime county supervisor, who fought for decades to preserve the tide pools at Moss Beach, and was rewarded by having his name put on the county reserve.

Bob Breen, the top ranger at Fitzgerald Marine Reserve, who with Ranger **Steve Durkin**, has taught generations about caretaking the marine pools of the Coastside.

The **Friends of the Fitzgerald Marine Reserve** and its members, directors and advisers.

Bill Barrett, developer of the Ocean Colony subdivision and golf course, who bought the land from Westinghouse and built the Coastside's first golf community. **Pat Fitzgerald,** who has run the golf course since it opened. And **Moon Mullins**, who has been the golf pro at the course for years.

Barbara Walsh, who has been feeding seafood and signature tempura to hungry Coastsiders and tourists the world over for more than three decades at Barbara's Fishtrap at Princeton-By-The-Sea, (formerly Hazel's) and whose daughter **Melody** is working toward a second generation of ownership.

The Pastorino, Repetto, Lemos, Bundgard, Cozzolino, Andretti, Silva, Figone families who have continued to make agriculture and floriculture San Mateo County's dominant industry, and provided a place for visitors to enjoy.

Jack Olsen and **Jack Pearlstine** and the other generations of leadership from the San Mateo County Farm Bureau and the Half Moon Bay Growers Association.

Hank Sciaroni, who served Coastside farmers as regional agent for the University of California Agricultural Extension Service for nearly 40 years before his retirement in 1986, and a decorated World War II hero.

The Giorgetti Family, whose generations have been community leaders from the earliest days of Half Moon Bay.

Charlie Nye, former owner of Nye's Reef, one of the Coastside's landmark restaurants and an early place to hide.

Herr Wagner, who first conceived of Montara as a colony for artists, setting in motion a tradition that remains true today.

J.F. Weinke, who named Moss Beach for the moss-covered cliffs of his 19th century hotel.

D.H. Burnham, who laid out the meandering streets of Granada, before it was called El Granada, a mistake in Spanish grammar brought about by the U.S. Post Office.

The Ocean Shore Railroad and its growth-minded executives, who failed to make a financial go of a Coastside rail line, but opened the way for many people to see and admire the Coastside.

The Debenedetti family, pioneers who came to the area from Italy at the turn of the 19th century and stayed to erect some of the early buildings downtown, including the historic Debenedetti Building at the corner of Main and Mill streets in 1903.

The Boitano Family, early arrivals from Italy, who also made major contributions to the growth of the community.

The Anderson family of Pacifica, which operated Anderson's store for the first 80 years of the 20th century and whose descendants still own the building that now houses **Deidre and Eric Edstrom's** Chez D Café.

Andres Oddstad, the developer who built the first subdivisions in what became Linda Mar in Pacifica.

Frank Brophy, the developer who named Princeton-By-The-Sea for his dog, Prince.

Chris Mickelsen, whose Harbor House Bed & Breakfast at Princeton helped initiate the Coastside as a weekend tourism destination for the Bay Area.

Mark Church, Rose Jacobs Gibson, Richard S. Gordon, Jerry Hill and **Michael D. Nevin,** San Mateo County Supervisors and all the past supervisors committed to keeping the Coastside beautiful.

Tom Lantos, first elected to the House of Representatuives in 1980, a loyal protector of the 12th District coast stretching from San Francisco to Moss Beach and fighter for funding the Devil's Slide tunnel.

The Romeo family, which has owned Romeo Pier for generations and worked to keep the harbor as a center for area fishermen.

The Furtado and **the Bruno families** and all the other fish buyers, who keep Pillar Point alive as a place for fresh seafood.

The Bettencourt family, Don and Jerry Pemberton and skipper Steve Caruso of the Melissa and all the generations of fishermen who have made their living from the sea.

Kristen and Stephanie Raugust, whose Whale City Bakery, Bar &

Grill provide Davenport with top-notch, hearty cuisine in a small town ambience.

Sandy and Paul Obester, who pioneered the Coastside as a place for wineries.

This Side of the Hill Players, bringing quality community theater to the Coastside through generations of performers who have trod the boards.

The countless Audubon Society members who volunteer their time to look after the Pescadero Marsh and all the Coastside feathered friends, both local and migratory.

John Hernandez and all the other volunteers who worked so diligently to establish and maintain the Coastal Trail and its unique greenbelt in Half Moon Bay.

Keet Nerhan, who has used his KN Properties to improve the Coastside.

Ken Paul Lozada, the Half Moon Bay artist whose mystical tree sculptures explore the inner lives of wood and ourselves.

Sharon Scott, the San Benito House's "Best on the Coast" for serving spirits.

Bill Webbe, Half Moon Bay contractor whose work includes the Giorgetti Building on Main Street.

Eric Jacobsen, former fixture on the Half Moon Bay Architectural Review Committee whose building designs grace the Coastside.

The dozens of Half Moon Bay city council members, county planning commissioners, harbor commissioners, water board and sewer board members and the members of the community advisory boards that have argued, fought, agreed, and disagreed over development, growth and the protection of natural resources.

The Coastside is a place of unrivaled beauty, and it is a community. All that the Coastside has become and all that it has remained is due to the community of people – some like-minded, some who enjoyed the ebb and flow of political and civic battles – that settled and populated the Coastside for more than a century.

The greatness of the Coastside with all its beauties and all that its people have accomplished guarantees that we have left out important and key players in preserving this region. Their omission is not a reflection of anything other than the authors' discovery that the Coastside is a place teeming with leaders and dedicated people too numerous to count, and the limitations of page space, not on their accomplishments, influence, stewardship and citizenship.

The Coastside would not be in its present unique state without the people and organizations mentioned here. Future generations will look back and salute them as "The Greatest Generation" in keeping our shoreline open for all people to enjoy

Bibliography
Books

Bell, Major Horace, *On The Old West Coast,* NY, 1930, William Morrow & Co.

Bright, William, *1500 California Place Names, Their Origin and Meaning,* Berkeley, CA, 1998, Univ. of California Press

Carner-Ribalta, J, *Gaspar de Portolá, Explorer of California,* San Diego, CA,1990, Tecolote Publications

Cleland, Robert Glass, *The Cattle on a Thousand Hills,* San Marino, CA, 1990, Huntington Library

Cloud, Roy W., *History of San Mateo County,* Chicago, IL,1928

Conant, Edward, *Memories of Gazos Creek & Pigeon Point,* Modesto, CA,1998, Glenhaven Press

Costanso, Miguel, *The Discovery of San Francisco Bay, The Diary of Miguel Costanso,* Lafayette, CA, 1992, Great West Books

De Lapp, Karen, *Trailside Plants of Año Nuevo,* Pescadero, CA, 1986, Año Nuevo Interpretive Assn.

Gualtieri, Kathryn, *Half Moon Bay, the Birth of A Coastside Town,* Half Moon Bay, CA, 1988, Historical Society

Hynding, Alan, *From Frontier to Suburb,* Belmont, CA,1982, Star Publications

James, George Wharton, *In and Out of the Old Missions of California,* Boston, MA, 1916, Little Brown & Co.

Lyons, Kathleen and Mary Beth Cuneo Lazano, *Plants of the Coast Redwood Region,* Boulder Creek, CA, 1988, Looking Glass Press

McConnaughey, Bayard and Evelyn McConnaughey. *Pacific Coast, A National Audubon Society Nature Guide,* NY, NY, 1998, Knopf

Moore & DePue, *Illustrated History of San Mateo County in 1878,* San Francisco, CA

Pitt, Leonard, *The Decline of the Californios, A Social History of the Spanish-Speaking Californians, 1846-1890,* Berkeley, CA, 1998, Univ. of California Press

Robinson, W.W., *Land in California,* Berkeley, CA, 1979, Univ. of California Press

Rosenus, Alan, *General Vallejo and the Advent of the Americans,* Berkeley, CA, 1999, Heyday Books/Orion Press

Stanger, Frank M., *Sawmills in the Redwoods, Logging on the San Francisco Peninsula, 1849-1967*, San Mateo, CA, 1967, San Mateo County Historical Assn,

Stanger, Frank M., *South from San Francisco*, San Mateo, CA, 1963, San Mateo County Historical Assn.

Walker, Clifford James, *One Eye Closed, The California Bootlegging Years*, Barstow, CA, 1999, Back Door Pub.

Wolfe, Tom, *The Electric Kool-Aid Acid Test*, NY, NY, 1969, Bantam

Newspapers

The Coast Side Comet, 1920-36, varied dates

Half Moon Bay Review, varied dates

The San Mateo County Gazette, varied dates

Acknowledgements

We wish to thank those unsung heroes and heroines, the research librarians at the Half Moon Bay, Burlingame, Redwood City and San Mateo libraries for their unstinting assistance. Likewise, the members of the Spanishtown Historical Society and the San Mateo County Historical Association have been most generous in their help. The Duarte family and Meredith Reynolds helped bring the Pescadero history alive. Credit for the illustrations on pages 32, 33 and 57 are from Moore & DePue's *Illustrated History of San Mateo County in 1878* courtesy of Gilbert Richards. The map of the Miramontes ranch on page 8 is taken from the files of the San Mateo County Recorder. Maps in the Nature Tour section are adapted from originals from the San Mateo County Parks and Recreation Department, the Midpeninsula Regional Open Space District and the California Department of Parks and Recreation; we thank these public servants for their assistance.

Index

A

A Taste of Pacifica 227
Ackerson, John 83
Acknowledgements 264
Acoustical Interiors 174
Agates 153
Agriculture 11, 185
Airport Street 175
Alders 109, 125
Alder Springs Trail 128-129
Alice's Restaurant 46
Allen Rd 88
Alpine Creek 127, 130, 131, 133,
    134, 136, 137
Alpine Pond 137, 139
Alpine Road
    47, 48, 100, 106, 111, 127, 128,
    130, 134, 135, 136 - 139,
    211, 250
Alvarado, Governor Juan Bautista
    181
Alviso, Jose Maria 42, 65
Anderson, James L., 15
Andy Korfal boat restoration 173
Anemones 191
Angel Island 6
Año Nuevo 60
Año Nuevo Beaches 214
Año Nuevo Island 78, 187, 213,
    215
Año Nuevo State Reserve 36, 177-
    187, 213, 214
Año Nuevo Trail 76, 77
Apple Jacks 45, 229
Arcangeli, Sante 157
Arroyo Cañada Verde 56
Arroyo de los Frijoles 78, 215-216
Arroyo de los Pilarcitos, 144
Arroyo en Medio 207

Arroyo Leon Creek 42, 66
Artichoke Golf Classic 3, 225
Artichoke soup 39, 167
Ascension, Fr. Antonio de la 177
ASSISTANCE 259-262
As You Like It 172
Audubon Society 11, 183, 185,
    187, 196, 209, 254
Azalea Flat 100
Azores 2, 39, 49, 160, 224

B

Bach Dancing and Dynamite
    Society 221
Bailey, August, 256
Baja California 185-186, 206
Bald Knob 125-127
Bald Ridge Trail 121, 125-127
Banana slugs 85
Bank of America, 150
Bank of Half Moon Bay, 150
Bank of Italy, 150
BANKS 259-260
Baquiano Trail 21
Barbara's Fish Trap 55, 171, 175
Bartlett V. Weeks House 157
Basketry 74
Bay Area Ridge Trail 24, 68, 123,
    139
Bay laurels 67, 126
Bay trees 107, 123
Beach Boulevard 202
Beach primrose 172
BEACHES & PICNIC SPOTS 203-
    218
Bead lily 74
Bean Creek 118
Bean Hollow Beach 36, 60, 215
Bear Creek Trail, 118
Bear Gulch Road 79, 85, 86, 88
Bear Ridge Trail 109
Bears, Black 9, 15, 16
    Brown 9, 15
    Grizzlies 9, 15, 42

BED & BREAKFASTS 248-251
Ben Ries Campground 71-73, 76
Benedetti, Norm 157
Bergano, Angelo, 150
Bering, Vitus Jonassen 5
Bernardo, Frank, 153
Bernardo, Manuel J., Jr., 153
Bibliography 264-65
Bidwell, Henry 144, 146
Big Basin Redwoods State Park 95
Big Tree 110-111, 115, 132
Big Tree Trail 133
Big Tree Loop Trail 131
BIKING TOURS 53-68
Binoculars 35, 175, 193
Blackbirds, redwing 138
Blacksmith 56, 165
Bloomquist Creek 95
Blue Blossom Trail 86
Boat projects 173
Bobcat tracks 76
Boitano, Angelo, 147, 152
Boitano, Emilo, 147
Bombay Boat & Bike Club 175
Bootlegging 44, 45, 172
Borden, George 126
Borden Hatch Mill 127, 128
Borden Hatch Mill Trail 121, 125-127
Borel Hill 128, 130
Bracken ferns 78
Braddock Weeks House 48
Bravo Road 109
Broadway 173
Brome grass 24
Brook Trail Loop 104-105
Brooks Creek 29
Brooks Falls 27, 28
Brooks Falls Overlook Trail 28
Brussels sprouts 18, 223
Buckeyes 138
Buelna, Antonio 79
Bueno, Jose Gonzales Cabrera 5
Buffalo Valley 47-48
Burleigh H. Murray State Park 42, 66, 188-189
Bushtits 182
Butano Creek 15, 38, 39, 61, 66, 192
Butano Fire Road 75
Butano Ridge 15, 49, 89, 91, 101, 102, 104, 105, 108 - 111, 116, 134
Butano Ridge Trail 109-110
Butano State Park 15, 38, 71-78, 95 140, 216, 248

C

Cabrillo, Juan Rodriguez 5
California box elder 103
California hazel 131
California nutmeg 75
California Parks Department 69, 177-178
California Street, 190
Californios 77, 142, 254
Calle Condado, 153
Calle de Molino 142
Calle Real 142
Camerons Inn 229
Campbell Soup 36
Campgrounds 95, 100, 111, 205
CAMPING 256-258
Camp Pomponio Road 108-109
Canyon Trail 75, 107
Capistrano Road 54, 169, 171
Captain John's 170
Carrier Pigeon 36, 70, 194-196
Carty House, 147
Carty, Martin, 147
Casa Grande 6
Cascade Creek 215
Cascade Creek Trail 215
Cascade Ranch 38, 213
Castiglione, Nat, 150
Castle Rock State Park 92, 135
Castro, Jose Simeon de Nepomuceno 180, 206
Cattle Hill, 21

Ceonothus, warty-leafed 116
Cermeno, Sebastian Rodriguez 5
Cetrella 154
Chamarita Festival 2, 153, 157,
    216
Chamise 78
Chaparral
    27, 29, 30, 64, 75, 76, 82, 84, 97,
    104, 124, 126, 127 136, -139,
    189
Chaparral-peas 137
Charcoal 14
Charlie's Cough Cure, 152
Cheese factory 153
Chili Cookoff 3, 228
Chinese laborers 38
Chinook campsite 133
Chinquapin 75, 119, 126
Chiton, mossy 191
Christmas tree farms 38, 136, 140,
    236
CHURCHES 260-262
Church Street 149, 150
Clarendon Road 209
Clarke, Jeremiah 181
Clothing 2, 14, 40, 45, 58, 70,
    103
Cloud, Roy W. 94
Cloverdale Coastal Ranch 38
Cloverdale Road 38, 48, 70, 249
Coastal Scenic Tour 53
Coastside Adult Health Care Center
    225
Coastside Associates 174
Coastside Comet 52, 172
Coastside Opportunity Center 228
Coburn, Loren 50, 163, 181
Coburn's Folly 50
Coffeeberry 30
Committee for Green Foothills 11
Common snowberry, 118
Cormorants 1
Coronado Street 204
Correas Street 152-153

Costanoan 19
Costanoan at Cascade Ranch
    36, 38, 60, 257
Costansó, Miguel 20, 21, 217
Cougars 9
Cowell Beach 31
Cowell, Henry 65, 208
Cowell Ranch 65, 120, 208
Coya 195
Coyote brush 172, 215
Coyote Ridge 116
Coyote Ridge Loop Trail 116
Crab cioppino 167
Crab, hermit and kelp 191
Creamery 153
Creek Trail 99
Creeping snowberry, 116-117
Crespi Drive 210, 229
Crespi, Father Juan 6 20, 44,
    221, 235
Cuhna, Ben 148, 149, 150
Cuhna, Bev 148
Cuhna Store, 148
Cuhna, William, 148
Cuneo-Lazano, Mary Beth 69-70
Cyclists 46
Cypress, Monterey
    14, 31, 32, 43, 47, 56, 180,
    206

D

Daisies, seaside 214
Dairies 38
Daly City 10
Daniel's Nature Center 138
Danieri, Emmanuelle 147
Dark Gulch 110
De Anza, Juan Buatista 6
De la Ascension, Father Antonio
    169
De Martini, Louis 149
Debenedetti Building 146, 147
Debenedetti, Joseph 147 - 149
Deciduous alder 103

Deer 8, 15, 17, 28, 107, 138
Deer fern 108
Denniston, James 146, 161
Denny, Joseph E., 1556
Devil's Slide 11, 26, 203, 204
Diarrhea 6, 7, 34, 44
Discovery Site 19 - 25, 69
Doe Ridge Trail 76
Doebbel, Kurt 32, 65, 208
Doggie Walk 114
Douglas fir 51, 68, 117-118, 124,
    126, 127, 130, 134, 137, 140
Drake 25, 26
Drake, Francis 5, 25
Drakes Bay 26
DRAMA, MUSIC & TALENT
    229; REGULAR WEEKEND
    GIGS 229
Dream Machines 3, 54, 217, 218
DRIVING TOURS 31
Druids, Pebble Beach Order of 165
Duarte, Emma 167
Duarte, Frank 167
Duarte, Ron 167
Duarte's Restaurant 39
Ducks, mallards 181
        pintails 181
Dunes Beach 204, 207
Dutra, A.P. "Mac" 148
Dutra, Manuel Phillips, 148
Dutsch, Christ 164

E

East Lambert Creek 139
EATERIES 230-239
Egrets, snowy 193
El Corte de Madera Creek 79-87
El Corte de Madera Creek Trail
    82, 83, 84
El Corte de Madera Open Space
    Preserve 51, 79-87
El Granada 55, 170
Elephant seals 177, 183-185
Elk clover 84

EMERGENCY 259
Empire Grade 47
Equestriennes 51
Eucalyptus 15, 29, 30, 38 - 40,
    44, 52, 58, 59, 61, 65,
        106, 181, 182, 186, 214, 215
Evans Creek 117
Exclusive Fresh Fish 175

F

Fall Creek 115
Farallons 23, 25, 26, 128
FARM BUREAU 260
Farmers
    11, 14, 42, 61, 65, 66, 101, 145,
    149, 192. 194
Fassler Boulevard 21, 203
Field mustard 21
Finches 182
Fir Trail 82, 87
Fire
    14, 19, 64, 65, 67, 71, 74, -
    76, 78, 96, 97, 100, 101, 105,
    108, 109, 111, 115, 116, 119,
    121, 123, 124, 131, 133, 149,
    153, 156, 163, 171, 216, 218,
    222, 240, 241, 242- 246, 248,
    249, 250, 251
First aid kit 16
First National Bank of Pescadero
    163
Fishing 2, 191
Fist, The 214
Fitzgerald, James V. 190
Fitzgerald Marine Reserve
    2, 54, 182, 190, 197, 245
Five-finger ferns 104, 108, 134
Fleas 7
Flower Market 224
Flowers
    7, 11, 15, 24, 27, 45, 68, 74,
    83, 89, 112, 115, 118, 122, 186
Fogarty Winery 47
Foothill sedge 24

Forest Loop Trail 133-135
Four Corners Restaurant 46
Fourth of July 225
Foxes 138, 205
    Gray fox tracks 76
Francis Beach 205, 206
Francis, Joseph M., 155
Francis, Manuel, 147, 155
Franciscans 3, 9
Franklin Point 214
Frenchman's Creek 206
Friendly Acres Horse Ranch 200
Fromont, Eugene 51, 62
Frontierland 226
FUN TIME ON THE COAST 221-258

G

Gabrielli, Apple Jack 45
Gadsen Purchase 10
Galli, Francisco 5
Garretson, John 48
Gazos Creek 38, 214
Gazos Creek Road 38, 71
Gazos Creek Trail 78
Geddes, Charles 155
Geology 171
Giannini House 149
Gilcrest, Andrew, 150
Gilcrest, George F., 153
Gilcrest, John 152
Giorgetti Building 152
Giorgetti, Federico 152
Giorgetti, Leo 152
Giorgetti, Marie 152
Goat Hill 71, 76
Goat Hill Trail 76, 78, 79
Gold Rush 42, 66, 188
Golden chinquapin 75
Golden Gate Bridge 24
Golden Gate National Recreation
    Area 209-210
Gomez, Asuncion Luis 150
Gonzales, Juan Jose 9, 160

Good Templars Associaion, 152
Good Workout Loop 85
Gordon's Chute 57
Gorge Creek 134
Goulson, Alfred. 165
Goulson, Douglas 165
Goulson, John 165
Grabtown 63
Grabtown Gulch 125
Grabtown Gulch Trail 63, 121, 125-127
Graham, Isaac 173
Grangers Bridge 105
Gray whale 180
Gray Whale Cove 203
Gray Whale Cove State Beach 210
Greasewood 14
Great Salamander Trail 85
Gregory I 44
Gualtieri, Kathryn 148
Guerrero, Francisco Palomares 144

H

HALF MOON BAY 142-156,
Half Moon Bay 2, 3, 7, 9 -11, 15,
    30, 31, 33, 34, 39, 44, 50, 52,
    54, 55, 56, 58, 61, 120, 123,
    142, 157, 149, 164, 165, 167,
    177, 180, 187, 193, 194, 196,
    197, 199, 200, 201, 209, 213,
    214, 216 - 219, 221, 222, 224,
    227, 228, 231, 234, 237, 239,
    240, 241, 242, 243, 244, 245 -
    248, 251, 253- 255
HMB Airport 54, 225
HMB Beaches 205-208
Half Moon Bay Bakery 151
HMB Brewing Co. 55, 171-172, 175
HMB Chamber of Commerce 150, 225-226
HMB Charity Golf Classic 226
Half Moon Bay City Hall 150-151
HMB Feed & Fuel Store 144

HMB Fishermen's Marketing Assn. 227
HMB Grammer School 150
HALF MOON BAY PUMPKIN FESTIVAL 2, 220-224
Half Moon Bay Review and Pescadero Pebble 260
HMB Yacht Club 167
Halloween 2
Hanson, Charles 83
Harbor House 173
Harbor Day 3, 227
Harbor Lights Ceremony 228
Harbor seals 179
Harkins, George 64
Harkins Ridge 120, 123, 126
Harkins Ridge Extension 64
Harkins Ridge Trail 67, 124, 126
Harrington Creek 88-90
Harrier, northern 182
Hartley, G.P. 85
Harvard Street 175
Harwood Creek 109
Hatch, Alvin, 154
Hatch, Rufus 126
Hawk, northern harrier 138
Hawk Ridge Trail 128-129
Hazelnut 30
Hazelnut Trail 29
Helhena, Jose C., 153
Hellespont 188
Heritage Grove 131, 136, 137
Heritage Grove Trail 133, 136, 137
Heritage Grove Loop 131, 134
Hernandez, John 206
Herons, blue 193
Hewlett Packard 40, 58
Hickory Oaks Trail 91
Higgins-Purisima Road 42, 66,119, 126, 188-189
Higgins-Purisima Tour 65
Hikers Hut 104, 134, 137
Hoffman, Carl 144
Hoffman Creek 95
Hoffman Creek Trailhead
103, 106, 109, 110
Hollywood Courts, 154
Holy Spirit Festival 224
Homestead Flats 97
Homestead Trail 99
Hooker Creek 110
Hopkins, Mark 71
Hopkins, Timothy 71
Horses
72, 77, 101, 108, 135, 138 - 140, 142, 193, 199, 250
Horseshoe Lake 139
Horsetail 75, 95
Hostelling International - American Youth Hostels 36, 54, 60, 197
HOSTELS 255
Hotel San Pedro 199
HOTELS & MOTELS 251-255
Huck Finn Sportfishing 170
Huckleberry (ies)
46, 60, 95, 96, 99, 108, 116, 119, 131, 210
Huckleberry Flat 98, 217
Hypothermia 203

I

I.D.E.S. Hall 153, 162, 225
I.O.O.F. Hall, 151, 161
Imandade do Divino Espirato Santo Society, 153
Index Saloon, 148
Indian paintbrush 24
Indian Trail 75
International Order of Odd Fellows 153
Iris, long-leafed 118
Irish Ridge 126-127
Italy 160
Iverson, Christian 112, 115
Iverson Trail 115-116

J

Jack Brook Horse Camp 133, 135
Jackscrew 64

Jackson Flats Trail 74, 75
Jail 156-157
James McCormick House 165
Janssen, J.L., 155
Johnston Foundation 43
Johnston House 43, 67
Johnston, James 42, 43, 66, 67,
    146, 155
Johnston Street 155-157
Johnston, William 42, 66, 116
Jones Gulch Bridge 104
Jones Gulch Trail 104, 106

K

Kelly, Charles E. 148
Kelly Avenue, 146-150, 156, 205
Kennebunkport, ME 165
Kesey, Ken 45, 90
Kestrels, American 182
Ketch Joanne 170
Keystone Creek, 110
KIDS WILL LOVE IT 177-201
Kingfisher, belted 138
King's Mountain Art Festival 219
King's Mountain Community
    Center 227
King Street, 14, 23
Kings Mountain Inn 51
Kings Mountain Road 51, 125
Kirkpatrick, Edward 199
Kites, black-shouldered 182
Knapp, Robert I. 148, 152
Krebs, Al 164

L

La Di Dah 229
Laguna Salada 209
La Honda 45, 132
La Honda Country Fair and Music
    Festival 225
Las Honda Creek 88-90
La Honda Creek Preserve 86-90
La Honda Garden 225
La Honda Road 34, 40, 58, 84, 94

130, 138, 217, 225
Lake Lucerne 216
La Piazza, 151, 152, 224
Lambert Creek 136-137, 139
Lawrence Creek 79
Lawrence Creek Trail 86, 87
Leon Creek 148, 155
Level Lea Farm 162
Levy Brothers, 150
LIBRARIES 260
Lilacs, California wild 30, 107, 108
Linda Mar Boulevard 27, 198
Linda Mar Valley 23
Linguica 223
Lintt Trout Farm 191
Little Butano Creek
    71-74, 76, 77, 78, 79
Lions Club 226
Lizard tail, 21
Lobitos
    32, 34, 40, 44, 52, 56, 61, 62, 126
Lobitos Creek 40, 56, 128
Lobitos Creek Cutoff 40
Lobitos Creek Road 40, 62
Lobitos-Purisima Tour 61
Loggers
    3, 11, 14, 43, 47, 48, 50, 51,
    74, 80, 82, 85, 86, 101, 112,
    114, 117, 119, 122, 134, 160
Loma Prieta earthquake 111
Long Ridge Preserve 90-93
Long Ridge Trail 91
Los Amigos Market & Taqueria
    163
Lucy Lane 40
Lupines 98, 172
    Silver 21
Lyme disease 17
Lyons, Kathleen 69

M

Madrones 47, 51, 68, 81, 82, 89,
    104, 118, 124, 126, 130, 131
Main Street 142

Manzanita 1, 14, 30, 75, 76, 95, 119
Manzanita burls 14
Maples, big leafed 127
Maria, Jose Alviso 62
Marine Radio Station KFS 32, 44, 61
Marsh, Antonio, 153
Martini Creek 25-27, 211
Martin's Beach 32
Mavericks 2, 169
Mavericks Roadhouse Cafe 55, 172
Mayer, Ollie 105
McArthur, Hugh 85
McConnaughey, Bayard 203
McConnaughey, Evelyn 203
McCormick Creek 95
McDonald, Sam 130
McMurtry, Larry 90
McNee Ranch State Park 26, 27
Meadowlark 182
Mel Mello Center for the Performing Arts 223
Memorial Grove 48
Memorial Park 48, 94-101, 109, 111, 217
Merry Prankster Cafe 45, 230
Methodist Episcopal Church 155, 156
Methuselah Trail 80, 87
Methuselah Tree 50, 79, 82, 85
Metzgar House 154
Metzgar, William 154
Mexican Army 41
Mezza Luna 54, 165
Midpeninsula Regional Open Space District 70, 79, 80, 87 - 90, 119, 127, 135
Milgra Ridge 5, 24
Mill Street 142, 145,146
Milliken, Dr. Albert 151
Mill Ox Trail 74, 75
Mills Barn 188-189
Mill Creek 42, 66, 189
Mills, Charles, 153

Mills, Robert 42, 66, 188
Mindego Creek 130
Mindego Hill 98, 99, 107, 129, 132, 136
Mindego Hill Trail 129
Mindego Ridge Trail 128
Miners lettuce 131
Mirada Road 55
Miramar Beach 204, 229
Miramar Drive 204
Miramontes Beach 207-208
Miramontes, Bernardo, 142
Miramontes, Candelario 9, 31, 66, 142, 144, 188
Miramontes, Jose de los Santos 147
Miramontes Point 10, 31, 43, 56, 63, 1203, 207, 244, 247, 248
Miramontes Point Road 31,42, 207
Miramontes Street 153-155
Mission Dolores 3, 6, 25, 28, 143-144, 169, 198
Mission Santa Cruz 180, 190
Missions 9, 173, 191, 206, 254
Mitchell Creek 51, 62
Modoc group camp 138
Monkey flowers 84
Monkey tree 165
Montara 10, 11, 23, 26, 27, 29, 30, 54, 190, 197, 204, 205, 226, 227, 241, 242, 247
Montara manzanita 30
Montara Mountain 23, 27, 30
Montara State Beach 10, 26, 211
Monterey 5
Monterey Bay 5, 6, 15, 20, 25-27, 38, 78, 180
Monterey Formation 179, 190
Moon Bay Restaurant 169
Moonshine whiskey 45
Moore, Alexander 160
Moore, Fisher & Troupe sawmill 107
Moore, Thomas W. 160-161

Morgan, Dr., Charles, 153
Mori Point 209
Mori Point Road 209
Mori Ridge 22-24
Mori Ridge Trail 22 - 24
Mosconi, James, 147
Moss Beach
  2, 10, 54, 190, 227, 228,
  238, 239, 245, 252
Moss Beach Distillery 54
Mount Diablo 51
Mount Hamilton 51
Mountain iris 21, 104, 108
Mountain lion 15, 16
Mt. Ellen 99
Mt. Ellen Nature Trail 97
Mt. Tamalpais 23
Mullen, Delores 154
Murray, Burleigh C. 188
Murray, Burleigh H. 188
Murray, Miranda 188
Mussels 191, 197
Muzzi, Joe, Jr. 164
Muzzi, Vince 164
Muzzi, Veronica 164
Muzzi's Market 164

N

Naples Beach 204
Narcotics 45
National Audobon Society 216
National Bell Foundary, 150
National Oceanic & Atmospheric
  Administration 210
Native Sons of the Golden West,
  161
NATURE TOURS 69
Nature Trail Loop 97, 116
Nettles, stinging 192
New Spain 5, 7
NEWSPAPERS 260
Nick's 230
Niles Canyon 130
Norm's Market & Arcangeli Bakery
164
NORTHERN BEACHES/
  MONTARA, PILLAR POINT
  210-217
North Leaf Trail 87
North Peak Access Road 27
North Pond Trail 193-194
North Ridge 124
North Ridge Trail 67, 125, 128
North Road 165
Nunzetti family 192
Nye's Rock 183

O

Oaks, Canyon 47, 130, 131, 138
  Live 14, 68, 117, 124, 130
  Maul 76
  Scrub 30
  Tan 14, 68, 76, 81, 99, 104
    117, 123, 124
Obsidian 180
Occidental Hotel 150
Occidental Hotel Annex 150
Oddstad Theater 229
Ohlone 5 -7, 9, 19, 23, 34,
  35, 44, 50, 69, 70, 74, 75,
  81, 82, 102, 109, 111, 136,
  169, 180, 194, 195, 213, 215
Oil 41, 106
Oil Creek 91
Oil wells 41
Old Haul Road
  95, 101, 103, 105, 109, 110, 112
Old Haul Road Trail 95
Old Page Mill Road 136-137
Old Pedro Mountain Road 27
Old Princeton Landing 172
Old Tree Trail 114
Old Trout Farm 28
Olhausen, Pam 191
Olmo Fire Road 76, 78
Our Lady of the Pillar Catholikc
  Church 149, 257

P

Pacifica
2, 4, 5, 10, 11, 21 - 24, 27,
28, 69, 191, 202 - 204, 210,
217 -222, 226, 230, 233 -240,
246, 248, 251, 252, 253
Pacifica Antique and Collectibles
Street Fair 226
Pacifica Chamber of Commerce
210
Pacifica Community Center 222
Pacifica Coast Fog Fest 228
Pacifica Co Op Nursery 222
Pacifica Spindrift Players 229
Pacifica Tribune 229
Page Mill Road 93, 113, 129, 137,
141
Page, William 92, 113, 135
Palmetto Avnue 226, 228
Paloma Avenue 202
Palomares, Guerrero 54, 169
Parasurfing 201
Pebble Beach 153, 163, 209, 216
Pedro Point 203
Pelicans 1, 164, 182, 187
Peninsula Open Space Trust 11,
36, 38, 58
Pescadero
2, 9, 10, 15, 35, 39, 48-
50, \59 - 60, 71, 90, 93, 95- 98,
99-105, 108-112, 114, 115,
130-132, 134, 135, 143,
146, 151, 158167, 160,
184, 185, 192, 216, 224, 227,
233, 236, 243, 247, 249,
250, 253, 254, 255
Pescadero Arts and Fun Faire 227
Pescadero Beach 58, 216
Pescadero Community Church 162,
164
Pescadero Creek 10, 35, 101, 103,
106, 115-118, 192-193
Pesadero Creek Canyon 135
Pescadero Creek County Park

47, 91, 95, 98, 100, 101, 108,
110-111, 130, 136, 140
Pescadero Creek Road 10, 39, 160,
191
Pescadero High School 39
Pescadero Hotel 160
Pescadero Marsh
15, 35, 49, 50, 60, 191, 216
Pescadero Road 10, 94, 99, 130-
131, 133
Pescadero State Beach 216
Pescadero Walkabout 156-167
Peter the Great 5
Peters Creek
91, 92, 93, 111, 113, 115-
118, 120
Peterson Creek 95
Pharis, Purdy 71, 83, 122
Pheasants, Asian 172
Picnic Sites 216-219
Pigeon Point
1, 2, 10, 36, 37, 50, 60, 71,
72, 94, 151, 173, 187, 188,
189, 207, 243, 247, 254
Pigeon Point Anchorage and Wharf
189
Pigeon Point Light Station 36, 37,
60, 194-197 , 247
Pilarcitos Creek
7, 9, 10, 142, 143 - 145, 199
Pillar Point
1, 2, 5, 10, 11, 14, 54, 55, 146,
168-175, 190, 196, 197,
212, 218-220, 226-228, 242,
244, 245, 247
Pillar Point Harbor 1, 14, 54,
168-175, 196, 203, 205, 219,
228, 242, 244, 245, 247
Pillar Point Inn 55
Pillar Point Walkabout 168-175
PILLOW FOR YOUR HEAD, A
248-258
Pines, Knobcone 75, 78, 118
Monterey 14, 24, 206, 208

Piney Creek 103
Plovers 1, 205-206
Plover Watch Volunteer Program
 206
Plow factory 148
Point Año Nuevo
 2, 5, 6, 10, 50, 54, 61, 206, 246,
 249
Point Año Nuevo Reserve 61
 See also Año Nuevo Reserve
Point Montara 54
Point Montara Fog Signal and Light
 Station 54, 197
Point Reyes 5, 23, 25
Poison oak 74, 95, 125
Pomponio Creek 35, 40, 58,
 60, 101
Pomponio Creek Road 40
Pomponio State Beach 58, 217
Pomponio Trail 97, 101, 103,
 104, 106-109
Poplar Avenue 55, 207
Poplar Beach 207
Poppies, Bush 137
Port of San Francisco 5
Portolá, Captain Gaspar de 2, 4-9,
 26, 29, 44, 172, 180, 217
Portola Creek 110
Portolá Expedition 211, 213, 215
Portola Redwoods State Park
 91, 92, 95, 102, 110-114,
 135, 137, 140, 81
Portugal 49, 160, 224
Portuguese 2, 60, 195, 216
Portuguese immigrants 60
Pottery 2, 239
Prickleback 191
Primrose, beach 214
Princeton Boat Storage 174
Princeton by the Sea 161, 169
Princeton Drive 166
Princeton Inn 54
Princeton Sea Food Market 170

Produce 34, 54, 160, 239
Prohibition
 11, 45, 149, 160, 172, 192, 228
Prohibition Party, 152
Prospect Road 172
PUMPKIN FESTIVAL 213
Punta de Año Nuevo 169
Purisima Creek 7, 33, 41, 51, 63 -
 65, 67, 68, 12 0 - 128, 142
Purisima Creek Redwoods Open
 Space Preserve 41, 42, 51, 65,
 119-127
Purisima Creek Trail 120
Purisima Creek Trail Extension 64
Purisima Road 41, 42, 63
Purisima Street 147, 152

Q

Quail 182
Quilla, Antone 1478
Quinlan, Pete 149, 155
Qurostes 172

R

Railroad 32, 169, 207
Railroad Avenue 56, 207
Ranch Spring Trail 92
Rancheria de las Pulgas 7
Rancheros 10, 77
Rancho Arroyo de los Pilarcitos
 9, 31, 42, 56, 66, 188
Rancho Buri Buri 199
Rancho Butano 10, 70, 77, 195
Rancho Cañada Verde y Arroyo de
 la Purissima 10, 62
Rancho Corral de Tierra Norte 54,
 169
Rancho Corral de Tierra Sud 10
Rancho de Punta de Año Nuevo 10,
 163, 213
Rancho El Pescadero 9, 160
Rancho San Benito 142
Rancho San Gregorio

10, 45, 79, 89, 243
Rancho San Pedro 10
Ranch Springs Trail 92
Rapley Ranch Road 127, 130
Rattlesnake 16, 74
Ravewns 205
Ray Linder Trail 76
Red elderberry 77
Redondo Beach 207
Redondo Beach Road 207
Redwood City 10, 51, 62, 80,
83, 255
Redwood sorrel 95, 1118, 131, 136
Redwoods
1, 2, 10, 11, 14, 29, 36, 38, 42, 43,
45 -51, 62 - 69, 73, 75, 80,
81-84, 86, 89, 90, 92, 95,
98-101, 103,104-107, 110 -117,
119-126, 131, 133-135, 137,140,
160, 206, 211, 218, 229, 254
Reina del Mar Ave 24
Resolution Loop 84
Resolution Trail 83, 84
Reynolds, Meredith 159
Rhododendron Creek 110
Ritz Carlton 207-208
Road Warrior 39, 59
Rockaway Beach 165, 209, 227
Rockaway Beach Avenue 209-210
Rockefeller, J.D. 106
Rolph, Governor James "Sunny
Jim" 136
Roosevelt, President Franklin D. 95
Rosehenge 162
Roses, California 118
Russian Ridge 47, 130
Russian Ridge Open Space Preserve
47, 127-130
Russo, Ron 191
RV PARKS 255-256

S

Saint Gregory 44
Salmon 9

Saltbox house 43, 67
Sam McDonald County Park
48, 94, 101, 130-135, 218
San Benito 10, 31,
142, 147, 224, 241
San Benito House 147
San Bruno Mountain 24, 25
San Carlos 20
San Diego 20
San Francisco
1 - 3, 5, 6, 9, 10, 19, 20,
23 - 26, 28, 31, 33, 34, 42,
44, 54 - 56, 61, 66, 69, 84,
95, 100, 101, 111, 112, 121,
127, 142, 145, 146, 148,
151, 161, 173, 181, 188, 191,
205, 206, 221, 254
San Francisco and Ocean Shore
Railroad 169
San Francisco Bay 2, 6, 19, 26,
28, 34, 69, 95, 121
127, 205, 254
San Francisco Presidio 9, 25, 31,
54, 143, 199
San Francisco Water Department
21
San Gregorio 10, 11, 15, 34,
38, 40, 41, 44, 45, 50, 52,
58, 60, 78, 79, 88, 89, 171,
210, 222, 233, 236, 237, 243
San Gregorio Creek 7, 34, 40, 44,
52, 58, 60, 88, 89, 180, 210
San Gregorio Fault 39, 77, 179
San Gregorio General Store 40, 44,
58, 230
San Gregorio Hotel 40
San Gregorio State Beach 217
San Mateo County 3
San Mateo County Board of
Supervisors 48, 94
San Mateo County Harbor District
212
San Mateo County Historical
Association 199

San Mateo County Jail Farm 47
San Mateo County Parks Dept. 69
San Mateo Road 191
San Pedro Beach 25, 210
San Pedro Creek 23, 26 - 30, 191
San Pedro Mountain 25, 144
San Pedro Valley 199
San Pedro Valley County Park
    27, 28, 30, 210
Sanchez Adobe 198-200
Sanchez, Francisco 10, 199
Sanchez, Ramona 70
Santa Cruz 3
Santa Cruz Mission 70, 120
Santa Cruz Mountains 54, 135, 174
Santos, Jorge 146
Saunders, Ambrose 84
Save the Redwoods League 114
Sawmills 10, 38
Scarpa, Teresa 147
Scaups 1
Schenly Creek 109
Schooners
    10, 11, 33, 56, 72, 145, 161
Sculpins 191
Scurvy 6, 7, 25, 210
Sea fig 172
Sea Horse Ranch 200, 206
Sea lions 1–3, 177
Sea otters 186
Sea rocket 172
Seals
    1, 2, 31, 169, 170, 171, 175,
    186-189, 201, 208
Seals, California 185
    Harbor 185
    Stellar 185
Seal Rock 63
Sea turtle tracks 214
Squoia Audobon Society 192
Sequoia Audubon Trail 193
Sequoia Flat 99
Sequoia Nature Trail 114

Serra, Father Junipero 9
Seton Coastside Medical Center
    226
Sharp Park 21
Sharp Park Beach 209
Sharp Park Golf Course 209
Sharp Park Road 21
Shaw Flat Trail 110
Shaw Flat Trail Camp 109
Shell Dance Nursery 24
Shell Oil Co. 52
Shingle Mill Creek 108
Shingles
    10, 11, 51, 52, 62, 72, 80, 83,
    85, 95, 112, 119, 121
Ship to Shore Fish Market 170
Shipwrecks 195-197
SHOPPING 241-248
Sierra Club 11, 105, 250
Sierra Morena 51
Simmons, William Adams, 157
Sir John Franklin 195
Six Bridges Trail 77
Skeggs Point 51, 79, 80, 84,
    85, 87
Skunk cabbage 74
Skyline Boulevard 90, 127, 135
Skyline College 25
Skyline Ranch 139
Skyline Ridge Preserve 113, 135-
    141
Skyline Trading Post 46
Skylonda 46, 103
Slate Creek 91, 92, 93, 95,
    111, 115 - 117
Slate Creek Trail 117
Slate Creek Trail Camp 119
Smithsonian Institution, 152
Smugglers 11
SNACK TIME 239-241
Snag Trail 110
Snails, brown turban 191
Snake-bite kit 16

Snakes 16, 28
Soda Gulch Creek 123
Soda Gulch Trail 122-127
South Coast Children's Center 228
SOUTHERN BEACHES/ SAN
    GREGORIO-AÑO NUEVO 213-
    217
Spanishtown, 31, 146
Spanishtown Historical Society 156
Spear points 180
Spring Board Trail 86
Spring Fest 3, 225
Squirrels 95
St Anthony's Church 157
St. Francis 20
St. Matthew 3
Stage coaches 40
Stage Road 15, 39, 40, 44, 57,
    58, 60, 151 -153, 155, 156,
    159-167, 225, 228, 243
Stage Road Shops 160
Stage Road Winter Faire 228
Stanford University 71
Stanger, Frank 86
Starfish, ochre 191
Star Hill 79
Starrs Hill Road 85
State Highway 84 34, 44
Steam Donkey Trail 86
Steele Brothers 38
Steele, Charles 38
Steele Brothers Dairy 181, 213
Steelhead 9, 95
Stellar jays 95
Stegner, Mary 90
Stegner, Wallace 90
Steller sea lions 179
Sticky monkey flower 99
Summit Springs 121
Summit Springs House 51, 52, 63
Summit Trail 118
Surfers Corner 204
Sutro Heights 24

Swallows 182
    barn 138
Swanton House 160-163
Swanton, Mrs. Charles 163
Sweeney Ridge 2, 6, 19, 209
Sweeney Ridge Trail 21, 24
Sweetwood Park 199
Swett Road 79
Swifts 192
Swimming 97, 99, 178, 203,
    217, 243, 245, 248
Sylvia's Curiosity Shop 172

T

Tafoni Trail 80-85, 87
Tan Oak Flat 100
Tan Oak Nature Trail 100, 101
Tanners 3, 14
Tarwater Canyon 108
Tarwater Creek 106-108
Tarwater Trail 107-108
Tarwater Trail Camp 106, 110
Tarwater Trail Loop 107
TAXIS & LIMOS 260
Teals, cinnamon 181
    green-winged 181
Teknova 173
Theodore J. Hoover Natural
    Preserve 201
Thimbleberry 77
This Side of the Hill Players 221
Thomas W. Moore House 165
Three Zero Café 54
Thrush 180
Tick 17, 18, 72, 149, 221
Tide pools 2, 178
Tie Camp 106
Tiger lilies 84
Timberview Trail 85, 86
Tiptoe Falls 115, 116
Tours des Fleurs 2, 226
Towhee 180
TOWING 260
Towne Creek 104, 105

Towne Fire Road 110
Towne Ridge 133-134
Towne Trail 131, 134-135
Toys 2, 153, 233
Tunitas Creek 10, 11, 32, 33,
    40, 44, 51, 52, 55 -57,
    61, 62, 63, 64, 121,
    125, 126, 160
Tunitas Creek Alternative 50
Tunitas Creek Road 10, 40, 127
Tunitas Ridge 119
Turkey Lane 62
Twinberries 193
Two Dreamers 175
Two-eyed violets 115

U

Urchins, purple sea 191
U.S. Coast Guard 36

V

Valle de los Cursos 34
Valley View Trail 29
Vasquez, Pablo, 145
Vasquez, Tiburcio 10, 145, 149
Vassar Street 167
Venice Beach 205
Venice Boulevard 205
Verbena, Sand 172
Verde Road 31, 32, 41, 44,
    52, 56, 61, 65, 119
Vidal, Estevan 151
Village of Purisima 31, 44, 56, 208
Violets 116
Vireos 182
Virginia Mill 85
Virginia Mill Trail 80, 85, 86
Vizcaino, Sebastian 5, 177,
    180, 213

W

Waddell Beach 2, 36, 38, 201
Waddell Creek 11, 109

Waddell, William 10, 36, 201, 206
Wake Robin 74
Walker, Clifford James 45
WALKING TOURS 142-175
Wally's Creek 108
Warbler 182
Ward Road Trail 91
Weather 1, 13, 14, 17, 25,
    29, 67, 70, 100, 101, 108,
    124, 164, 183, 196, 197
Weiler Ranch Road 29, 30
Wells Fargo Express 149
Welsh pasties 223
West Point Drive 175-176
Western coltsfoot 73
Western wake robin 116, 134
Whales, Gray 186, 195-196
    humpbacks 195
Whaling stations 2, 195
Wharf 10, 36, 189, 206
Whitehouse Creek 215
Whittemore Gulch 64, 120-123
Whittemore Gulch Trail 123
Wigeons 181
Wild cucumber 77
Wild pigs 10
Windsurfers 2, 194
Windy Hill 46
Winter storms 2, 205
Wolfe, Tom 45
Woodhams, Alfred 161
Woodhams House 161
Woodpeckers 95
Woodruff Creek 46
Woodruff Inn 46
Work Projects Administration 95
Workout Loop 86
Worley Flat 103
Wrens, marsh 138, 182
Wrentits 182
Wurr Flat 94, 96
Wurr Road 98, 103, 109
Wurr School 94

Wurr Trail 101

Y

Yarrow. Golden   24
Yerba Buena 10, 25, 47, 118
Young Avenue 204
Yurok 58

Z

Zaballa, Estanislao 145
Zaballa House 146